AF800824

Palgrave Studies in the History of Finance

Series Editors
D'Maris Coffman, Bartlett Faculty of Built Environment, University College London, London, UK
Tony K. Moore, ICMA Centre, Henley Business School, University of Reading, Reading, UK
Martin Allen, Department of Coins and Medals, Fitzwilliam Museum, University of Cambridge, Cambridge, UK
Sophus Reinert, Harvard Business School, Cambridge, MA, USA

The study of the history of financial institutions, markets, instruments and concepts is vital if we are to understand the role played by finance today. At the same time, the methodologies developed by finance academics can provide a new perspective for historical studies. Palgrave Studies in the History of Finance is a multi-disciplinary effort to emphasise the role played by finance in the past, and what lessons historical experiences have for us. It presents original research, in both authored monographs and edited collections, from historians, finance academics and economists, as well as financial practitioners.

More information about this series at
http://www.palgrave.com/gp/series/14583

Craig McMahon

Taming the Fringe

The Regulation and Development of the British Payday Lending and Pawnbroking Markets since 1870

palgrave
macmillan

Craig McMahon
Economics
Villanova University
Villanova, PA, USA

ISSN 2662-5164 ISSN 2662-5172 (electronic)
Palgrave Studies in the History of Finance
ISBN 978-3-030-70614-2 ISBN 978-3-030-70615-9 (eBook)
https://doi.org/10.1007/978-3-030-70615-9

© The Editor(s) (if applicable) and The Author(s), under exclusive license to Springer Nature Switzerland AG 2021
This work is subject to copyright. All rights are solely and exclusively licensed by the Publisher, whether the whole or part of the material is concerned, specifically the rights of translation, reprinting, reuse of illustrations, recitation, broadcasting, reproduction on microfilms or in any other physical way, and transmission or information storage and retrieval, electronic adaptation, computer software, or by similar or dissimilar methodology now known or hereafter developed.
The use of general descriptive names, registered names, trademarks, service marks, etc. in this publication does not imply, even in the absence of a specific statement, that such names are exempt from the relevant protective laws and regulations and therefore free for general use.
The publisher, the authors and the editors are safe to assume that the advice and information in this book are believed to be true and accurate at the date of publication. Neither the publisher nor the authors or the editors give a warranty, expressed or implied, with respect to the material contained herein or for any errors or omissions that may have been made. The publisher remains neutral with regard to jurisdictional claims in published maps and institutional affiliations.

Cover credit: Goerge Marks

This Palgrave Macmillan imprint is published by the registered company Springer Nature Switzerland AG
The registered company address is: Gewerbestrasse 11, 6330 Cham, Switzerland

To Francis J. Doyle

Contents

1 Introduction: Fair Price and Sufficient Profit 1

2 Victorian Pawnbrokers: Cancerous Worms of Ruin or the Poor Man's Banker? 17

3 Moneylenders: Deeply Rooted Evil or Providers of Quick Cash? 57

4 Legitimate Bankers: Pawnbrokers and Moneylenders Join the Premier League 99

5 Small-Loan Providers: Sent Back to the Fringe 139

6 Fintech to the Rescue or Predators in Disguise? 185

7 Conclusion: Perceptions Matter 213

Principal Persons 219

Index 221

Abbreviations

ACCA	Association of Chartered Certified Accountants
ADR	Alternative Dispute Resolution
APR	Annual Percentage Rate
CCA 1974	The Consumer Credit Act 1974, c. 39
CCA 2006	The Consumer Credit Act 2006, c.14
CMA	Competition and Markets Authority
Crowther	The Crowther Report on Consumer Credit 1968–1971
DTI	The Department of Trade and Industry
EBITDA	Earnings Before Interest, Tax, Depreciation and Amortisation
FCA	Financial Conduct Authority
FOS	Financial Ombudsman Service
FSA	Financial Services Authority
HC deb.	House of Commons Debate
HC	House of Commons
HCSTC	High-Cost Short-Term Credit
HL deb.	House of Lords debate
HL	House of Lords
HM	Her (His) Majesty
MLA 1900	The Moneylenders Act 1900: 63 & 64 Vic. c. 51
MLA 1927	The Moneylenders Act 1927: 8 Geo. 5 c. 21
MLSC 1897	The Moneylenders Select Committee 1897
MLSC 1898	The Moneylenders Select Committee 1898
MLSC 1925	The Moneylenders Select Committee 1925
MPPS	Metropolitan Pawnbroker Protection Society
NPA	National Pawnbrokers Association
OFT	Office of Fair Trading

PBA 1872	The Pawnbrokers Act 1872: 35 & 36 Vic. c. 93
PBG	*Pawnbrokers' Gazette*
PBSC 1870	The Pawnbrokers Select Committee 1870
PBSC 1872	The Pawnbrokers Select Committee 1872
pcpa	Per Cent Per Annum
pcpm	Per Cent Per Month
PPRA	Pawnbroking Parliamentary Reform Association
ROCE	Return on Capital Employed
ROE	Return on Equity

List of Figures

Fig. 2.1	Pawnbrokers per one million capita 1909 (*Source* HC, Local Taxation Licences, 1909 [London: HMSO])	22
Fig. 2.2	Pawnbroking licences, 1870–1930 (*Source* Annual report of the Commissioners of HM Inland Revenue, 1870–1909 and HM Customs & Excise thereafter)	48
Fig. 4.1	Pawnbroking licences, 1800–1970 (*Source* Annual report of the Commissioners of HM Inland Revenue and HM Customs & Excise, 1870–1970; Crowther testimony; National Pawnbrokers Association; and the PBSC 1870)	102
Fig. 4.2	Moneylending licences, 1925–1970 (*Source* [NOP Research; and author estimates using data from the MLSC 1925 and Customs & Excise, England and Wales])	104
Fig. 5.1	Three-part price control (*Source* "FCA Confirms Price Cap Rules for Payday Lenders," FCA press release, 11 November 2014)	165

List of Tables

Table 1.1	Regulatory episodes	6
Table 2.1	Estimated annual pledges by location, 1870s	23
Table 2.2	John Dicker, transactions for the week ending 7 May 1870	23
Table 2.3	The Derby scale	30
Table 2.4	John Dicker business analysis, June 1870	37
Table 2.5	Summary returns of six testifying pawnbrokers	38
Table 2.6	Pledges redeemed on Saturday 7 May 1870	40
Table 2.7	Estimated redemption rates	45
Table 3.1	Schedule of guidance interest rate	70
Table 3.2	Financial data on fifteen moneylenders	82
Table 4.1	Pawnbroking and moneylending licensing, 1969	101
Table 4.2	Pawnbroking market estimates, 1970	103
Table 4.3	Pledge analysis, 1970	103
Table 4.4	Pawnbroking and moneylending licences, 1942–1970	105
Table 4.5	Average rates on unsecured loans	106
Table 4.6	Unsecured loan profile	106
Table 4.7	Actual versus effective rates	126
Table 5.1	Payday loan market growth	154
Table 5.2	M&A and market expansion	155
Table 5.3	Cash America estimated UK loan p/l	160
Table 5.4	2012 Payday loan repayment	160
Table 5.5	Total cost of credit for the largest high street lenders	161

Table 6.1 Pre- and post-cap average revenue per loan 190
Table 6.2 Debt held by high-cost credit borrowers as of November 2016 191
Table 6.3 Other credit usage in same period as denied payday loan 191
Table 6.4 Average pawnbroker in 2018 192

CHAPTER 1

Introduction: Fair Price and Sufficient Profit

'I lose by every pledge that goes out of my house, which is pledged for 5 shillings and under, which does not remain with me more than a month', lamented a London based pawnbroker in 1870.[1] Thanks to government caps on interest rates and fees, pawnbrokers were losing money, and fast. The price cap schedule was devised in 1800, and seventy years later expenses had risen considerably. Price controls threatened the financial viability of this crucial lifeline for poor families in need of quick cash. The pawnbroker's plight drew little sympathy from policymakers, some of whom wanted to curtail the 'evil' of small loans further still. The core issue was not especially complex: 'plenty of poor people would starve' without cash loans.[2] The difficulty dwelt in figuring out how to supply reasonably priced credit to vulnerable borrowers.

Over one hundred and fifty years later, the British small-loan market has evolved. The lived experiences of borrowers have changed too. While in the past, a family might find themselves on the streets for want of a few shillings, today's consumer society, higher standards of living and the welfare state have, for the most part, eliminated outright destitution. Those gains conceal the fact that nearly half of the British population have less than £100 in savings and live with almost no financial buffer.[3] The household savings rate has collapsed from around 13% in the mid-1990s to just over 6% in the fourth quarter of 2019. The reality is that low-income households use small loans to avoid having to choose between

© The Author(s), under exclusive license to Springer Nature Switzerland AG 2021
C. McMahon, *Taming the Fringe*, Palgrave Studies in the History of Finance, https://doi.org/10.1007/978-3-030-70615-9_1

'putting the heating on and putting food on the table'.[4] What was once limited to pawnbrokers and moneylenders, is now a multi-billion-pound high-cost fringe credit sector offering an array of options for those most in need of goods, services and cash. Access comes at a high cost and it is paid by those least able to afford it.

Once self-funded proprietorships, today's fringe lenders enjoy corporate status and are backed by capital market and bank financing. The moneylenders of yesteryear are now commonly known as payday lenders. Along with pawnbrokers, these providers of small-value cash loans occupy a controversial, if not notorious, niche within the credit markets. Following the 2007–2008 financial crises, dodgy business practices and a rapid expansion drew attention onto payday lenders, none more so than the now infamous Wonga. Wonga was once considered a rising fintech disruptor with the potential for a billion-pound stock flotation. In a crowded field, Wonga stood tall as the industry leader and raised its profile through sponsorship of the football club Newcastle United. Lose lending standards, high interest rates and an avalanche of advertisements caught up with Wonga and its peers. Policymakers and the media began questioning whether loans with annual percentage rates (APRs) reaching into the thousands did more harm than good. Entering the fray, the Church of England believed that payday lenders 'purposely' put customers in debt to 'farm their assets and milk them dry' (Merrill 2014). Finding themselves at the intersection of capitalism and economic justice, policymakers pondered why the poor were charged so dearly for credit. Still, it was unclear what measures could alleviate borrowers from the 'devastating impact' caused by these 'legal loan sharks' (Watt 2012).[5]

A significant step was taken in 2015 when the newly created Financial Conduct Authority (FCA) implemented price controls on payday lenders. Capped by the Government, no longer could Wonga and the like determine the cost of their loans. Economists and trade groups warned that the extreme measure would drive participants out of the market leaving those most in need without access to cash (Goff 2014; Osborne 2014). Paying off a high-cost loan is one thing, but missing a utility payment or primary school fees has ramifications too. Dozens of lenders did exit the market. This was the first instance of implementing new price caps on a consumer credit product since usury was repealed in 1854. Since 1900 parliament had rejected similar measures on at least eight occasions. Lord Glasman, a Labour peer and academic, referred to the price control measure as 'an absolutely exceptional moment'.[6]

Even pawnbrokers, once the lone exception to usury's 1854 repeal, were operating quite cheerfully, as their price caps were rescinded in 1974. Pawnbroking also benefitted from the financial upheaval of 2007–2008. The sector grew from approximately 800 outlets in 2003 to over 2000 in 2014, with a market value of £930 million.[7] This trend did not go unnoticed. In 2016, the *Guardian* reported, '£75.06 interest on £180 over six months. That is 41.7 per cent. Extortionate, you might think, and surely one of the reasons why pawnbrokers, a ubiquitous feature of every working-class district 50-odd years ago, died out. Except they didn't' (Boggan 2016). Phil Murphy, the founder of Albemarle & Bond, a major UK pawnbroker, argued that 'in a funny way we don't create indebtedness; we pick up the pieces when people have got into debt. In fact, we're absolutely lovely' (Warren 1988). Over a century earlier, John McKay, a pawnbroker in Glasgow, said that during times of great need pawnbrokers 'help people on in the world'.[8] While twenty-first-century pawnbrokers have slipped through a tightening of the regulatory net, they are never far from regulatory crosshairs nor is their position in the lending hierarchy settled. Are they 'proper' and legitimate financial service providers or should pawnbrokers be treated differently by virtue of their vulnerable client base?

British policymakers have struggled with small loans because they raise broader issues pertaining to poverty, capitalism and financial regulation. Concerns over the high cost and burdensome terms of small loans remains a troublesome and contentious topic amongst policymakers. The values of easily accessible credit and financial independence compete with society's desire to protect people from what many believe are predatory lenders.[9] Again and again, policymakers have pondered whether regulatory tools can lower the cost of credit without reducing access for those most in need of cash loans. Can the government set a just and fair price for money that protects borrowers while also providing sufficient profit for lenders?

This book analyses the development of high-cost small loans through the lens of the policies aimed at *Taming the Fringe*. It analyses the motivation, content and outcome of critical regulatory episodes that have shaped pawnbroking and money-payday lending (Grossman 2010).[10] The objective is to understand both the policy and market evolution of two credit products that were, and remain, vital to the working poor. *Taming the Fringe* is an extended study of Britain's small-loan market, and the only one to examine over 160 years of financial results and market data. It adds to our knowledge of fringe banking and the evolving role of financial regulation to protect vulnerable people. More ambitiously, it is about how successive generations of British policymakers have defined fairness within capitalism for the poor and vulnerable (Fleming 2018).[11]

Why begin this book with a quotation from a pawnbroker? Surely recounting an eye-catching and heart-tugging tale concerning a down-and-out borrower paying 1000% annual interest on a loan offers a far more compelling hook? Yes, probably so; but the answer is that often the vantage point of the lenders is neglected by a literature and popular press that too easily vilifies a product that millions of people rely on to make ends meet. To be fair, Wonga and many others broke various laws and harmed untold thousands of consumers along the way. By and large, however, customers are quite happy with the service and products offered by these small-time capitalists. Whatever their actions, since the 1870s, small-value lenders have shaped regulation—a viewpoint that the existing literature does not address adequately. While the market pales in comparison with the vast sums of government and corporate debt, these loans help low-income families cope with emergency and vital household expenditures. These lenders are an important component of the lives of the poor and are worthy of our consideration and study.

By narrowing on moneylending and pawnbroking, the development of policy and market outcomes is more apparent than an evaluation of the entire spectrum of fringe banking. This method helps uncover why policymakers have sought protection of poor borrowers from small cash loans. While in the decades since the 1870s, the government is more willing to interfere in market outcomes on behalf of borrowers, the process is more complex than a linear evolution from the so-called Victorian laissez-faire attitude towards a modern state. The Victorian period was not a triumph of laissez-faire over moral economic principles (Daunton 2008). The main issue then and now, was in determining the appropriate relationship and boundaries between the 'public' government and 'private' business (Alborn 1998).

This book evaluates a range of material including business, charity, legal and political archives, along with parliamentary papers, government reports, securities filings, newspapers and periodicals. It incorporates and builds on the existing histories of borrowing and lending to appreciate why policymakers regulated small-value loans (Finn 2003; Tebbutt 1983; Johnson 1985; O'Connell 2009). Engaging accounting and financial data open new avenues of exploring the development of small-value lending.

Detailing the revenues, expenses and how the market has worked since the 1870s helps us to understand the perspective of policymakers and their divergent viewpoints concerning borrowers, lenders and the conditions of poverty (Balleisen and Moss 2010; Hatton 2007; Lanzalaco 2009; Hall and Soskice 2001; Anderson 2008).[12] It also adds a new dimension to the literature concerning the tools that have been considered and implemented by parliament in its decades-long quest to protect borrowers without unduly restricting market activity. In other words, which market features were policymakers most concerned with, and what were their proposed solutions.

Historians have examined working-class credit from a variety of perspectives. Shop credit, cheque traders, tallymen, hire-purchase friendly societies and other savings institutions are familiar ground for economic and financial historians (Johnson 1985, 1993; O'Connell 2009; Rubin 1986; Horne 1947; Scott 2003). This study focuses on pawnbrokers and unsecured moneylenders. These businesses provide small sums with no expectation as to how the money is spent. Shop credit, tallymen, cheque traders and hire purchase can be understood as purchase-money-credit, that is, credit issued as deferment of payment for the acquisition of goods. Shop credit was extended to regular customers and was limited to the goods of that shop. Credit advanced by cheque traders was limited to goods found in shops that accepted their cheques. These and other lenders limited and controlled the use of loan proceeds. Pawnbrokers, unsecured moneylenders and later payday lenders issue non-purchase-money-credit, that is, a straight loan of money without restriction. Unlike other high-cost credit providers, pawnbrokers and moneylenders deal in cash loans that in one way or another found their way back into the economy at the borrower's discretion. In 1870, Benjamin Blackwood, a Bradford pawnbroker, recounted that, 'I have a neighbour, a grocer, who tells me that the principal part of the money which he takes on a Monday comes from my shop … he has opened another shop about a mile away, and wishes I would open a branch shop there …'.[13] The demand for cash and the channels through which small values of it were supplied focuses this work and delineates it from the existing scholarship.

Decades have passed since Tebbutt's carefully researched account of British pawnbroking (Tebbutt 1983). O'Connell's investigation into working-class credit is broader than this work and ends before the 2007 Global Financial Crises reinvigorated fringe banking (O'Connell 2009). While the first few chapters of this book build on their contribution,

Table 1.1 Regulatory episodes

Regulation	*Key feature(s)*
The Pawnbrokers Act 1872	Raised the price ceiling on PB loans
The Moneylenders Act 1900	No price controls; guidance rate rejected; ML registry
The Moneylenders Act 1927	No price controls; guidance rate implemented; advertising restricted; ML licensing system
The Consumer Credit Act 1974	No price controls; advertising restrictions lifted; guidance rate removed; ML & PB legitimised
The Consumer Credit Act 2006	Licensing segmented by risk category; payday lenders targeted
FCA price controls 2015	Three-part price control on payday lenders

Note ML = Moneylender; PB = Pawnbroker

neither answers how policymakers have tamed the rough edges of small-time capitalism only to see the industry roar back to life. This is a battle that started with Henry VIII's 1546 capping of pawnbroker pledged-back credit and intensified as wage labour became dependent on unsecured cash loans from moneylenders in the late 1800 s. As Chapter 5 recounts, payday lenders picked up where moneylenders left off and by doing so they tested parliament's willingness to limit the everyday financial transactions of the lower working-classes that form the bulk of the small-loan market.

Table 1.1 shows the episodes explored by this work. Starting with the Pawnbroking Select Committee 1870 and ending with recent regulation implementation by the FCA reveals a consistent pattern of key issues, debates, concerns and policy tools meant to level the playing field between borrowers and lenders. Five main areas of concern surfaced: the high cost of loans, advertising, the use of an APR, the legitimacy of small-value lenders in the financial system and regulatory enforcement. In each period, policymakers debated three main policy responses: price controls, information disclosure and licensing.

The consistency of the concerns reveals much about why protection was sought in the first place and the conditions under which certain policies were enacted and others discarded. The objective is not to analyse regulatory theory, the history of usury or the legislative procedures by which the laws were enacted, but to use the episodes as inflection points to examine how concerns over poverty and capitalism have informed policy and the evolution of the small-loan market (Geisst 2013, 2017).

Origins and Themes

This book's origin lies in a simple question: Why did the FCA implement price controls on payday loans in 2015? If British payday lending began in the early 1990s, what prompted the government to implement a two-tiered price of money, one for the poorer classes in need of cash and another for everyone else. Why wait over twenty-five years before enacting such strict regulation, had the industry or the lives of the poor markedly changed? From the lending perspective, the answer is no—while loan volumes increased, not much had changed operationally when compared to the 1990s. A long-term perspective provides a more definitive answer, payday lending differs little from the legal moneylending industry which traces its roots to the passage of the 1900 Moneylenders Act. The loan product is essentially the same, namely, unsecured, small-value cash loans issued on the borrower's ability to repay from future wages. These loans are not attached to purchasing any particular good or service. These lenders offer quick cash at convenient hours designed for people living on inadequate and unpredictable income.

Chapter 5 of this book shows that enough similarities exist between money and payday lending that policy debates date not to the 1990s, but to the 1890s. Since pawnbrokers were the leading provider of small sums at that time, policymakers crafting Britain's first moneylending law used pawn regulation as a starting point, which in turn, guides this book's beginnings. Pawnbroking reigned over the small-loan market at the turn of the twentieth century, while payday lenders earn the twenty-first-century high-cost crown. The controversies surrounding these products varied little overtime and throughout one finds passionate, if not crusading, policymakers bent on improving the lives of vulnerable borrowers.

The many attempts at doing so reveal the difficulty of safeguarding the needs of people who have experienced financial trouble before seeking a loan. Often, the root cause of financial distress occurs irrespective of any credit product. Low-income households regularly balance competing financial priorities such as utility bills, medical expenses and basic household expenses. Living on low and varying income is difficult, small-value loans are just one of the tools engaged to make it through the monthly financial cycle. Demonizing 1700% interest rates is easier than understanding the expense and difficulties involved in lending to high-risk borrowers. Even if well deserved, condemning a loan product is far easier than addressing the underlying conditions of financial insecurity experienced by so many British citizens.

The assumption that high interest rates generate high profits is incorrect. The data shows that pawnbrokers and money-payday lenders are not always and everywhere an extremely profitably industry. Financial results depend on the economy and the expertise of any given business or enterprise. High interest rates draw attention onto the small-loan market. Since cost is the main issue, why not cap it? In the world of credits, debts and profits, price controls are the nuclear option. Literally, the government picks a price point past which it considers the cost of money harmful. After more than a century of considering price caps too harsh a measure, in 2015, the government implemented price caps on unsecured small loans. The question is: why did the government reverse its policy.

Taming the Fringe recounts the nitty-gritty of the policy debates and market's evolution revealing several themes of historical significance. This method provides insights to whether decision makers believed small loans 'made poverty worse', how they understood the ability of borrowers to manage their financial affairs, and whether small-loan lenders were considered predatory or a necessary, albeit regrettable, component of the economic system. Readers are introduced to how issues such as freedom of contract, perceptions of borrower rationality, bargaining inequity, market segmentation and credit rationing influenced the six episodes under consideration. Chronicling small-loan policy demonstrates the market's evolution in response to how the government intended to influence lending decisions, borrower outcomes and the conditions of poverty.

Three broad themes are found in the development of small-loan policy and consequent market outcomes. Two of the themes, that is, the appropriate role of the government within a market economy and poverty debates are nothing new. However, analysing how varying perspectives impacted small loans adds to this rich literature. Pawnbrokers in the late 1800 s navigated an environment both fearful of, and concerned over, poverty-stricken borrowers (Himmelfarb 1984; Stedman Jones 2004, 2013). In 1870, Archibald Orr-Ewing MP (Conservative) led an eradication campaign of the small-loan evil. For him, pawn loans drove the 'degenerate' poor towards destitution and government welfare. Hard work and upright living, it was argued, propelled one towards the vibrant middle classes, while small loans provided fuel for the immoral passions of lazy men. 'Clever' pawnbrokers knowingly took advantage of an entire class of people without enough reason or control to protect themselves, or so the story went. Those with a more intimate knowledge of the lives of poor countered those attacks. Charity workers and some law enforcement suggested that the poor managed their finances remarkably well considering unpredictable and insufficient income. For them, market competition free from a paternalistic state afforded far better protection than punitive legislation.

The mostly unexplored story in the 1870s reform is the role pawnbrokers played during the policy formation process. Even by today's standards, pawnbrokers formed an impressive lobbying network. The archives detail their priorities and how pawnbrokers settled differences amongst themselves before seeking an adjustment to the existing regulation. Their organizational prowess leaves a trail of details allowing for a long-term comparison of loan volumes, revenues, expenses and redemption rates between the Victorian era through to today. Parliament never settled whether poverty was self-inflicted or resulted from the structural features of the urban economy, nor did they conclude whether small loans worsened the conditions of poverty. Better to allow the industry some profit than to upset the delicate balance of the lives of poor in either direction—freely competitive markets or more authoritarian regulation. The 1870s Parliament concluded that pawnbrokers served a needed function for people with few other options.

Taming the Fringe offers evidence that the small-loan market development cannot be understood as a confrontation between lenders and regulators. This third theme explores how policymakers viewed the place of small lenders within the financial system and the intimately bound question of whether borrowers were equipped to tangle with them on equal footing. Pawnbrokers and money-payday lenders viewed a degree of regulation as a step towards legitimacy, and as an avenue for joining the ranks of 'proper' banks and financiers (Saleuddin 2018). Few shared these goals, and for the most part these lenders find no home in the financial hierarchy. The lenders' narrative concerning how their business works, how much they profit, and why borrowers frequent their shops has not changed much since the late 1800 s. Few people then or now listen to what they have to say. Even accountancy certified financial statements are viewed suspiciously. Perceptions matter, and high annual interest rates along with aggressive advertisements invite hostility against the industry.

In 1900 and again in the 1920 s, as loan volumes increased and advertising blanketed newspapers and letterboxes, concerns over moneylending led to parliamentary enquiries. Few questioned the government's ability to improve the economic and social conditions on behalf of the people (Taylor 2005; Fraser 2009; Dorey 2011; Ball 2013). Chapter 3 finds a relatively unorganized moneylending trade facing an 1897 Select Committee bent on fencing in what was then an unregulated credit product. Few doubted the 'miserable ruin and terrible evils brought upon tens of thousands of innocent and easily deluded men and women in Great Britain by the heartless of usurious moneylenders'.[14] Many policymakers wondered if these loans provided any good whatsoever. Protecting hapless borrowers meant considering a full spectrum of controls including advertising restrictions, licensing requirements and price caps.

Chapter 3 examines those issues, all of which were considered in pursuit of fairness through state intervention in the economy. An obvious, but not so easily obtained requirement of regulating the fringe, is defining what, exactly, constitutes it in the first place. How do moneylenders differ from banks? Both lend money. Should interest rates or the type of borrower define the industry? Regulating the industry without defined boundaries is an impossible task. At the centre is a wider question concerning the appropriate place of small-value lenders within the financial system. Examining the period from the late 1890 s to the 1920 s provides a starting point of policymakers' attempt to define and segment 'right' from 'wrong' finance, a process later manifest in twenty-first century attempts at constructing a more inclusive financial system. More immediately, Parliament's failure to ringfence moneylenders in the 1927 Act generated a host of problems that came to breaking point in the late 1960s.

By the mid-twentieth century accessing consumer credit was an important component of the British economy. Outdated and restrictive regulation hindered a growing and increasingly complex credit system. None more so than the 1927 Moneylenders Act. The rise of nonbank financing left many companies unsure whether they needed a licence under the 1927 Act. Operating without a licence meant these lenders had no legal recourse to seek funds from defaulting debtors. Serious amounts of money were at risk. Not only did these companies have nothing at all to do with small loans, the punitive nature of the existing regulation hampered the efficient allocation of credit throughout the economy.

The Consumer Credit Act 1974 sought competitive markets, assumed capable borrowers and appreciated that access to credit benefitted society and improved standards of living. While past regulation attempted to restrict credit access, the 1970 s ushered in regulation seeking increased market efficiency. Chapters 4 and 5 find that it is unlikely that the fringe sector would have been as well capitalized or grown as quickly during the decades that followed without the 1974 framework. Policymakers spent a considerable amount of time researching small loans. Many hoped that competition-enhancing regulation would bring down costs and encourage product innovation across the entire spectrum of consumer credit. In a best-case scenario, traditional banks would dip into the low-end of the market and compete moneylenders and pawnbrokers out of existence. Chapters 5 shows that they were half right. Fringe banking became highly competitive, with providers offering all sorts of products under a one-stop-shop model. Borrowers had more options than ever, yet costs remained prohibitive when compared to products issued by credit unions, community development financial institutions and high street banks. Chapter 6 explores why other financial institutions have failed to drive high-cost credit providers from the market. Lending small sums is risky and expensive. Like them or not, their products meet the unique needs of poor borrowers in a way that other institutions cannot service profitably or sustainably.

Do small loans make poverty worse? Can borrowers protect themselves without help from the state? Should the government curtail market operations? By 2015, the answers were clear: payday loans made poverty worse, many borrowers suffer from poverty through no fault of their own and loan volumes should be far smaller than what was tolerated in the past. The market's tremendous growth and the government's interest in constructing an inclusive financial system paved the way for strict regulation. Connecting how Britain's financial inclusion agenda tipped the scales towards severe regulation is a major contribution of this book and fills a missing component in the consumer credit literature.

Financial inclusion coupled with the aspirant goal of economic social justice encouraged, if not enabled, the current hard-line approach towards small-value loans. The impact of financial inclusion and economic social justice are all the more apparent considering that even with gigabytes of data and elaborate financial modelling, the FCA admitted that it does not know whether high-cost small loans harm borrowers. The FCA is not alone. Reams of research offer conflicting evidence as to the impact of small loans on borrowers. As has been the case for centuries, small-loan policy is driven by 'feel'—as in, the cost of small loans 'feels high'.

For centuries, private lenders have fulfilled a market need and priced their loans according to the risks involved. Fringe providers have played an essential, albeit high-cost role, in the daily life of the poor and vulnerable. In response, small-loan policy balances concern over poverty and a primarily market-based system of capital allocation. The fact is financial regulation does not lessen the demands for funds. Unless policy addresses the underlying reasons why people need small loans in the first place, high-cost credit providers will continue responding to the unique demands of high-risk borrowers including convenient operating hours, predictable loan approvals and quick access to loan proceeds. This makes understanding the long-run development of this industry all the more important, as it is unlikely to disappear anytime soon. Instincts aimed at protecting the poor from small loans are understandable. Avoiding the regularly applied rhetoric of lenders as evil, bloodsucking, cancerous predators facilitates an historical objectivity that better informs future policy. While what happens next will differ from the past, future reformers will likely believe, as have their forbearers, they are but a few modifications away from creating a fair and just small-loan market (Fleming 2018). Though history demonstrates the difficulty in doing so, this should not deter the pursuit of so noble a goal.

Notes

1. Pawnbroker Select Committee (PBSC) (1870, 720–721).
2. PBSC (1870, 3505).
3. "Tackling Financial Exclusion: A Country that Works for Everyone?" House of Lords (HL) Select Committee on Financial Exclusion Report of 2016–2017 Session, HL Paper 132, 25 March 2017; "The Financial Lives of Consumers Across the UK," Financial Conduct Authority, 20 June 2018, updated January 2020.
4. House of Commons Debate (HC deb.), 3 February 2011, vol. 522.
5. "Payday Loans Campaign," Citizens Advice Bureau, 2014.
6. HL debate, 28 November 2012, vol. 741.
7. As of 12 December 2015, www.thenpa.com; "Pawnbroking Customers in 2010," A report for the National Pawnbrokers Association prepared by the Personal Finance Research Centre, University of Bristol (2010), 7.

8. PBSC (1870, 2165–2168, 2177).
9. Anne Fleming finds similar dynamics in the history and development of fringe finance in the United States and especially in the State of New York, see *City of Debtors* (2018).
10. This is a similar approach to Grossman (2010). As detailed in Chapter 5, Victorian-era unsecured, small-sum moneylending morphs into modern payday lending. This work covers pawnbrokers, moneylending and payday lending.
11. Unknown to either of us at the time, Anne Fleming and this author pursued similar lines of research concerning small loans, albeit in two different national markets. Anne and I intended to collaborate on a project comparing the British and American markets. Unfortunately, Anne passed away unexpectedly in September 2020. Her intellect and scholarly achievements were surpassed only by her kindness and consideration.
12. This research defines policymakers in a general way without recourse to political or regulatory theory to include politicians, the judiciary, government agencies, law enforcement, business interests, think-tanks, academics and charitable entities that have influenced the regulatory process.
13. PBSC (1870, 393–406, 1807).
14. "Money lending: How to Deal with Usurers," *Melbourne Punch*, 25 August 1898.

Bibliography

Archives

Official Publications.

The Consumer Credit Act 1974, c. 39.
The House of Lords Debate Sessions.
The Pawnbrokers Select Committee 1870 (377).
The Pawnbrokers Select Committee 1872 (288).
The Pawnbrokers Act 1872: 35 & 36 Vic. c. 93.
The Moneylenders Act 1900: 63 & 64 Vic. c. 51.
The Moneylenders Act 1927: 17 & 18 Geo. 5 c. 21.

Sources

Alborn, Timothy. 1998. *Conceiving Companies: Joint Stock Politics in Victorian England*. New York: Routledge.

Anderson, Elisabeth. 2008. Experts, Ideas and Policy Change: The Russell Sage Foundation and Small Loan Reform, 1909–1941. *Theory and Society* 37 (3): 271–310.

Ball, Stuart. 2013. *Portrait of a Party: The Conservative Party in Britain 1918–1945*. Oxford: Oxford University Press.

Balleisen, Edward, and David Moss. 2010. Introduction. In *Government and Markets: Toward a New Theory of Regulation*, ed. Edward Balleisen and David Moss, 1–10. New York: Cambridge University Press.

Boggan, Steve. 2016. "Pawn Again." *Guardian*, 20 October.

Daunton, Martin. 2008. *State and Market in Victorian Britain: War, Welfare and Capitalism*. Woodbridge: Boydell Press.

Dorey, Peter. 2011. *British Conservatism: The Politics and Philosophy of Inequality*. London: IB Tauris.

Fleming, Anne. 2018. *City of Debtors: A Century of Fringe Finance*. Harvard, MA: Harvard University Press.

Finn, Margot. 2003. *The Character of Credit: Personal Debt in English Culture, 1740–1914*. Cambridge: Cambridge University Press.

Fraser, Derek. 2009. *The Evolution of the British Welfare State: A History of Social Policy Since the Industrial Revolution*. London: Palgrave Macmillan.

———. 2013. *Outcast London: A Study in the Relationship Between Classes in Victorian Society*. London: Verso.

Geisst, Charles. 2013. *Beggar Thy Neighbour: A History of Usury and Debt*. Philadelphia: University of Pennsylvania Press.

———. 2017. *Loan Sharks: The Birth of Predatory Lending*. Washington, DC: Brookings Institute Press.

Goff, Sharlene. 2014. "Tougher UK Rules Drive Payday Lenders Away." *Financial Times*, 20 May.

Grossman, Richard. 2010. *Unsettled Account: The Evolution of Banking in the Industrialized World Since 1800*. Princeton, NJ: Princeton University Press.

Hall, Peter, and David Soskice. 2001. Introduction. In *Varieties of Capitalism: The Institutional Foundations of Comparative Advantage*, ed. Peter Hall and David Soskice, 1–68. Oxford: Oxford University Press.

Hatton, Thomas. 2007. *The New Comparative Economic History: Essays in Honor of Jeffrey G. Williamson*. Cambridge, MA: MIT Press.

Himmelfarb, Gertrude. 1984. *The Idea of Poverty: England in the Early Industrial Age*. London: Faber.

Horne, Oliver. 1947. *A History of Savings Banks*. London: Oxford University Press.

Johnson, Paul. 1985. *Saving and Spending: The Working-Class Economy in Britain 1870–1939*. Oxford: Clarendon Press.

Johnson, Paul. 1993. "Small-Debt and Economic Distress in England and Wales, 1857–1913." *The Economic History Review* 46 (1): 65–87.

Lanzalaco, Luca. 2009. Business Interest Associations. In *The Oxford Handbook of Business History*, ed. Geoffrey Jones and Jonathan Zeitlin, 293–318. Oxford: Oxford University Press.

Merrill, Jamie. 2014. "Church of England to Open Credit Union in Its 'War' on Wonga." *Independent*, 20 June.

"Money lending: How to Deal with Usurers." 1898. *Melbourne Punch*, 25 August.

O'Connell, Sean. 2009. *Credit and Community: Working-Class Debt in the UK since 1880*. Oxford: Oxford University Press.

Osborne, Hillary. 2014 "Payday Lenders May Vanish Within Year as Result of Price Cap, Says Economist." *Guardian*, 10 November.

"Payday Loans Campaign." 2014. Citizens Advice Bureau.

Rubin, Gerry. 1986. From Packman, Tallymen, and 'Preambulating Scotchmen' to Credit Drapers' Association, 1840–1914. *Business History Review* 28 (9): 206–233.

Saleuddin, Rasheed. 2018. *The Government of Markets: How Interwar Collaborations Between the CBOT and the State Created Modern Futures Trading*. New York: Palgrave Macmillan.

Scott, Peter. 2003. The Twilight World of Interwar British Hire Purchase. *Economic History Review* 56 (2): 195–225.

Stedman Jones, Gareth. 2004. *An End to Poverty: A Historical Debate*. London: Profile Books.

Taylor, Andrew. 2005. Stanley Baldwin, Heresthetics and the Realignment of British Politics. *British Journal of Political Sciences* 35 (3): 429–463.

Tebbutt, Melanie. 1983. *Making Ends Meet: Pawnbroking & Working-Class Credit*. Leicester: Leicester University Press.

Watt, Nicolas. 2012. "Payday Loan Firms Face Cap After Government U-turn." *Guardian*, 28 November.

Warren, Rachel. 1988. "Uncle Breaks Loose: Pawnbrokers; Family Money." *The Times*, 24 September.

CHAPTER 2

Victorian Pawnbrokers: Cancerous Worms of Ruin or the Poor Man's Banker?

> I think it would be a most desirable thing to have a law even to prevent people from making themselves and their children so poor and miserable as they are at present
>
> William Miller, Magistrate of the City of Glasgow[1]

> The poor are able to detect for themselves very well they are very intelligent with regard to the amount which they have to pay
>
> Sir Thomas Henry, Chief Magistrate of the Metropolitan Police Courts[2]

Mrs Vincent's anxious demeanour suggested that something was seriously amiss.[3] And indeed there was—her dying husband needed food and medicine. In desperate need of cash, she pawned a family heirloom. Mrs Vincent's was just one of the hundreds of millions of pawns that year. Families like hers had few cash savings from which to draw or access to the banking system. Some needed money for emergencies, while others borrowed on a weekly basis—a pawn ritual by which bills were paid, and food was placed on the table. It was all rather elementary; poor people needed cash and in the 1870s pawnbrokers were one of the few financial institutions willing to lend. It would be mistaken, however, to assume that it was without controversy.

© The Author(s), under exclusive license to Springer Nature Switzerland AG 2021

C. McMahon, *Taming the Fringe*, Palgrave Studies in the History of Finance, https://doi.org/10.1007/978-3-030-70615-9_2

In the latter half of the nineteenth century pawnbroking was a massive industry, issuing over 250 million loans a year to the urban poor. Busy city pawnbrokers contracted over 5000 times a week.[4] Despite high loan volumes pawnbrokers were struggling to make a profit because the amount they could charge was restricted by the Pawnbroker Act 1800 (PBA 1800). In other words, revenue was capped, but expenses were not. For pawnbrokers it was simple: costs in the 1870s were higher than costs in the 1800s. Beginning in the late 1860s, Pawnbrokers lobbied Parliament for increased interest rates and fewer restrictions. Engaging parliament was a risky strategy. Much of the public held the industry in low regard, and many policymakers felt duty-bound to protect the poor from predatory lending.

This chapter analyses the business of Victorian pawnbroking and the driving forces behind regulatory reform. It details the in-and-outs of how the pawn market functioned under the PBA 1800, the process through which the pawnbroking lobby developed its reform strategy and examines the conflicting viewpoints of whether pawn loans helped or harmed borrowers. Notwithstanding the tale of Mrs Vincent and her ill husband, for the most part it avoids framing the industry in such personalized terms. It does so for two reasons. First, Melanie Tebbutt's *Making Ends Meet* masterfully recounts the social and cultural history of Victorian pawnbroking. She provides a far more intimate historical account than offered here. This chapter focuses on what we know about the business on a more aggregated level and asks why and through what methods policymakers attempted to tame it. It relies heavily on trade association documents, providing a relatively unexplored perspective of the lenders themselves and their policy goals. Second, the back-and-forth debates and the financial details offer a baseline of comparison for later periods concerning business operations and policy formation related to price controls, how lenders and borrowers were understood by policymakers, disclosure terms, and the like. Analysing and categorizing the main issues of contention and how those concerns interacted with the formation of policy is one of the major contributions of this chapter and its main differentiator from the existing literature.

Lenders, borrowers and policymakers found themselves balancing the various, if not competing, priorities concerning small-time capitalism and financial regulation. Some viewed small-loan providers as 'bloodsuckers and canker-worms of ruin' whose harmful loans trapped the poor in a debt spiral and encouraged crime, drinking and gambling. They argued that most poverty resulted from a lack of individual responsibility, and immoral and lazy behaviours. Pawnbrokers cash loans drove the undeserving masses into a debt spiral of destitution and government welfare threatening the very core of Victorian self-help ideology (Tebbutt 1983; Himmelfarb 1984; Stedman Jones 2013). Whether driven by guilt or fear of the urban masses, small loans made poverty worse and many believed the state should curtail, if not abolish, 'evil' pawnbroking.

Alternatively, low wages and labour market instability created an economic situation where cash was desperately needed. This was not a question of morality, but one where reasonable people managed unpredictable budgets and low incomes, often ranging from 18 s.0d to 21 s.0d a week (Tebbutt 1983, 11; Rowntree 1901; Reeves 1914). For their part, pawnbrokers wanted to be considered respectable businessmen, and like other credit issuers, operate free of burdensome regulation and price restrictions. They and others argued that ample and unfettered competition provided far more borrower protection than an Act of Parliament.

Neither the 'total abolish' nor 'complete free-trade' camps won the day. The everyday realities of the urban economy influenced the Pawnbrokers Act 1870 (PBA 1870) more than moral rhetoric or laissez-faire ideology. Millions of people needed cash for everyday expenses and turned to pawnbrokers for small loans. The data shows that even with high loan volumes, most pawnbrokers struggled to earn a profit under the PBA 1800 and its seventy plus year-old price controls. For all of the talk of crime and punishment, and while certainly there were a few sinners mixed among the saints, most pawnbrokers conducted their business honestly.[5] These highly organized and well-networked small-business owners were well-positioned to lobby parliament in achieving their goal of more favourable regulation. In the end, whether they liked the industry or not, Parliamentarians of all stripes recognized that the poor had few other borrowing options. Since lawmakers were not at all interested in dealing with the root causes of poverty, or in offering an alternative lending source, they raised the legal price limit on loans and eased certain regulatory burdens to help ensure a viable and profitable pawnbroking market.

A Regulated Trade Under Distress

British pawnbroking regulations originated in the thirteenth century and by the nineteenth century had evolved into a strict framework of processes, procedures and price controls. The millions of pawn tickets issued reveal the operations of thousands of pawnbrokers, who collectively provided credit on a massive scale. From regulated pawn tickets and accountancy books, a paper trail can be followed detailing the operations and financial landscape of these small business owners who lent cash on low-value collateral. This section explains how the pawn market operated up to the 1870s, demonstrating how the highly organized and sophisticated pawnbroker network approached parliament with a unified and coherent reform message.

Pawning is a simple transaction, whereby moveable personal property is given as collateral for a loan.[6] Pawning does not require a credit application, nor does it question why the borrower wants funds. After appraisal, the pawnbroker offers a loan, to be repaid in a single sum on redemption of the collateral. The transaction is for money lent and is not payment for the transfer of property. The pledger retains ownership of the collateral. If an agreement is reached, a pawn ticket is issued and the good is stored on the pawnbroker's premises. The contract is an agreement to pay a ticket fee and repay the principal and interest. The interest is calculated from the day of the pledge until the day of redemption. If the loan went unpaid, the good was forfeited.[7] In 1870, the *Pawnbrokers Gazette* (PBG) suggested that 'the object of the borrower is not to get what he wants in the cheapest market, but to get the largest loan with the least trouble. The lender's interest is also to get as much capital out as he can … so long as he is assured of its redemption'.[8] This contradicted the widespread belief that pawnbrokers sought possession of borrowers' goods in order to sell them on. Though certainly sales of new and used goods were common and supported the ebbs and flows of the pledged goods, first and foremost, pawnbrokers viewed themselves as lenders (Tebbutt 1983, 134). They considered ticket fees as compensation for appraisal, administrative and labour costs, while interest charges related to the loan itself. Pawnbrokers incurred considerable operating expenses in addition to risk of loan default.

A pawn transaction occurred with impressive speed. In 1870, transaction times averaged two minutes to pledge and between thirty seconds and two minutes for redemption.[9] These quick cash loans were in high demand. Estimates from the Royal Statistical Society indicated that, in 1851, the ratio of pawnbroking licences to 100,000 of the population was 8.9. By 1871, this had increased to 13.2, with approximately 3450 pawnbroking establishments operating in England, Scotland and Wales.[10] The rise of casual urban employment with its irregular wage cycle coupled with low incomes coincided with the industry's growth (Tebbutt 1983, 13). Throughout the 1860s and 1870s, licensed pawnbrokers received approximately eight pledges for every person in Britain.

Urban density provided the potential loan volumes necessary for a business characterized by high fixed-costs and low-margins. Approximately 85% of pawnshops were found in city and borough boundaries.[11] Fig. 2.1 shows that pawnbrokers were concentrated in the industrial North and the Midlands, as well as in Middlesex (London).[12]

Most of these pawnbrokers lent very small sums to the urban poor and working class. The majority of pawn loans were for less than 10 shillings and in many areas the average loan was half that. The trade was customarily divided into three segments: the low trade of 5 shillings and less, the medium trade of 5 to 10 shillings and the high end 10 shillings and more. The majority of pledges were in the low and medium trade. In 1870, John May, a Salford pawnbroker, estimated that 80–90% of his 76,603 loans issued in 1867–1868 were for less than 10 shillings, with an average pledge of 4s 3d.[13] In 1869, Liverpool pawnbrokers received an estimated 9,088,000 pledges, 49.5% of which were less than or equal to 2 shillings, and 99.4% were for less than 42 shillings.[14] The average pledge in Liverpool in 1869 was 4s 11/2d, placing that city's average in the low range of the trade.[15] William Hector, a public prosecutor in Renfrewshire, estimated that 50% of the families in his district engaged in 100 pledge transactions annually.[16] George Gillman, a London City Missionary charity worker, concurred with Hector, estimating that 50% of his working-class constituency in Peckham frequented pawnbrokers with an average loan size of 5 shillings.[17] Table 2.1 shows that larger cities dominated what was primarily a small-value credit model. Considering that by the early 1870s, the population of Greater London approached 4 million, 30 million loans was quite significant.

Most of these transactions occurred in a regular weekly pledge cycle coinciding with the day wages were paid (Tebbutt 1983, 6–7). Seasonal trends meant heavier volumes in the summer and autumn months when pledgers could more readily turn unneeded winter items into hard cash. Table 2.2 represents a typical London shop, Saturday being the

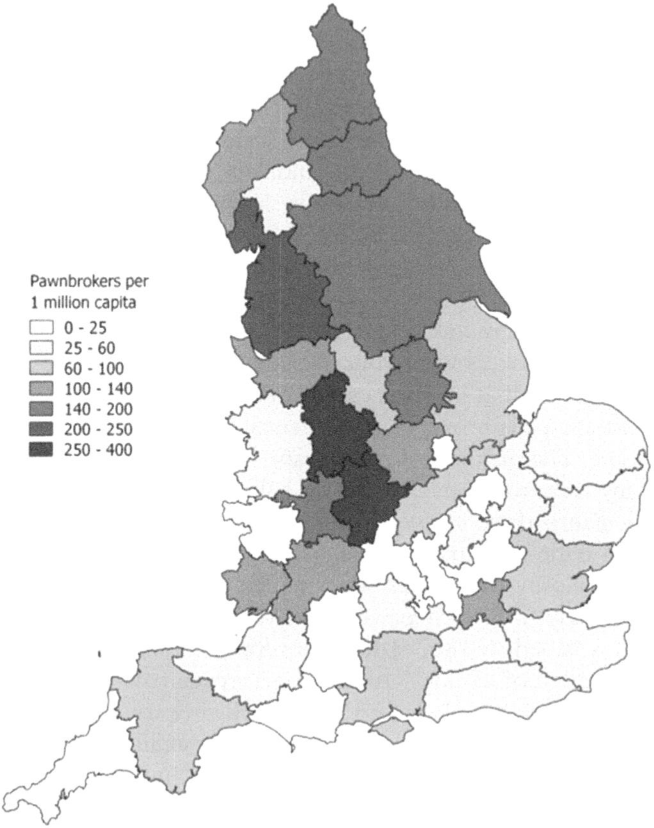

Fig. 2.1 Pawnbrokers per one million capita 1909 (*Source* HC, Local Taxation Licences, 1909 [London: HMSO])

busiest redemption day and Monday the highest volume of pledging. By the week's end, the shop's owner, John Dicker, had advanced £522, redeemed £582, collected £36 in interest and £6 in ticket fees. From a revenue standpoint, he earned only £42 in interest and fees. Pawnbrokers argued that price controls failed to provide sufficient remuneration to cover the expenses associated with the high-volume, low-value, weekly pledge cycle.

Table 2.1 Estimated annual pledges by location, 1870s

Location	*Est. annual pledges*	*Business type*
London	30,000,000	–
Liverpool	9,088,000	50% less than 2s
Glasgow	6,690,000	90% less than 10s; avg. 4s.
Edinburgh	1,426,800	–
Pollokshaws	96,000	85% less than 10s
Salford	76,603	25% less than 2s
Exeter	36,000	–

Source PBSC 1870, 129, 934, 1215, 1252, 1851, 4863). Geographic boundaries determined by the Board of Inland Revenue Licensing Division

Table 2.2 John Dicker, transactions for the week ending 7 May 1870

	Pledges	*Pledges*
	out	**in**
Monday	249	725
Tuesday	163	482
Wednesday	134	437
Thursday	130	446
Friday	189	371
Saturday	1899	225
Total	2764	2686

Source PBSC 1870, Appendix 14

At the other end of the spectrum were loan defaults. Under the PBA 1800, a borrower had fifteen months (twelve months with three months' grace) to redeem pledged collateral. Following default, items with loan values of 10 shillings or less became the immediate property of the pawnbroker. As a protection against aggressive undervaluation forfeited items valued at 10 shillings and more were sold at public auction. If the sale value exceeded the amount due plus auction expenses, the surplus was returned to the borrower. Even though the data reveals otherwise, it was a matter of common repute that pawnbrokers earned significant profits from forfeited and auctioned goods. During the PBSC 1870, Robert Carter MP (Liberal) was stunned to find that George Attenborough, a London pawnbroker, lost £356 on twelve articles at auction. Attenborough replied, 'You must remember that a pawnbroker standing behind his counter has to advance money upon every description of article … between a flat iron and a diamond … and know its value … and the consequence is that he only gets a smattering of judgement … so that he very frequently loses his money'.[18] Explaining the complexities of how a one-minute transaction then tied up capital for fifteen months were lost on most observers.

While regulation limited interest rates and ticket fees, the amount lent on any one object was not limited—this resulted in fierce competition among pawn shops. For pawnbrokers' high loan advances brought both risk and reward. While higher advanced sums benefited pawnbrokers by increasing their capital turnover, inflated collateral value also meant higher losses in the case of default. Word spread quickly among the tightly bound networks of borrowers who would become well aware of a pawnbroker willing to lend even a shilling more on an overcoat, a wedding ring or a household good. An over-generous pawnbroker could lose considerable money if a resold forfeited good went for less than the principal lent. Owing to seasonality, and during economic downturns, pawnbrokers found it almost impossible to sell last year's stock during a year of unseasonable weather.[19] But if a pawnbroker offered too stingy an advance, the customer and their items took their business elsewhere.

Pawnbrokers earned revenue from ticket fees, interest on loans and from selling forfeited goods. These funds had to provide for all expenses incurred, including valuation, wages, employee board, rent, rates, duties, salary for services and a return on invested capital. The amount of interest earned was determined by how long a good was held in pawn. The pawnbroker had no control over when an item would be redeemed. An early redemption meant the accrued loan interest failed to cover the fixed and variable transaction costs. In the 1870s, this scenario was especially problematic for low pledges held in pawn for less than a month. Attenborough testified that, 'I lose by every pledge that goes out of my house, which is pledged for 5 shillings and under, which does not remain with me more than a month'.[20] John Telfer, a Whitechapel pawnbroker, suggested that if all his business was from the low end and retained pledges for less than a month, he would 'not realise three-quarters above the 2.5d it takes' in labour for a pledge.[21]

In a worst-case scenario, pawnbrokers risked a total financial loss if a good was counterfeit or stolen. Dealing with the counterfeit market was one of the most difficult aspects of pawnbroking at the time.[22] London and Manchester were known production centres for counterfeit goods. From there products were sent round the country for resale or pledging.[23] During a gathering of the Bouverie Society, a pawnbroking and dining club, pawnbrokers discussed the innovative ways criminals traded fraudulent goods.[24] Rampant fraud drove some less scrupulous pawnbrokers towards their own deceptive methods of ridding themselves of duffed goods (Tebbutt 1983, 88) Even so, the majority of pledgers operated within the boundaries of the law and most pawnbrokers avoided criminal elements as best they could. Pawnbrokers were far more likely to fall victim to crime than the other way around.

Fraud was not the only legal issue entangling pawnbrokers as an entire unlicensed and illegal pledge trade existed. Price caps kept pawnbrokers from taking items that they could not possibly profit from such as heavy goods requiring significant manual labour and bulky items that took up significant shop space. The government also dictated operating hours and prohibited trading on Sunday which forced some needy borrowers into the black market. These traders known as dolly-shops, leaving shops and, in Scotland, wee-pawns, provided quick cash on demand and operated well outside the restrictions placed on pawnbrokers.[25] Estimates suggest that unlicensed lenders charged twice as much as their legal counterparts (Johnson 1985, 186). By some accounts, there were more illegal lenders in London than there were licensed pawnbrokers (Hancock 1850). Though pawnbrokers readily assigned many of their ills to the lower caste of unlicensed lenders, the vibrant illegal market existed in large part because of the government's strict regulation and price caps. The policy question at hand was whether the legal protections provided were worth the trade-off of incentivizing an illegal trade.

By the late 1860s, the PBA 1800 was unfit for purpose. In addition to burdensome administrative procedures, price controls failed to reflect market conditions and supported unlicensed lending. The trade itself debated the best path towards parliamentary reform. The next section examines the conflicts and compromises that developed within the industry before parliament was approached to revise the PBA 1800.

Conflict, Compromise and the Case for Reform

Some sixty some odd years later, most pawnbrokers agreed that the economy had changed markedly since the enactment of the PBA 1800. Its price caps threatened the survival of the low-end weekly trade. Conflict centred on whether pawnbrokers should pursue a laissez-faire agenda or propose targeted reforms bringing with it a higher likelihood of getting through parliament. On the one hand, these small business owners understood themselves to be little different from other trades and saw no reason for burdensome regulation. On the other hand, pawnbrokers recognized that society held them in such low regard that proposing a free-trade agenda might scupper much-needed reform. The deliberations reveal much about their economic preferences and show the existence of a sophisticated national network of small-business owners willing to comprise to achieve a common end.

Pawnbrokers were an organized trade. Although a national association was not founded until 1892, large regional groups had successfully ushered previous legislation through parliament. While many outsiders held that pawnbrokers were unsophisticated 'back alley' businesses, readers of the PBG were kept well informed of economic, political and business trends. Domestic and foreign newspaper stories and articles in *The Economist* were reprinted alongside industry news. By the late 1860s, many pawnbrokers found the economic and political signals were clear—now was the time for reform.[26] They hoped that parliament would 'remove all trade restrictions which are proved to be … unnecessary … as usury laws have been repealed, and remuneration which was once thought excessive now scarcely draws attention' (Hardacker 1892, 119–120). Loosening the regulatory net fitted nicely into a narrative supporting the normalization of free trade after the repeal of the Usury Act in 1854.

Whatever the favourable headwinds, pawnbrokers suffered longstanding prejudice and were often associated with criminal and illicit activities.[27] They did the best they could keeping informed of their reputation, protecting it when necessary and enhancing it where possible. Networking with other industries occurred with some regularity. In 1869, the MPPS told the Goldsmith Company that large numbers of electroplated goods bearing imitation silver hallmarks were being produced. The Goldsmith Company, one of the Great Twelve Livery Companies of the City of London, agreed to prosecute the parties if they were arrested. The instrument manufacturer Messrs. Chappell & Co. wrote to the MPPS offering to certify any musical instrument bearing its name (Egginton 2016).[28] Improved public relations played a key role in building up the case for reform.

The question was how far to push for deregulation. A segment of the sector wanted 'pure free trade' with the ability to set loan prices and conduct business without government oversight.[29] Pawnbrokers were frustrated and insulted that their trade was exempted from the repeal of the Usury Act 1854. Lobbying for the ability to operate without a price cap was a tall order. Even Jeremy Bentham, the intellectual foundation behind the 1854 repeal, believed exempting pawnbrokers was a worthwhile consideration. In *Discourse upon Usury* letter VIII.6, he wrote, 'If there be a case in which the allowing of extraordinary interest is attended with more danger than another, it [pawnbroking] must be this'. Since collateral remained in their possession, Bentham saw no reason why pawnbroking rates should take advantage of the 'lowest poor'. Interestingly though, Bentham suggested that the government need not actually regulate pricing because competitive markets would keep prices from rising too high.

This, in fact, was and remains the inherent tension in the small-loan market: How best to protect the poor from high-cost credit: government regulation or competitive markets? Mr Heys, a Manchester pawnbroker, left no doubt as to his position:

> [I] am in favour of free trade and freedom of contract ... there exists no other the profits of which were fixed by Act of Parliament, and if all other trades were free to follow the natural laws of Commerce, why should the pawnbrokers be prevented from doing so too? As for protecting the working classes, they [are] well qualified to protect themselves.

For Heys and others the very idea of credit price restrictions was at odds with British values not to mention the unfairness that some commerce operated under regulation and others did not.[30] Competition, after all, best regulated all business behaviour and prices.[31] In this market, 'buyer and seller having opposite interests stand face-to-face ... competition is considered to hold the balance between the two parties' and 'everything was up for negotiation'.[32] Justice dictated that nothing short of a complete removal of all regulation, licensing and restrictions sufficed.[33] Proponents believed this framework would drive out unsavoury operators and prevent prices from rising to unreasonable levels. Freeing pawnbrokers from regulation not only treated them on equal terms to other British business, but competitive market pricing offered the best form of borrower protection. For them and their poor borrowers the unfettered market was not the problem, but the solution.

Practical realities weighted heavily on their beliefs—having been regulated for centuries, there was almost no chance parliament would completely repeal the entire PBA 1800 (Weir 1952, 22). For all of the rhetoric, pawnbrokers, if nothing else, were practical. They needed another plan.[34] In what would become known as the 'Nottingham Sessions', fifty-six pawnbrokers delegated from twenty-three regional trade associations met in Nottingham on 23 April 1868 to draft a bill that would remedy the industry's ills without compromising borrower protection.[35] Victorian pawnbrokers grappled with the very same question that policymakers had for centuries before and after, at what point is the price of money excessive and dangerous for poor borrowers? Can fixed pricing provide both borrower protection and ample profits?

Delegates from Manchester and Liverpool presented two competing answers (Hardaker 1892, 123–125).[36] Manchester's proposal sought to remove all interest and ticket fee restrictions but kept a minimum forfeiture period. Since theirs was a somewhat radical departure from the 1800 legislation, they suggested lobbying for a parliamentary select committee of inquiry to present their case and garner support. Liverpool's competing plan offered a two-tiered fixed and flexible pricing scheme. Under this plan fixed pricing would be for the smallest loans of less than 40 shillings. As long as the fixed amount compensated pawnbrokers for their time, effort and cost of capital, many saw an advantage in not having to negotiate for every single common item that came through their doors. Above 40 shillings the pawnbroker had two options. Either he could enact an 'implied contract' and operate under the price cap or he could proceed under negotiated terms. This hybrid pricing scheme walked a fine line between offering protection for the lowest-end borrowers while leaving room for negotiations should both parties consent to a separate agreement.

The price-cap free Manchester proposal, by 31 to 25 votes, carried the day.[37] Almost immediately opponents from Liverpool, London, Sheffield and Nottingham questioned whether a majority of six was to 'be the means of bringing disaster upon upwards of the three thousand pawnbrokers in Great Britain' (Hardaker 1892, pp. 126–143). In an open letter received by thousands of pawnbrokers, the 'non-free-traders' believed it unlikely that parliament would release the trade from restrictive pricing leaving the reform effort in shambles.[38] Too much was on the line for the low-end weekly trade and even passionate free traders admitted that a combination of fixed and flexible pricing increased their chances of a new law. Practical realities had prevailed over the much-admired laissez-faire theory and a two-tiered pricing plan was agreed. Having settled their differences, 594 guarantors and 164 subscribers pledged in excess of £2200 in funding to create lobbying entity called the Pawnbroker Parliamentary Reform Association (PPRA) (Hardaker 1892, p. 144).[39] That Manchester pawnbrokers provided almost a quarter of the funding comes as no surprise as they were mostly a low-value pledge city and had long held that profits needed to be increased.[40]

Almost a year after its foundation, the PPRA circulated a complete draft bill seeking a higher interest rate, the ability to negotiate special contracts and a shorten forfeiture period to six from twelve months. In large part the draft reflected a combination of the original Manchester and Liverpool proposals from the Nottingham Session. On 11 February 1869, 161 pawnbrokers from forty-three towns and cities met in Derby to discuss the draft (Hardaker 1892, 152–156).[41] Delegates entertained six different options, five were rejected as too complicated requiring fractional calculations and for continuing the industry's reliance on farthings—a coinage which were increasingly difficult to obtain.[42] Balancing the practical realities of the business with the more abstract process of determining the appropriate price of a cash loan was no easy task. Since a busy pawnbroker transacted thousands of times weekly, simple pricing was vital for easy calculations and speedy service. The delegates settled on a point-to-point scale of charging a 1/2d for every 2 shillings lent under 42 shillings and 1/2d for every 2.6 shillings above 42 shillings. Both charges amounted to a 5% increase over the PBA 1800 rates. The rate was monthly, or any part of a month, excluding a period of grace. Table 2.3 illustrates the agreed Derby scale.

At the very least the details reveal the complexities of designing price controls—and breakpoints, scales and calculations are an expected part of the process. By definition, price controls require a cut-off point at which they will or will not be applied. Price caps demand a definitive judgement concerning the point at which the cost of money warrants a government response. After the haggling and discussion, whatever their previous disagreements, the trade rallied around what they viewed as a reasonable price scale and a bill that stood a good chance of passage in parliament.[43] Leaving nothing to chance, the PPRA lobbied the Home Office and individual MPs (Hardaker 1892, 168–178).[44] Finally, on 9 May 1870 seventeen MPs were nominated to sit on a government select committee of inquiry into the pawnbroking industry (Hardaker 1892,

Table 2.3 The Derby scale

Principal < 42s in shillings (s)			*Interest in dimes (d)*	*Principal 42s < £10 (in s.d)*			*Interest*
–	–	2	0.5	42	<	42.6	8.5d
2	<	4	1	42.6	<	45	9d
4	<	6	1.5	45	<	47.6	9.5d
6	<	8	2	47.6	<	50	10d
...		...	...	...		...	...
36	<	38	9.5	90	<	92.6	1s 6.5d
38	<	40	10	92.6	<	95	1s 7d
40	<	42	10.5	95	<	97.6	1s 7.5d
42	–	–	11	1/2d monthly for every 2s 6d < £10			

Source PPRA, 2–3 July 1868; PBG, 15 March 1869

179–189).[45] After two years of compromise pawnbrokers won a small victory—parliament had finally taken up their cause.

With the select committee appointed, the industry closed ranks, with the PBG urging its readers to refrain from criticizing the bill or the work of the PPRA going forward.[46] Pawnbrokers found a less co-operative and sceptical public.[47] An editorial from the *Daily Telegraph* claimed that the pawnbrokers' greed would lead them to the same 'evil example of Overend, Gurney and Company' a well-known bank whose ambitions led to financial disaster. The *Latest News* was more optimistic: 'Not long ago the public ignored prostitution ... but now, however unpleasant the topic may be, recognises it', and that even though pawnbroking is the 'evil of the day', it did benefit the poor.[48] The *Spectator* criticized the pawnbrokers for: 'In their distress ... like everybody else, turn[ing] to the House of Commons for relief'.[49] Even before the first witness testimony, the select committee news coverage converged around the appropriate role of regulation when financing the poor.

For Victorian pawnbrokers, competitive markets within an accommodative regulatory framework seemed a reasonable path forward. The detailed price tables, forfeiture rules, disclosure norms and the like show the complex and interrelated nuances that need consideration when regulating small-value collateralized loans. Even with all of the data and details, convincing parliament that theirs was not an especially profitable business often fell on deaf ears as many viewed them as financial predators.

Pushing Reform Through Parliament

Pawnbrokers had a sense of urgency as the Select Committee's findings would impact the business for decades to come. Given their vast network and paper trail, ample and reliable financial information could be found. According to one PPRA member, 'balance sheets were copied, books checked, and everything was put in order'.[50] The PPRA leadership considered it imprudent to have a pawnbroker testify without accurate financial statements. Pawnbrokers hoped that a data-driven process would, at worst, help them overcome negative attitudes to the industry. At best, if the public understood how they operated, the data could provide a much-desired entry way into the ranks of respectable lenders and businessmen.

This gets to the heart of the matter: were pawnbrokers 'proper' financial service providers or were they somehow different because of their poor clients. How one answers that question has influenced centuries of small-loan regulation.[51] During the PBSC 1870, strong, divergent and at times passionate views concerning the trade and its impact on the poor were voiced. Heated exchanges reveal that poverty, capitalism and financial regulation were on trial as much as the pawnbrokers and their small-value loans. A range of witnesses including pawnbrokers, magistrates, barristers, newspaper editors, high-ranking law enforcement officers, independent experts, auctioneers and charity workers recounted their experiences with small sum lending.

At one end of the spectrum were industry sympathizers who viewed pawnbrokers as no different from the banking industry as a whole. A Glasgow pawnbroker reversed the analogy and argued that 'bankers are but pawnbrokers on a larger scale ... I hold that the poor man in distress has as much right to borrow money on his watch, or coat, as the rich have to borrow on their lands, and very often a much better excuse for so doing'.[52] Often, that better excuse included borrowing for medical expenses, lodging and basic necessities relieving those suffering from illness or temporary unemployment.[53] Still, few policymakers considered pawnbrokers as 'real' bankers.[54] The critical feature was not so much that pawnbrokers lent money, but to whom they lent that money, and why the money was needed in the first place. However necessary a service, providing loans to the poor in desperate need of cash did not qualify one as a banker.

Archibald Orr-Ewing MP (Conservative) immediately went on the attack, seeking nothing short of totally eradicating the evil and immoral business.[55] He said, 'this system of pawnbroking for these small sums is a black spot upon our social system. It is degrading and demoralizing to the people who deal in it; it does not limit any suffering; it only increases those gross passions which we all wish to see improved' (Hardaker 1892, 264).[56] For him and others, economic failure resulted from irrational and immorality. Since cash loans prolonged, if not facilitated, such disastrous behaviour they made the conditions of the poor even worse.

The battle-lines were established early—pawnbrokers were either financiers providing loans to hard-working adults who found themselves in poverty through no fault of their own, or they preyed on the irrational and immoral poor, driving them into destitution. Supporters of loosening government regulation believed pawnbrokers were a private market solution to a demand for cash and kept people from seeking charity and relief under the Poor Law. Detractors sought to tighten the regulatory net. For such small amounts of cash, much was at stake. Severely restricting the market could lead to millions of people struggling for survival. Loosen the pricing system too far could line the pockets of these small-time capitalists at the expense of a vulnerable and poor population.

There was little dispute that the demand for small loans was driven by poverty. Only a poor family would need to borrow three or four shillings to make both ends meet. What mattered for policy was the source of that poverty. Whether the conditions of poverty were created by unstable labour markets and low wages or were the result of improvidence and irrational behaviour was debated. Those seeking to keep or enhance regulation saw pawn borrowers as 'the undeserving poor'. They argued, like indiscriminate charity, pawnbrokers contributed to the demoralization of the lower classes which burden the whole of British society. Correcting the poor's tendency towards harmful behaviour, and the loans that encouraged such harm, fell squarely within the government's purview. Supporters, however, believed freeing pawnbrokers from government regulation provided borrowers with far more protection than any law or act—history had demonstrated that competitive markets would keep reasonably priced credit flowing to those who need it most.

Debates centred on whether the working poor had the ability to negotiate freely in their best interest. A minority argued that pawnbrokers held an unfair advantage since the poor were in such desperate need of funds.[57] Regulation was meant to level the playing field. Another perspective demanded regulation but held that the working poor were intellectually inferior and morally improvident, harming themselves and burdening the entire nation as a result.[58] Hambro argued that pawning added fuel to the immoral fire of the urban masses.[59] For them, regulation could and should correct societally deviant behaviour, especially if economic outcomes were at stake.

Influential MPs and testifying witnesses such as Orr-Ewing, Hambro, Stubbs and Alexander McCall, the Chief Constable of Glasgow, believed poverty resulted from decaying morality, a lack of thrift, irrationality, drunkenness and crime. They closely associated extreme poverty or pauperism, with 'the irregularly employed and semi-criminal elements', which were distinguished from the 'authentic' and self-supporting working class (Englander 2013, 58). While many within the working class had improved their standard of living, paupers 'chose' not to (Stedman Jones 2013, 6–12). Regulation then was less geared to relieving the poor of their immediate needs, and more for reversing self-inflicted pauperism (Johnson 1985; Searle 1998; Bigelow 2003).

If friendly societies were an indication of the working class striving for the higher values and economic stability, the 'destructive' pawn system provided easy cash to the 'degenerate poor', allowing them to avoid honest and hard work (Fraser 2009, 130; Winstanley 1992, 8; Atiyah 1979, 509; Lee 1998, 163). Pawnbroking credit was considered as especially problematic since the acquired cash could be spent freely in a public house or gambled away. Industry antagonists considered Victorian pawnbrokers as no better than providers of indiscriminate charity, a phrase and idea introduced decades prior but made popular by social reformers such as Helen Bosanquet.

Under her leadership, the Charitable Organisation Society (COS), founded in 1869, strove to 'check the evils' of indiscriminate charity and the 'inculcation of habits of providence and self-dependence' among the poor. Bosanquet believed pawn loans encouraged the poor to forgo savings and indulge irresponsibly, saying, 'A very small want today looms large enough to obscure a great necessity in the future, and it is useless to point out how the price of a few pots of beer would pay the sick-club subscription' (Bosanquet 1896).[60] She was particularly critical of the weekly pawn cycle, calling it a 'pathetic absurdity'. This attitude to small loans fitted into the poverty—morality argument articulated, if not co-opted, by Orr-Ewing and the like during the PBSC.

Alcohol consumption doubly threatened these crusaders, as it ruined financial stability and morality (Lee 2004, pp. 166–177). McCall testified that one 'drunken wife' had pawned 'every article of furniture and every stitch of clothing' the family owned.[61] He believed that there were 'very few cases of provident well-behaved people' living in such destitution that they had to pledge low-value household goods.[62] Pawning low-value goods was evidence enough of improvidence.[63] Johnston suggested that even the poorest person owned articles worth more than 3 shillings.[64] This point failed to appreciate that the working poor pawned only what they could manage without. There was little reason to pawn the family's only frying pan to purchase food that required cooking or the father's tools if he is to work. However insignificant an item's value to the middle and upper classes, the household goods of lower income families were treated as assets to be held in pawn for cash when the need arose (Tebbutt 1983).

Harsh criticism was levelled at those who could work but opted not to. Able-bodied men that pawned regularly were especially irksome, as those were precisely the type of poor that should have no need for charity or cash loans. The 1834 Poor Law concept of 'less eligible' attempted to eliminate indiscriminate charity and replace it with a system of sanctions to encourage thrift and hard work (Stedman Jones 2013). Pawnbrokers afforded the working poor to avoid those sanctions creating a type of spiralling dependency, which in part is why they were dubbed evil and received such harsh criticism. Regulation was viewed as the only way to tame the child-like poor's improvident and irresponsible behaviour.[65]

Charity workers in London who mixed with the poor regularly challenged the very notion of linking economic outcomes with immoral behaviour.[66] James Parker, sixteen years a London City missionary, said those taking small loans were not intemperate, but were irregularly employed or 'under pressure from sickness'.[67] This and similar rebuttals shed light on the operations of the market with detailed testimony. From creative credit usage, to budget management skills, pawnbroker supporters invoked imagery of competent, intelligent and capable borrowers who managed their poverty remarkable well.[68] Their loans provided a much-needed service to borrowers fully capable of managing their affairs.[69]

Orr-Ewing remained unimpressed, asking John May, a pawnbroker: 'Do you think that the poor people who come to you and pledge their articles for small sums ... are in a ... position to deal with the clever men in your profession?' Absolutely he did, and not only that, but some of the 'sharpest bargains' were to be found among working people.[70] Pawnbroking challenged Orr-Ewing's narrowly defined understanding of rationality, and even more so any deviation therefrom was considered grounds for corrective action, without which the immoral poor would never recover, much less obtain entry into the middle class (Stedman Jones 2004, 26; 2013, 268).[71]

Arguing for the opposite position, in 1867 the *Manchester Examiner and Times* suggested that 'commercial depression' affected even the 'best workers' and that pawnbroker loans enabled them to maintain their independence and equalize their wages.[72] These hard-working families lived-on under casual employment and a fluctuating labour market.[73] Far from wasteful extravagance and public house spending sprees, small loans met the reasonable requirements of the working classes.[74]

If the working poor could in fact handle their own affairs, and pawnbrokers helped them on in the world, then it was not too far of step to argue for fewer regulations. Ayrton and William Hancock, an independent expert on pawnbroking worked through this logic:

> *Hancock*: I think that the poorer people, on the whole would get fairer terms, and more money and more convenient arrangements, and that the contracts, if worked out under a perfectly free system, would be better suited to both parties.
> *Chair*: Then would you reply upon competition to enable the parties to get the most they could and at the lowest rate of interest?
> *Hancock*: Yes, certainly.[75]

These exchanges piece together a different picture of borrowers, who were considered rational, intelligent and able to cope with unpredictable wages and expenses. William Knight, an assistant judge of the Middlesex Court of Session, who was antagonistic to the industry, said that certain people 'would be dreadfully distressed if they could not raise even 1 shilling on an article of dress to provide them [with] food'.[76] William Shaw, an assistant pawnbroker: believed that 'plenty of poor people would starve' without pawn loans.[77] Medicines, food and household expenses and other necessities were acquired through cash loans. Convincing sceptics of this reality was an altogether different scenario, as Robert Johnston and others simply refused to believe that one's 'necessities can be so great as they can possibly be relieved ... by so paltry an advance as 2 s 6d'.[78]

For many in the upper classes, the make or break scenario of a shilling here or there was unimaginable.

Divergent views of poverty and the impact of small loans on borrowers led to different preferences for the government's role in the market. One side held that borrowers were independent decision-makers who had the ability to maximize their welfare without state interference. The pawnbroker, far from being evil, simply fulfilled a needed service. The other side sought strict regulation to control immoral behaviour that pawnbrokers indiscriminately supported by providing cash loans. These arguments took on a heightened importance when the select committee took on the issue of how far the government should restrict loan pricing.

Price Controls

Seventy years of government limitations had taken a toll on industry profits. Price controls under the PBA 1800 afforded insufficient compensation and a low return on invested capital. Low-value pledges redeemed in less than a month were especially problematic since the related expenses often exceeded the accrued interest. The details provided the select committee much-needed insight behind the finances of lenders serving the urban masses. Pawnbrokers hoped that a dispassionate presentation of the matter-of-fact evidence would sway MP votes in their favour.

John Dicker, who owned pawn houses in Poplar, Limehouse, Commercial Road East and Clerkenwell in London, presented the limitations of the PBA 1800's price control mechanism:

> seventy years ago the expenses connected with the pawnbroking business were entirely different ... expenses with the staff are now very much increased. In addition to that, one's rent and every other thing is altered; and either the profit must have been excessive at the time when the law was adopted, or else the business having grown in one direction, whilst being tied in the other.[79]

Fixed revenue with rising expenses left Dicker with what he felt was an inadequate return on his invested capital. In the 1870s, he had £11,182 of invested capital, generating a net profit of £629 or 5.6% ROE and a 2.6% return on a sum advanced of £23,594 collateralized by 69,656 pledges.[80] Pawnbrokers argued that a 5% return on passive investment capital was widely available.[81] Considering the amount of work involved in running a pawn shop, a fair return ought to exceed the ordinary rate of 5%. A summary of his financial position is found in Table 2.4.

Lending on 70,000 pledges was no small accomplishment. One can appreciate the accompanying buzz of activity with appraisal, ticket writing, storage and managing employees. It was hard work and with expenses creeping ever upward, pawnbrokers needed some relief from restrictive price controls. Though pawnbrokers bookkeeping was less than perfect, especially under the burdensome PBA 1800, in aggregate, the select committee data provides a relatively accurate picture of the Victorian industry. There is no indication of cherry-picking data to achieve their reform goals. Pawnbrokers were not deceiving Parliament, expenses in the 1870s were higher than in the 1800s.

Table 2.4 John Dicker business analysis, June 1870

Pledges taken in				*69,656*
Sum advanced				£23,594
Capital turnover (a)				2.6x
Average pledge				6 s 11d
Capital investment	*£*	*s*	*d*	*% total*
Pledge stock	£8919	0	7	62.7%
Premium on stock (b)	800	0	0	5.6%
Lease on premise	890	0	0	6.3%
Cash	573	11	0	4.0%
Pawnbroker capital	£11,182	11	7	78.7%
Sale stock	3034	14	5	21.3%
Invested capital	£14,217	6	0	100.0%
	£	**s**	**d**	**% total**
Interest fee	£1406	15	1	87.9%
Ticket fee	193	2	5	12.1%
Total	1599	17	6	100.0%
Expenses	970	5	3	
Total	£629	12	3	
Return on capital	*5.6%*			
Return on sum advanced	*2.6%*			

Source PBSC 1870, 426–483, Appendix 14 and author calculations. It represents twelve months of business. **a** Sum advanced /capital investment in pledged stock. **b** Capitalized interest. It is unclear if the expense category included Dicker's salary

Table 2.5 shows the results of six pawnbrokers. Dicker and Telfer's 70,000 loans averaged near the same amount. The consistency in their pledge stock, interest and ticket fees again demonstrates some level of data reliability. The six pawnbrokers were more or less operating at 5% return on invested capital. Low loan averages earned less than higher volume brokers with higher average loans. Comparing McKay's low-end business with Russell and Telfer's (higher average loan size) and Barnett's (high volume and loan average), the returns varied as expected, with McKay earning less than the other six pawnbrokers. The results bring forth an

Table 2.5 Summary returns of six testifying pawnbrokers

	Barnett	*Russell*	*Dicker*	*Dicker*	*Telfer*	*Blackwood*	*McKay*
	Lambeth	*Edinburgh*	*London 1*	*London 2*	*London*	Bradford	Glasgow
Pledges in	134,505	72,000	69,656	65,824	69,784	58,601	53,884
Average loan	4s 3d	11s 3d	6s 11d	5s 9d	6s 3d	5s	3s 1d
Sum advanced	£28,608	–	£23,594	£18,840	£21,663	£16,821	£8372
Pledge stock	£8726		£8919	£7897	£8201	–	£3500
Total capital	£11,896	£27,000	£11,182	£10,560	–	–	£4482
Capital turnover	3.3x	–	2.6x	2.4x	–	–	5.6x
Interest fee	£1706	–	£1406	£1180	£1146	£647	£477
Ticket fee	£320	–	£193	£164	£195	£138	£136
Capital return	6.4%	7.2%	5.6%	6.1%	7.1%	–	3.6%
Est. fair return	5.0%	5.0%	5.0%	5.0%	5.0%	–	5.0%
Adjusted return	1.4%	2.2%	0.6%	1.1%	2.1%	–	−1.4%

Source Compiled by the author from PBSC 1870. Unless noted otherwise, it is unclear whether the adjusted return included an owner-operator salary expense. (Barnett). Financial information submitted anonymously to parliament. The pawnbroker was later identified as Mr Barnett. (McKay) Expenses exclude deductions for McKay's salary and that of his two sons, both key managers, thus overstating profitability important point of consideration that manifests throughout this study that whatever the legal constraints, profitability is impacted by the business mix and the individual operating acumen of the owner/managers. Some lenders thrive while others languish, but at this point in the story, few if any, seemed to be making excessive returns.

The largest PBSC pawn sample covered over 1.4 million loans issued in 1869 by thirty pawnbrokers representing approximately 15.6% of the 9 million total loan volume in Liverpool that year. Approximately 95% or 1.3 million of the pledges were for less than 10 shillings, and over 50% or approximately 702,000 pledges were for less than 2s 6d. Only 5% of the 1.4 million pledges were valued above 10 shillings. Like other urban centres, the majority of Liverpool pawnbrokers participated in the weekly cycle of the low-end trade, which earned a smaller ROE than the high-pledge businesses. Excluding four outlier pawnbrokers, the adjusted average ROE was 4%.[82] Of the fifteen pawnbrokers that earned ROEs greater than the adjusted average, thirteen experienced 3% or more of loan volumes above 10 shillings. Of the eleven pawnbrokers with below-average returns, six experienced above-average loan volumes in the lowest category below 2s 6d. Though thousands of mostly small transactions came in and out each week, it was the one-off higher valued good that pushed a pawnbroker towards profitability. Even a small percentage of high-pledge business substantially improved financial returns.

Pawnbrokers' principal complaint was the rising expense of labour. Since pledges required the same amount of effort and administration regardless of the loan size, high-volume and low-average loan pawnshops were at a distinct disadvantage. It was estimated that six or seven employees were needed for every 1000 pledges received daily. One of the employees would be a manager or a 'First'. In busy pawnshops a First was charged with managing the other employees, who might include a Second, a Third and boys performing menial tasks.[83] A First earned approximately £2 a week and in some cases a profit dividend. In 1867, a First working in South London at a shop taking in 96,000 pledges annually earned £100 in annual salary and £26 in kind for room and board.[84]

Demonstrating the labour employed on 7 May 1870, a typical Saturday, Dicker produced 1899 strung-together pawn tickets transacted on that day with an average loan size of 3s 11d (Hardaker 1892, p. 199).[85] It measured approximately 58 feet long and was dubbed 'the serpent'. It spoke to the fact that only 346 (18%) of 1889 loans were

Table 2.6 Pledges redeemed on Saturday 7 May 1870

Time in Pledge		*Principal*			*Interest*			*Ticket fees*			*Total*			*% of principal*	
														Intake expense	*Loan profit*
	Pledges	*£*	*s*	*d*	*£*	*s*	*d*	*£*	*s*	*d*	*£*	*s*	*d*		
1 month	1553	304	17	4	5	18	8.5	3	8	0.5	9	6	9	4.36%	−3.05%
>1 month	346	72	8	2	8	6	2.5	0	14	11.5	9	1	2	4.36%	12.57%
	1889	377	5	6	14	4	11	4	3	0	18	7	11	4.36%	4.88%
														Gain	0.52%

Sources PBSC 1870, 524–526 and Hardaker (1892, pp. 199–200)

profitable. Gross remuneration was equal to 4.88% on loans, totalling approximately £304. The business expense of 4.36% or approximately 2 1/4d per pledge absorbed nearly all the remuneration. Table 2.6 shows that low-value pledges held for less than one month were unprofitable. Dicker earned £9 6s 9d on 1553 pledges in house for less than one month, which failed to cover his costs associated with those pledges. He earned profit through higher interest charges from 346 pledges held for more than one month. If a handful of the 346 pledges had been pulled out earlier and the pattern repeated a few times a month, much of his profit would have been vanished. It was a time-gamble that worried pawnbrokers to no end and an increasingly untenable one as they watched expenses rise while the price ceiling remained stuck in the year 1800.

The industry was not reaping vast sums on the back of the poor. A few pounds in any one direction could make or break the pawnbroker's business. Even so, long and deeply held suspensions of predatory behaviour and profiteering were not easily countered by facts and figures. Few, if any, MPs challenged the data itself. Many simply believed that pawnbroking was an extremely profitable affair. Miller could not understand why a pawnbroker who had 'good security for the money advanced' needed to charge the rates authorized by the PBA 1800, even calling for a reduction in those rates.[86] He was not alone.[87] Hector could not 'conceive that carrying on a business with forty thousand pledges a year should not yield a sufficient livelihood' and that it was a 'matter of common repute' that pawnbrokers have a 'very good trade'.[88] An article in the *Dudley Herald and Wednesbury Borough News* repeated the widespread belief, 'What we are certain of is ... they either get it back with interest, or get more than double its value often, in the goods that are forfeited'.[89] Some of the misunderstanding resulted from treating the headline annual '20 per cent' interest rate as a profit margin.[90] This is an ongoing feature of the small-loan market—namely, that interest rates reflect the amount of earned revenue, whereas in reality the revenue relates to the amount of interest and fees above and beyond the principal lent. Recall that Dicker earned only £18 of revenue on 1899 pledges, which had to cover all of his expenses and provide a sufficient return on capital.

Pawnbrokers cautioned against thinking in percentages terms.[91] While the PBA 1800 maximum chargeable rate for loans of less than 42 shillings was approximately 20% per annum (pcpa), and at or more than 42 shillings was approximately 15 pcpa, these rates were misleading. The 1800 Act stated a monetary not a percentage limit. If an article were redeemed the day it was pledged it would pay a rate of approximately 600 pcpa, and if the loan was only 6d, the protective statute allowed 3000 pcpa.[92] Whether annual percentage rates are an appropriate measure of cost for small-value loans issued for short periods was and remains a subject of continued debate. Certainly, it is the eye-popping interest rates draw attention to the industry and few antagonists bother to dig deeper. Shifting the narrative away from annual rates towards monetary charges was, and remains, a losing battle.

For all of the top line focus it remained an open question whether British pawnbrokers in the 1870s were operating efficiently. When compared to *non-profit* pawnbrokers in Ireland and France, with an average cost per pawn of 3 s 71/2d, and no less than 9d, British providers had a lower expense structure.[93] It was estimated that if a weekly 6d pledge was to be profitable, a minimum of 11/2d was required in compensation per transaction.[94] No matter how frequently pawnbrokers proclaimed that theirs was a business like any another, naysayers shifted the conversation towards the high interest rates charges and the financial burdens of their poor and needy clients.

At times, even the generally supportive chairman, Ayrton, did not fully agree with the pawnbrokers:

> *Mr May*: Everybody has an idea that pawnbroking is exceedingly remunerative and they do it because in the Pawnbrokers' Act, a pawnbroker's profits are laid down. For instance, I, as a pawnbroker would lend a pound for a month or for five weeks, which is the legal time for 4d. If I were to lend a man 30s on a watch for a month

> or five weeks (for there are seven days' grace), I should get 6d for that transaction. The butcher says you are getting rare profits, you pawnbrokers, but I have said you bought a sheep for 30s would you like to have all the trouble with that sheep and to sell it at the end of a month for 30s 6d? Would you like to say on Saturday night when you had cut up that sheep and weighed it that you got 6d for your investment?
>
> *Chairman*: Do you know any butcher that kills 76,603 sheep in a year?[95]

The sheer scale and volume of Victorian lending made lobbying for increased profits a difficult task. While they were self-interested, their argument reveals a major complication of static price controls in an ever-evolving market. With rising expenses and shifting currency norms, outdated price controls detrimentally impacted their business. One of the strongest arguments against price controls is that a single rate cannot be applied across an entire credit class. Having to apply a single rate leads to credit rationing and market segmentation. The types of goods that pawnbrokers could work with were limited because the government pricing structure did not account for different risks, processing expenses and storage costs. Without adequate compensation pawnbrokers refused certain goods.[96]

Bulky items were especially awkward, as they required increased labour and warehouse storage. Under price controls these large goods were charged at the same rate as a pocket watch or overcoat. In many instances a porter was paid more to carry the good to the shop than a pawnbroker who would value, ticket, store and lend money on the item.[97] Dicker explained:

> I have two instances here which will show how inconveniently it works; I have here a ticket for £6 for a pianoforte, which was taken in by a pawnbroker, the interest and all that he would be allowed to charge for warehouse-room and other things, would be 1 s 6d a month. Before that pianoforte was redeemed 15 months had expired, and the interest that he would be allowed to charge, and which he did charge was 22 s 6d (£1 1 s 6d). I have a bill here from Peachey of Bishopsgate street for warehousing a pianoforte for the same time and it is £3.[98]

Yet those rationed out of the market still needed cash and while it is unlikely that the poor owned something as large as a pianoforte, larger household goods and lesser value items could not find their way into the licensed pawn market. More than mere speculation, regulatory-induced market segmentation led to a large illegal trade. These unlicensed shops operated outside price controls and regulated trading hours. Pawnbrokers argued that, along with second-hand dealers, these shops exploited the needy.[99] Price controls segmented the market and resulted in some borrowers resorting to transact illegally.

Even with these negative effects, many considered price controls a necessary measure to protect the 'irrational' working poor from 'sophisticated' pawnbrokers.[100] Perceived power imbalances between lender and borrower or, more formally, the presence of bargaining inequity, directly challenged the notion that borrowers freely engaged and negotiated with pawnbrokers. Price controls were meant to protect 'some poor creature with an empty stomach, who has denuded herself of every rag of clothing that decency will permit ... to raise a few pence to provide food. How can she bargain with any chance of equity?'[101] Desperation, it was thought, left poor borrowers as price-takers with no room or leverage for negotiation.

A more subtle motivation was also at work. If price controls protected the poor from themselves, then perhaps credit rationing was welcomed. Any reduction in the credit supply for the undeserving poor would have been viewed favourably by some. Borrowers rationed out of the market were better off without a loan as the indulgent poor could avoid the debt and moral spiral into pauperism and destitution. If certain poor borrowers with respectable needs went unfilled, so be it, the greater societal good required limiting the ravenous desires of the undeserving poor—or so the argument went.

In moments of calm when the rhetoric around poverty lessened, Committee members queried why pawnbrokers were petitioning parliament when they could refuse the unprofitable business or simply advance less on frequently pawned, low-value goods.[102] Pawnbrokers relied on loyal customer relationships and repeat business. McKay suggested that if a pawner was refused once, next time, perhaps with a more profitable item, the pledger would go elsewhere.[103] Time uncertainty also mattered. On more than one occasion a pawnbroker stated that if he were to refuse a pledge because it could go out in a few weeks, he would never have any pledges for longer.[104] Customer relations, timing factors and the sheer number of pawn shops determined how much money a pawner received. Dicker indicated that 'competition regulates' which shop people frequent and the shop with the highest advances attracted more customers.[105] Gillman agreed: ‘It would be generally known among the people where the best bargain was to be had’.[106] With sixty-four pawnbrokers operating in the London borough of Stepney, which included Whitechapel, St George-in-the-East and Mile End Old Town, one can appreciate the ease with which information was exchanged among customers.[107]

Price controls sparked widespread debate concerning the sources and remedies of poverty, the impacts of government interference in the marketplace and how pawn loans affected the lives of the urban poor. Free-market-oriented MPs took particular offence at price controls and market segmentation. The idea that the government limited what a private person could do with his or her property went against basic British freedoms. Ayrton believed that the public should have ‘every convenience of having money advanced on every conceivable article’.[108] Pawnbrokers agreed, it was ‘undeniable’ that negotiations between buyer and seller produced fair results in a way that regulation could not (Searle 1998, 27).[109] Despite this support, pawnbrokers remained committed to the PPRA’s two-tiered fixed and flexible price schedule. Ever practical, securing the industry’s future outweighed the perfection of complete de-regulation.

Forfeiture

Parliament was alarmed by default terms and the point at which pawnbrokers could take ownership of forfeitures. Rules governing the transfer of ownership were considered a basic form of borrower protection. For pawnbrokers, holding a good but one day longer cut into working capital and likely reduced resale values. Their plan for reducing the holding period was met with great reluctancy. An often-repeated narrative accused pawnbrokers of offering low principal loan amounts, only to acquire the good in default and sell it at a much higher retail price. Hector believed that ‘the number of articles that are forfeited is very large and the loss to the poor through forfeiture is very great’.[110]

Table 2.7, which includes PBSC testimony and information reported in the PBG, challenges this. Annual redemption rates for pawned goods ranged from 93 to 98%. Two pawnbrokers testified that 80% of items were redeemed within three months and 85% redeemed within six months. Data from a low-end business revealed that 92% were redeemed within six months and an additional 6% were redeemed between six and twelve

Table 2.7 Estimated redemption rates

Location	*Pawnbroker*	*Period*	*Redemption rate (%)*
Liverpool	Hardaker	<3 months	80
Glasgow	A. McKay	<6 months	85
Liverpool	Hardaker	1870	90–95
Liverpool	Hardaker	1856–1869	95.5
Bradford	Blackwood	Annually	98
Edinburgh	Russell	Annually	90–95
Glasgow	A. McKay	Annually	93
Glasgow	Scoular	Annually	90–95
Leeds	Scotson	Annually	93
London	G. Attenborough	Annually	95
London	R. Attenborough	Annually	95
Pollokshaws	G. McKay	Annually	93–95
Salford	May	Annually	96

Source PBSC 1870, 191, 203, 696, 946, 1685, 2030, 2040–8, 2731, 4278, 4527, 4738, 5027

months.[111] Gillman claimed: 'A great number of pledges are redeemed within a week'.[112] Redemption rates were relatively uniform across the low-, medium- and high-end trade. Accusations that pawnbrokers aggressively sought borrower property for resale were unfounded. Given that upwards of 90% of goods were redeemed within six months, halving the PBA 1800 twelve-month restriction would free up some working capital while having only a small negative effect on relatively few borrowers.

Slim profit margins meant even small losses on resold goods depressed the bottom line. In addition to the 1.5 million pledges in the 1869 Liverpool sample, which in total lost £859 on auction resales, during that same year Hardaker (£117), Lambeth (£147) and Telfer (£167) incurred losses.[113] According to Dicker, 'it is a mistake altogether to imagine that pawnbrokers look to unredeemed pledges for profit'.[114] Despite the evidence showing losses on the resale of forfeited items, John Simon MP (Liberal) questioned this: 'You [Dicker] generally make gains on your sales, do you not?'[115] MPs focused on a few book entries showing profitable resales such as a £7 pledged item sold for £17 and the sale of a telescope at £2 on which 15 shillings had been lent.[116] On higher-value goods, it was suggested that pawnbrokers rigged auction sales in their favour only to acquire and later resell goods for a gain.[117] Orr-Ewing asked whether pawnbrokers 'send a stranger to purchase' auction goods on their behalf. Raynor Storr, a London auctioneer, made it clear that the majority of items were purchased by the general public.[118]

Pawnbrokers were also concerned over the deflationary impact of new waves of mass-produced retails goods and clothing made of 'shoddy wool' which quickly lost its value (Tebbutt 1983, 81).[119] Seasonality complicated matters even further. Pawners understandably raised cash on the most valuable good needed the least. A winter coat pawned in the summer was financially valuable and not otherwise in use. From the pawnbroker's perspective, the holding cycle put their sale into the depressed portion of a seasonal market. Attenborough remarked, 'I have seventeen month goods in my house … unsold, because from December last I have been unable to sell any of the winter goods, and I cannot touch them until about September'.[120] Though a pawnbroker could hold on and sell in seasonally-driven demand cycles, this tactic tied up working capital, decreased the supply of loanable funds and reduced capital turnover. From the borrower's perspective, a shorter holding period would lead to higher loan sums per article as forfeited goods could be resold at a higher price later.[121] The downside is that borrowers would have to pay their loan sooner but having accrued less interest. Just this one aspect regulation, the holding period, shows how borrower protection methods ripple through pawnbroker's financial positions.

Even with accurate financial information and seasonality, rumours and widely held beliefs about the industry remained at the fore. Considered a basic form of borrower protection, even those generally well disposed to the trade were reluctant to reduce the twelve-month holding period. If cash were raised to cover an immediate emergency need, as was often argued, and goods were redeemed 'when work was plentiful and wages decent', a one-year period plus three months' grace was better suited the working poor and was difficult to refute.[122] On this point the majority opinion was against pawnbrokers.

The Final Result: The Pawnbrokers Act 1872

In August 1871 the Select Committee reported that, though necessary, regulation should 'be kept within the narrowest limits' and that lending money on items should be left to the individual actors as they saw fit.[123] Both the spirit and in the letter of the new law expressed a business-friendly attitude and met most of the PPRA's goals.[124] Price caps were lifted, special contracts were permitted, and burdensome paperwork reduced.

The Pawnbrokers Act 1872 applied to any loan of less than £10, unless a special contract was executed. Special contracts were permitted for loans of more than 40 shillings, which were to be signed by both parties and the borrower provided with a duplicate contract.[125] In a victory for the pawnbrokers, the PBA 1800 clause mandating a total financial loss owing to minor clerical infractions was removed from the 1870 Act. The law also contained a schedule detailing the information that a pawn ticket contract had to include.

The Derby scale of 1/2d for every 2 shillings lent became law. The rates were just over 2% monthly or 25 pcpa on loans up to 40 shillings and 1 2/3% monthly or 20 pcpa on loans of more than 40 shillings. Although the raise may seem insignificant, for Dicker and the many thousands of similar businesses, a 5% increase might have made his low-value business profitable. Moreover, while regulation alone did not determine the industry's development from 1872 to 1914, licensing grew year on year in 38 of the 40 years, with an overall CAGR of 70%.[126] Though some evidence suggests overall pledge volumes were starting to decline by the early 1900s, such growth in market participation would have been hard to achieve if low-value businesses did not in some way gain from the increased rates. Figure 2.2 shows the number of pawnbroking licences issued from 1870 to 1930. The series shows an upward trend until the First World War and a decline thereafter.[127] The fate of the industry after the nineteenth century is examined in Chapter 4.

Conclusion

Victorian pawnbrokers provided loans to the urban poor in need of quick cash. They did so on a tremendous scale, issuing over 200 million loans annually. While market reform did not generate as much interest as the Poor Law or Factory Acts had, examining the debate reveals much about the intersection of poverty, capitalism and financial regulation. There was little doubt that many urban families struggled to obtain an acceptable standard of living. In an emergency, these families had few savings from which to draw or access to the banking system. There was also widespread agreement that the poor required protection from small-scale capitalism. The issue was whether the government or the market offered

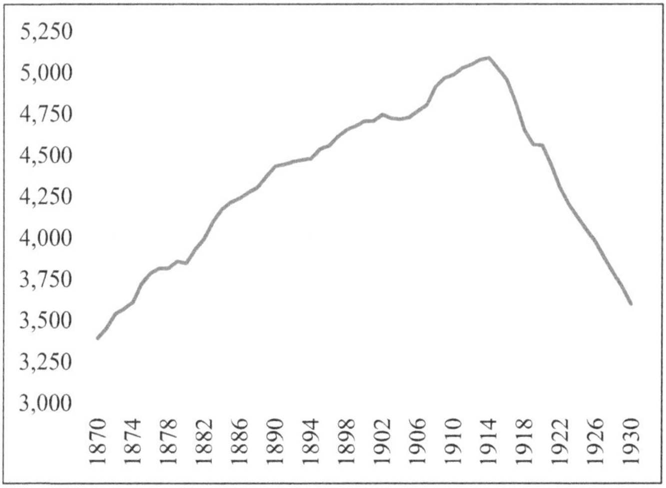

Fig. 2.2 Pawnbroking licences, 1870–1930 (*Source* Annual report of the Commissioners of HM Inland Revenue, 1870–1909 and HM Customs & Excise thereafter)

the better form of protection. Policy responses depended in part on one's understanding of how small loans related to poverty.

For many the conclusion was that those with the capital—pawnbrokers—took advantage of those who desperately needed it—the urban poor. For them, financial regulation was the appropriate response. Distinctions were being made between the 'undeserving' and the 'deserving' poor, with many considering that pawnbrokers served the former. Resolving the 'problem of poverty' meant controlling the immoral temptations of pauperism by encouraging 'right behaviour' by limiting the pawn market (Himmelfarb 1984). McCall went so far as to say that people who pawn for more than 10 shillings were from a different moral class from those that pawned for 10 shillings or less.[128] Supporters of strict financial regulation believed pawnbrokers' cash loans encouraged degenerate behaviour, causing a tailspin into moral and financial ruin.

Pro-regulators believed small loans made poverty worse. At times their advocacy demonstrated great intensity. Whether their poverty policy was primarily driven by guilt or fear is debatable. In the case of pawnbroking, it is likely that both were at play. The *Daily Telegraph* suggested that pawnbrokers invoked guilt in the wealthy, as the shops reminded them of the 'painful necessities amongst the poor'.[129] However, fear of the rising urban masses better explains both the visceral anti-pawnbroking reaction and doubt about the financial evidence. These people believed that borrowers were irrational and irresponsible, and that pawn credit led to pauperism. It was irrational to need small sums and pay such high rates for them. They wanted to limit the industry and protect borrowers 'from themselves'.[130] Those with deeply held beliefs about the link between debt and morality were not likely to have their mind changed by others in favour of business-friendly reforms.

Pawnbrokers and their allies understood the situation completely differently. The ever-evolving urban economy, offering irregular employment and low wages drove the demand for small loans. This was not about morals, but about a rational strategy utilized to overcome unavoidable budget shortfalls (Daunton 2007, p. 396). Though some of the more cynical members of the upper classes simply wanted to leave well-enough alone, fearing any disruption of the poorer classes could backfire, most supporters of the trade viewed lenders and borrowers as responsible and considered pawn credit as useful against grinding poverty (Tebbutt 1983, 117).

In the end, practical concerns and compromise carried the day. Neither free-marketers nor those wanting to shut down the industry won out. While many preferred unfettered markets they recognized that there was little political will for such a framework. Removing existing regulations would be an entirely different process from updating aspects of a 72-year-old law. Passionate objections to the bill were overcome by the reality that the poor needed cash. Since Parliament was unwilling to provide an alternative lending source or tackle the root causes of poverty, a regulated but viable pawn industry was the best worst solution.[131]

Notes

1. Pawnbrokers Select Committee (PBSC) 1870, 1476–1551.
2. PBSC 1870, 3588–3589.
3. "A Pawnbroking Incident," *Chambers' Journal*, 1 May 1875.
4. PBSC 1870, 1862.
5. See Chapter 4 and pages 95–96 of *Making Ends Meet*, Tebbutt recounts how certain members of the trade regularly broke the law.
6. See *Coggs v. Bernard*, Ld. Raymond, 909, 1 Smith's *Leading Cases*, 5th edition, 171, 182. Pawn's origins are disputed, with founding credit

given to such a diverse set of characters as to include St Nicholas, the Medicis and fifth-century Chinese Buddhist monks. See Oeltken (1998), Schwed (1975), and Walsh (2009).

7. Under the PBA 1800 the minimum holding time was twelve months and a three-month grace period.
8. PBG, 13 June 1870. The importance of transaction speed to the borrower is a recurring theme throughout the period covered by this research.
9. PBSC 1870, 2311–2313.
10. *Journal of the Statistical Society of London* 1872, 35 (4): 541–545. Each licence represented one location. It was possible for a person to hold more than one licence.
11. Data compiled from PBSC 1870, Appendix 14. Metropolitan and borough boundaries determined by the Board of Inland Revenue Licensing Division.
12. HC, Local Taxation Licences, 1909 (London: HMSO). Disaggregated tax return data is limited to English counties, 1890–1909.
13. PBSC 1870, 1012–1013.
14. PBSC 1870, 129.
15. PBSC 1870, Appendix 9.
16. PBSC 1870, 1857–1858; In Scotland, a procurator fiscal was similar to a public prosecutor. Hector's district was located near the City of Glasgow.
17. PBSC 1872, 46, 66–68.
18. PBSC 1870, 769–770.
19. PBG, 29 March 1869.
20. PBSC 1870, 720–721.
21. PBSC 1870, 867–873.
22. PBSC 1870, 952.
23. PBSC 1870, 700–701, 2844–2845, 2866.
24. The Bouverie Society, Minute Book, 7 January 1870, London Metropolitan Archives CLC/034/MS22322. The Bouverie Society (hereafter Bouverie) was a social club and professional society for pawnbrokers.
25. PBG, 24 August 1868; Metropolitan Pawnbrokers' Protection Society, Society Minutes 1863, The London Metropolitan Archives CLC/093/MS22329 (MPPS).
26. Pawnbroking Parliamentary Reform Association, Minute Book 23 April 1868, London Metropolitan Archive*s* CLC/097/MS22331 (PPRA); PBG, 28 January 1867, 3 June 1867, and 10 February 1868. For example, pawnbrokers cited a report authored by Dr Neilson Hancock concerning the Irish pawnbroking market. He argued that price controls on pawn should be lifted as they did not provide a sufficient remuneration and encouraged a black market.

27. PBSC 1870, 3053–3055, 4201), MPPS (1870–1871), PBG, 16 October 1871, MPPS (1864).
28. MPPS, 1869, 1870, 1906.
29. Often what was meant by free trade was the freedom to enter a pawn negotiation without government control over the interest rate, fees or forfeiture term.
30. PBG, 12 June 1871.
31. George Attenborough opened his first pawnshop in 1835. As of this writing the third generation operates two shops in London. See PBSC 1870, 682 and PBSC 1870, 2234–2249.
32. PBG, 13 January 1868, 1 February 1869, 5 April 1869, 13 June 1870.
33. PBG, 5 April 1869.
34. MPPS, 1869.
35. PPRA, 23 April 1868.
36. PPRA, 23 April 1868.
37. PPRA, 23 April 1868.
38. PBG, 1 February 1869 and 3 February 1869.
39. PPRA, 26 October 1870. Guaranteed funding was committed over time, whereas subscription constituted one-off donations.
40. PBG, 18 May 1868.
41. PBG, 15 February 1869; PPRA, January and February 1869.
42. PPRA, 2–3 July 1868; PBSC 1870, 1712.
43. PBG, 15 February 1869.
44. The PPRA received assistance from Sheffield MP Anthony Mundella (Liberal), Leeds MP William Wheelhouse (Conservative) and Dudley MP Henry Sheridan (Liberal). See PPRA, 22 April 1869, 26 October 1870.
45. PPRA, 22 April 1869. Hambro was appointed to the select committee.
46. PBG, 24 March 1870.
47. *Daily Telegraph*, 9 April 1870.
48. "Pawnbrokers," *The Latest News*, 25 April 1870.
49. "Mr Plimsoll's Pawnbroking Bill," *Spectator*, 2 May 1870.
50. PPRA, May 1870.
51. In 1546 H VIII capped the pawn interest rate at 10%, James I reduced the rate to 8%, Charles II to 6% and under Queen Anne the rate was reduced even further to 5%. In 1603 the first comprehensive regulatory framework was enacted to cover stolen goods and redemption procedures.
52. PBG, 18 February 1867.
53. PBSC 1872, 374.
54. PBSC 1870, 1791, 1803. Emphasis added.
55. PBSC 1870, 1537–1551, 3666–3671.
56. HC deb. 15 July 1872, vol. 212.
57. PBSC 1870, 3579.

58. PBSC 1870, 394–406.
59. PBSC 1870, 1357.
60. "Administrative History," Family Welfare Association formerly Charity Organisation Society, A/FWA, London Metropolitan Archives.
61. PBSC 1870, 1380–1388.
62. PBSC 1870, 1320–1332.
63. PBSC 1870, 1791–1807.
64. PBSC 1870, 3087, 4022–4025.
65. PBSC 1870, 1547–1555, 3133–3148.
66. PBSC 1872, 283.
67. PBSC 1870, 314–315; 1872, 370–374.
68. PBSC 1870, 4547–4558.
69. PBSC 1870, 526, 588.
70. PBSC 1870, 1034–1035.
71. Steadman Jones argued that Marshall, Toynbee and Green were optimistic in their hopes for the working class. This optimism departed from Malthusian pessimism.
72. As reprinted in PBG, 2 February 1867.
73. PBSC 1870, 3042–3045.
74. PBSC 1870, 2111–2112.
75. PBSC 1870, 2238–2241.
76. PBSC 1870, 4685–4689.
77. PBSC 1870, 3505.
78. PBSC 1870, 3087, 4022–4025.
79. PBSC 1870, 435–436.
80. PBSC 1870, 426–483, Appendix 14, and author calculations.
81. In 1870 the Bank rate was 2.5%, in 1871 3% and in 1872 5%. See "Three centuries of data" available for download from the Bank of England website.
82. Data compiled from PBSC 1870, Appendix 9. Pawnbrokers 5, 14 and 21 were excluded owing to incomplete expense data. Pawnbroker 12 was excluded owing to low-pledge volume accompanied by an abnormally high percentage of over 10 shillings pledges. Note: The total loss from the sale of forfeits was £859. Owing to missing data, the column summation of £835 is £24 lower. Finally, it is unclear whether the estimated ROE included an owner-operator salary expense.
83. PBSC 1870, 373, 461–483, 520, 4822.
84. PBG, 18 November 1867.
85. PBSC 1870, 524.
86. PBSC 1870, 1503–1517, 1551.
87. PBSC 1870, 1680, 3885–3886.
88. PBSC 1870, 1958–1963, 3583–3585.
89. Reprinted in PBG, 1 July 1872.

90. PBG, 6 February and 13 February 1871.
91. PBSC 1870, 437–439.
92. PBG, 27 April 1868.
93. PBG, 16 and 30 September 1867.
94. PBSC 1870, 321–322, 437–439.
95. PBSC 1870, 982–983.
96. PBG, 4 May 1868.
97. PBSC 1870, 20, 596–599, 2208.
98. PBSC 1870, 592–593.
99. PBSC 1870, 53–54, 2707.
100. "Pawnbrokers," *Daily Telegraph*, 21 August 1871.
101. "Pawnbrokers," *The Sheffield and Rotherham Independent*, 28 August 1871.
102. PBSC 1870, 596–597.
103. PBSC 1870, 2078.
104. PBSC 1870, 526, 720.
105. PBSC 1870, 562–563.
106. PBSC 1872, 174, 177, 260.
107. W. Kelly & Co., Post Office London Directories, 1851–1873.
108. PBSC 1870, 2702.
109. PBG, 24 February 1868, 13 June 1870.
110. PBSC 1870, 1971–1974.
111. PBG, 29 June 1868.
112. PBSC 1872, 17–22.
113. PBSC 1870, 141, 834, 2901, Appendix C.
114. PBSC 1870, 560–563.
115. PBSC 1870, 750–756.
116. PBSC 1870, 653–655, 783.
117. PBSC 1870, 1213–1225.
118. PBSC 1870, 3196–3214.
119. PBSC 1870, 223–30, 5017, 5105.
120. PBSC 1870, 725–726.
121. PBSC 1870, 201
122. PBSC 1872, 6–11, 26–29.
123. HC Report from the Select Committee on Pawnbrokers, vol. 419, 1870.
124. PPRA, "Draft of a Bill to Amend the Law Relating to Pawnbrokers of Great Britain," written by F. S. Reilly, 27 October 1868. The draft bill focused on the areas where reform was sought but did not repeal any clauses that pawnbrokers believed should remain in effect.
125. The record is unclear why the 40 shillings rate and not the PPRA proposed 42 shillings was selected. Recall that during the Nottingham Sessions Liverpool proposed the 40 shillings rate and their MP, Lord Sandon, was a member of the Select Committee. Perhaps the Liverpool delegation had lobbied behind the scenes. Alternatively, a simple explanation is that 40 shillings, or £2, was easy to work with.

126. Annual report of the Commissioners of HM Inland Revenue, 1870–1909 and HM Customs & Excise thereafter.
127. The reasons for this decline are analysed in Chapter 4.
128. PBSC 1870, 1434–1435.
129. *Daily Telegraph*, reprinted in PBG, 5 August 1872.
130. This motivation differed from efforts to regulate the railways. The impetus for the Railway Regulation Act 1844 was to counter monopolistic pricing power and subsidize travel for the working class.
131. HL deb. 6 August 1872, vol. 213.

References

Archives

The British Library, London.
M78445–55 Pawnbrokers Gazette and Trade Circular, 1867–1894.
The Guildhall & City Business Library, City of London.
MSS295 Pawnbrokers Gazette and Trade Circular, 1895–1941.
The London Metropolitan Archives.
CLC/034 The Bouverie Society.
MS22321 Rules of the Society 1885, 1889 and 1934.
MS22322 Minutes 1801–1811, 1841–1948.
MS22323 Visitors' Book.
MS22324 Society Papers and Invoices.
MS22325 List of Sons of Members on Active Duty in the First World War.
MS22326 Photographs.
CLC/063 The Eastern Society of Master Pawnbrokers.
MS22327 Society Minutes, 1813–1821, 1824–1831.
MS22328 Society Papers, 1821–1830.
Family Welfare Association (Charity Organisation Society).
A/FWA Administrative History.
CLC/093 Metropolitan Pawnbrokers' Protection Society.
MS22329 Society Minutes, 1863–1913.
MS22330 Society Papers and Correspondence.
CLC/097 Parliamentary Pawnbrokers' Reform Association.
MS22331 Minutes and Executive Reports, 1868–1871.
MS22332 Telegraphs, Alfred Hardaker.
MS22333 Photographs.
Official Publications.
The House of Commons Debate Sessions.
The House of Commons Local Taxation Licenses. 1909. HMSO.
The House of Lords Debate Sessions.

The Pawnbrokers Select Committee 1870 (377).
The Pawnbrokers Select Committee 1872 (288).
The Pawnbrokers Act 1872: 35 & 36 Vic. c. 93.

Sources

Atiyah, Patrick. 1979. *The Rise and Fall of Freedom of Contract*. Oxford: Oxford University Press.

Bigelow, Gordon. 2003. *Fiction, Famine, and the Rise of Economics in Victorian Britain and Ireland*. Cambridge: Cambridge University Press.

Bosanquet, Helen. 1896. The Burden of Small Debts. *The Economic Journal* 6 (22): 212–25.

Daunton, Martin. 2007. *Wealth and Welfare: An Economic and Social History of Britain, 1851–1951*. Oxford: Oxford University Press.

Egginton, Heidi. 2016. "Popular Antique Collecting and the Second-hand Trade in Britain." PhD diss., University of Cambridge.

Englander, David. 2013. *Poverty and Poor Law Reform In 19th Century Britain, 1834–1914: From Chadwick to Booth*. London: Routledge.

Fraser, Derek. 2009. *The Evolution of the British Welfare State: A History of Social Policy since the Industrial Revolution*. London: Palgrave Macmillan.

Hancock, W. Neilson. 1850. "The Usury Laws and the Trend of Lending Money to the Poor in Ireland." Paper presented at the Dublin Statistical Society, Dublin, 18 February.

Hardaker, Alfred. 1892. *A Brief History of Pawnbroking*. London: Jackson, Ruston & Keeson.

Himmelfarb, Gertrude. 1984. *The Idea of Poverty: England in the Early Industrial Age*. London: Faber.

Johnson, Paul. 1985. *Saving and Spending: The Working-Class Economy in Britain 1870–1939*. Oxford: Clarendon Press.

Journal of the Statistical Society of London. 1872. 35 (4): 541–545.

Lee, Stephen. 2004. *Aspects of British Political History, 1815–1914*. London: Routledge.

"Mr Plimsoll's Pawnbroking Bill." 1870. *The Spectator*, 2 May.

Oeltken, Jarret. 1998. "Pawnbroking on Parade." *Buffalo Law Review* 35.

"Pawnbrokers." 1882. *Chamber's Journal* 19:158–61.

"Pawnbrokers." 1871. *Daily Telegraph*, 21 August.

"Pawnbrokers." 1870. *The Latest News*, 25 April.

"Pawnbrokers." 1871. *The Sheffield and Rotherham Independent*, 28 August.

"Pawns, Pawners and Pawnbrokers." 1864. *Once a Week* 10 (247): 340–345.

Reeves, Maud Pember. 1914. *Round About a Pound a Week*. London: George Beel & Sons.

Rowntree, Seebohm. 1901. *Poverty, A Study of Town Life*. London: Macmillan and Company.
Searle, Geoffrey. 1998. *Morality and the Market in Victorian Britain*. Oxford: Oxford University Press.
Schwed, Peter. 1975. *God Bless Pawnbrokers*. New York: Dodd Mead.
Stedman Jones, Gareth. 2004. *An End to Poverty: A Historical Debate*. London: Profile Books.
Stedman Jones, Gareth. 2013. *Outcast London: A Study in the Relationship Between Classes in Victorian Society*. London: Verso.
Tebbutt, Melanie. 1983. *Making Ends Meet: Pawnbroking and Working-Class Credit*. Leicester: Leicester University Press.
"Uncle's Bill." 1870. *Daily Telegraph*, 9 April.
W. Kelly & Co. Post Office London Directories. 1851–1873.
Walsh, Michael. 2009. *Sacred Economics: Buddhist Monasticism and Territoriality in Medieval China*. New York: Columbia University Press.
Weir, William. 1952. *The First Hundred Years, 1851–1951: A Sketch of the History of the Glasgow Pawnbrokers Association*. Glasgow: Glasgow Pawnbrokers Association.
Winstanley, Michael. 1992. *Gladstone and the Liberal Party*. London: Routledge.

CHAPTER 3

Moneylenders: Deeply Rooted Evil or Providers of Quick Cash?

After diligent enquiry and long research, I am bound to come to the conclusion that a deeply rooted evil exists in our midst – an evil that eats into the bone and sinew of the poorer class, an evil that corrodes the happiness and comfort of many working men.

"Victims of usury," *Sheffield Independent*, 8 January 1896

Finding themselves at the end of their financial tether the working classes sought cash from moneylenders. Unlike pawnbrokers, moneylenders operated without regulatory supervision. Free from restrictive price controls, they charged whatever the market would bear. What the market would bear, however, was quite different from what the public found acceptable. Prolific advertising and sensational newspaper coverage drew attention to moneylenders and their high-interest loans. Twice—first in the late 1890s and again in the 1920s—public outcry encouraged Parliament to curtail 'evil' moneylenders.

Moneylenders conjured images of greedy capitalists preying on the downtrodden needy, and of slick salesmen coaxing well-to-do borrowers into oppressive loan contracts. In fact, the wide spectrum of borrowers and their varied needs complicated reform efforts. Whereas larger moneylending businesses served genteel borrowers along with a growing demand from the middle class, small-time lenders provide cash to the lower ends of the social spectrum. In the end, all sorts of people were indebted to moneylenders. Gender roles, the 1854 repeal of the usury

© The Author(s), under exclusive license to Springer Nature Switzerland AG 2021

C. McMahon, *Taming the Fringe*, Palgrave Studies in the History of Finance, https://doi.org/10.1007/978-3-030-70615-9_3

law and anti-Semitic prejudices further complicated reform. (O'Connell 2009, pp. 132–6; Tebbutt 1983, p. 131).

This chapter examines moneylending reform in 1900 and again in 1927. It pieces together financial information on the business model, analyses the rationale behind reform and studies the policy tools considered to tame the many grievances against the industry. Bringing down the cost of loans was a main priority followed closely by non-price issues including advertisements, contract disclosure terms and whether moneylenders should use the term 'bank' in their company names. These issues raised deeper questions of whether Parliament should regulate the price of money, how borrowers use information in making their decisions, how to define moneylending as opposed to banking, and how to limit the damaging impact of the supposed debt spiral.

The two episodes provide a baseline for comparing the long-term development of moneylending and the trends in British policy towards unsecured cash loans. In part, the 1900 process began as a result of conflicting judicial approaches concerning the rewriting of credit contracts. Activists held that the government had every right to alter oppressive moneylending contracts on behalf of the downtrodden working classes and wealthy borrowers bamboozled by sophisticated moneylenders. Initial reform momentum suggested that the government's protective ethic would override an otherwise deferential preference for laissez-faire business relations.

While much of these early efforts focused on limiting the impact of high-cost loans issued to wealthy clients, the regulatory tools under consideration impacted the rich and poor alike. Price controls were front and centre. While most policymakers found high interest rates abhorrent, the idea of capping the cost of money ran afoul of free-market principles and a belief that usury laws were administratively burdensome. Parliament considered the ability to engage in commerce freely as a sacrosanct British value. Initiating a price cap on the cost of unsecured cash loans was ideologically and practically a step too far.

Adamant resistance towards price controls limited Parliament's ability to bring down loan costs. A complicated series of alternative options was considered. The concern was that too few borrowers were in a position to bargain for better loan terms. The government sought a way to relieve borrowers from abusive contracts without restricting credit access. Since all of the proposed measures too closely resembled price controls they too were left out of the 1900 Act. Parliament provided no guidance on when the cost of money became abusive and harmful.

From advertising to a moneylender registry, the tepid 1900 reforms failed to tame lenders or protect borrowers. What started as an all-out assault on the industry had sputtered when MPs inclined towards fewer restrictions weakened many of the 1897 Select Committee's recommendations. No one specific measure of the Act can be considered successful. The most that can be said of the 1900 Act is that it established a precedent for government intervention in the industry. More subtly, the act of regulating also confirmed that the industry, however minimal, performed some useful function. In an indirect way, the 1900 Act legitimized moneylending.

Twenty-five years later, Parliament again rejected price controls but this time administrative concerns were at the fore. It was unclear how the government would set and enforce a maximum interest rate across the entire moneylending industry. Since each loan carried different risks, a single rate could not accommodate the entire market. Without a means to select an interest rate cap, much less enforce it, plans for price controls fell by the wayside. The 1920s saw a less dogmatic perspective concerning economic reform (Taylor 2005; Ball 2013). A thinner boundary between the state and the market encouraged broad-based social programmes and a protective ethic unseen in earlier reform (Dorey 2011).

In the background was an almost unquestioned belief that the government can and should limit the damage caused by small loans on behalf of those who needed help (Fraser 2009). Earlier concerns over free-markets and a paternalistic state gave way to a confidence that practical solutions existed to the small-loan problem. 1920s policymakers intended to restrain loan volumes and drive down costs through moneylender licensing, advertising restrictions, mandated disclosure requirements and interest rate guidelines (though not outright price caps) empowering judges to relieve borrowers from extortionate loans. Licensing would filter ill-qualified persons from the business, fewer and less sensational advertisement would dampen demand, cost disclosures would make borrowers think twice before taking out a loan, and if all else failed, judges could rewrite individual loan contracts on a case-by-case basis.

The tools were in place for a more subdued and tamed moneylending environment. After an initial burst of licensing, these expectations fell flat, and in the immediate decades following the 1927 Act it was not much more than a dead letter. Neither the central government nor the police enforced the law and without adequate boundaries it was unclear what, precisely, constituted moneylending. Fears of legitimizing moneylending and the unintended impact regulation might have on 'proper' banking were balanced against a strong desire to rein in loan volumes. It spent a great deal of time ensuring that moneylenders not be considered bankers, yet they neglected to effectively define the industry or its role within the financial system, leaving the policy tools scattered about without a unified enforcement mechanism or sector focus. Most of all, concerns over system-wide price controls forced Parliament to rely on a judicial case-by-case approach to relieve borrowers from high-cost loans. This and the next chapter chronicles why that method failed to protect borrowers.

What follows analyses two periods, the first from 1897 to 1900 including the MLSC 1897 and the MLA 1900, and the second from 1925 to 1927, including the Moneylenders Select Committee (MLSC 1925) and the Moneylenders Act 1927 (MLA 1927).

Judiciary Controversy

In the 1890s, the media concentrated on the industry's growth, high interest rates and moneylenders extensive use of advertising.[1] For many, the enormous number of advertisements was proof enough that the industry had grown. The *Daily Telegraph* and *Standard* carried an estimated 18,000 moneylending advertisements annually.[2] Profiting seeking newspapers that willingly carried the advertisements also sensationalized the industry with headlines reporting extortionate moneylending contracts such as 'Interest at 400 per cent' and 'Ruined by Exorbitant Interest' (Church 2000).[3] The latter article reported that in 1897 Simpson and Co. lent £5 16s to Arthur Slater, a railway fitter earning approximately £84 annually. Slater had borrowed the money to pay medical bills. After paying £9 12s, a balance of £9 10s remained. Such stories hardened the public mood against moneylenders.[4] A consensus formed that 'there is not one of the numerous class which preys upon society in general either so numerous or so aggressive as the unscrupulous moneylender'. Thomas Farrow's and his book, *The Moneylender Unmasked*, capitalized on the public's anxiety and growing resentment towards the industry. As Parliamentary insider, his disdain for the industry and his push for an investigation did not go unnoticed.[5] As early as June 1895, calls mounted for restraining the 'evil' industry.[6]

Moneylenders pursuing debts through small claims court worsened their already dire public image. Their use of the court generated interest in their affairs and the role of court system in protecting borrowers from unfair lending practices.[7] Attacks against two of the largest moneylending concerns, which were heavy users of the courts, were magnified owing to their owner's Jewish faith and heritage (O'Connell 2009). Isaac Samuel, a moneylender estimated that over six years he had issued 34,344 loans and had sued 4694 debtors.[8] On average, he pursued legal recourse on two loans every day. While lenders were unlikely to take their poorest borrowers to court, activity in the judicial system galvanized efforts at curtailing their activities.

In the absence of existing regulation, the court system had emerged as the battleground for protecting borrowers. In that system two completely different protective approaches emerged, one reliant on market principles, and the other based on economic social justice, created tension and discord within the county courts overseeing small debt claims. In certain respects, the MLSC 1897 was as much a vehicle to solve judiciary debates as it was to create order and fairness in the small-loan market.

The Judiciary and Market Intervention

With the repeal of the Usury Act in 1854, a legal, profitable and vibrant moneylending industry came into being. As the borrower promised nothing more than an ability to repay the loan based on future wages, these unsecured cash loans were riskier than pawnbroking. Comprehensive loan applicants mitigated some of that risk. Lenders asked about an applicant's marital status, annual income, rent owed, rent accrued, employment details, an estimated value of furniture and effects, any debts and liabilities owed and past borrowing history (Farrow 1895, p. 213).[9] Successful applicants received cash on site and repayment occurred through a series of small, regular payments over many months. Between the loan application, repayment process and to say nothing of default rates, moneylending was expensive and risky. Whatever their costs, the highest rates of 400, 500 and even APR rates into the thousands found moneylenders with few allies.

At the lowest end of the market, the repeal of the usury law had very little, if anything, to do with small loans. One suggestion is that, at the time of repeal, the demand for small loans was insignificant, but it is more likely few policymakers considered the impact on the working poor following repeal.[10] Whatever Parliament's intention, the repeal contributed to the development of a legal moneylending market. One county court judge reflected that 'the repeal of usury laws has brought into existence these swarms of moneylenders, who like parasites breed on animals, injure their vital power, and impair the health of the commercial body' (Farrow 1895, prefatory).

Without moneylending-specific legislation, the court system arbitrated debt disputes. Moneylenders, along with retailers, wholesalers and their customers pleaded their grievances in front of small claims county court judges. These judges were on the front line of the nascent consumer- and contractual-based society (Finn 2003). Judicial actions generated much debate about to how best protect poor borrowers from abusive moneylenders. On the one hand, were 'liberal' judges who refused to interfere with contracts executed by able-minded adults and on the other, activist 'revisionist' judges who amended contracts in favour of the borrower. While classical theorists championed the 'freedom of contract', revisionists argued that the daily hardships of the working classes and the complexities of the urban economy compelled them towards judicial intervention.

Revisionist judges sought a balance between the debts owed to lenders against the economic hardship of the borrower (Finn 2003, p. 262). Judge James Mathew feared that without intervention, the judicial system's enforcement of unjust and unfair contracts acted as a 'lever of oppression' against borrowers.[11] In rewriting contracts judges relied on the concept of 'equitable jurisdiction'. Originating in the Court of Chancery, equitable jurisdiction enjoyed powers regarding 'fiduciary relations, protecting persons who were unable to protect themselves'.[12] Previously, such powers relieved wealthy heirs from burdensome loans, often when collateralized by a future inheritance. Revisionist judges applied the same legal device in the county court system on behalf of society's less fortunate.

While interfering with private loan contracts for wealthy folks was widely accepted, doing so for the working classes generated much controversy.[13] Whether 'ordinary' transactions executed by the 'poor and ignorant' should be dealt with in the same way as the upper classes challenged the normal boundaries of state interference in the market economy. Revisionist challenged the once clear legal distinction between wealthy and poor borrowers.[14] The debate brought forth major questions of how far the judiciary should go in protecting lower class borrowers from the harsher conditions of capitalism. Still, these judges could only go so far.[15] A judge could not, for example, hear a debt-complaint based solely on the interest rate or because a borrower had incurred excessive loan renewal fees, nor could judges fully annul a moneylending contract. Even if a judge found some costs to be excessive, such as default terms or rollover fees, he could not set them aside. He could, however, rewrite the instalment terms. By decreasing the instalment to a nugatory amount, in practice the contract became worthless.[16] In one case the judge decreased the instalment to one penny a month, thereby extending the loan maturity to more than 140 years.[17] These interventions had nothing to do with fraudulent activity, but simply a belief that the contract took advantage of the borrower's circumstances.[18]

From the revisionist point of view, borrowers engaged with moneylenders 'under duress' and were de facto entering a moneylending contract with no bargaining power.[19] The aim was protecting persons incapable of protecting themselves.[20] This case-by-case approach implemented market 'reform' based on their vision of fairness. Nor were these judges alone in advocating for justice within the market system. Farrow sought reform because the moneylending system 'gnaws at the vitals of our social economy'.[21] These powerful judicial actors intervened citing a protective obligation to the working classes from wider economic forces. Left to their own devices, revisionist judges widened the rules of engagement between the market and state power.

On the other side were judges believing that industry and commerce should be free from government regulation.[22] Proponents of this classical school of economic theory found meddling in contracts particularly offensive and asked why if judges interfered with moneylending, what was to stop them from rewriting other agreement?[23] Reflecting this, *The Spectator* wrote:

> the right of the Judge, if he thinks the contract oppressive or unreasonable, to tear it up and substitute another of his own. That is ... a very dangerous principle to introduce into our laws; and in the case of moneylending, is it either just or wise? A moneylender is not only a human being, but a citizen as much as a dealer in bric-a-brac; and if he commits no fraud ... and writes out ... a clear contract with truthful details, why is that contract not to be enforced ...?[24]

It was argued that criminal law dealing with fraud gave borrowers sufficient protection and that moneylending should be treated no differently than other businesses. Whatever jurists thought or felt about high-interest loans was irrelevant; the judiciary had no role in rewriting a legally binding contract and nor should the government expect to produce better outcomes than the market.

Both revisionists and free-market-oriented judges relied on legal precedent and theory. The judicial debates added to the public outcry against moneylenders. As the pressured mounted, moneylenders faced a backlash against their business and treatment of borrowers. Since some judges had already pushed the legal boundaries to the edge, it was Parliament's turn to decide just how far the state should regulate finance on behalf of poor and rich borrowers alike.

Victorian Regulators Have Their Say, 1897–1900

Every cause needs a champion, and as early as 1894, Robert Yerburgh MP (Conservative) and his political secretary, Thomas Farrow led the political campaign against moneylenders. Their initial strategy of curtailing abusive lending fell on deaf ears. Policing moneylenders fell outside the scope of the Board of Trade and other similar government agencies.[25] While perhaps distasteful, high-interest small loans were not illegal. Even more sympathetic ears doubted if regulation could prevent moneylenders from making victims of people in desperate need. This idea found company over the decades. It is rather difficult for regulation to safeguard the needs of people who have experienced financial trouble before seeking a high-cost loan. Often the cause of financial distress occurred irrespective of any credit product. Undeterred, Yerburgh pressed for a political investigation into the 'grave abuses' of moneylenders whose 'victims' were the working class.[26]

After years of groundwork, in 1897 Parliament appointed a select committee to uncover the 'alleged evils' of high-interest loans and alleviate the 'oppressive' conditions of repayments.[27] After concluding slightly more than half of its twenty-six scheduled hearings, the Committee issued a strongly worded condemnation,

> The Committee unhesitatingly come to the conclusion that the system of money lending by professional money lenders at high rates of interest is productive of crime, bankruptcy, unfair advantage over other creditors of the borrower, extortion from the borrower's family and friends, and other serious injuries to the community and although your Committee

> are satisfied that the system is sometimes honestly conducted they are of opinion that only in rare cases is a person benefited by a loan obtained from a professional money-lender and that the evil attendant upon the system far outweighs the good.[28]

So strong was the anti-moneylending sentiment that George Lewis, with forty years of 'great' judicial experience, argued that he '[had] never known a single instance in which the borrower has benefitted'.[29] Farrow claimed that no man had 'righted' himself by borrowing from a moneylender.[30] Policymakers such as Henry Marks MP (Conservative), who believed that the recent exposure of 'money-lending vampires' demanded urgent attention, dominated the hearings.[31] During that same debate, it was argued that 'depriving the poor amongst the working class of all moneylenders' would be 'distinctly good'. Even before the Committee's conclusion, the verdict was clear: these loans were of no benefit to the borrower. However, the perennial question remained: How far was Parliament willing to control the moneylending 'evil'? The following explores the Committee's official investigation into the moneylending industry, revealing details about how the industry operated and the various methods Parliament considered for regulation.

High Interest Rates

With nineteenth-century newspaper headlines reporting annual rates of 200 and 300% and even rising into the thousands, disparaging and disliking moneylenders was a popular pastime. The problem for policymakers was to determine why rates were so high, and the best form of government regulation. Victorian moneylenders issued two different loan products. Less commonly, moneylenders issued bills of sale, which resembled a pawn contract. Unlike pawn, the collateralized good remained the possession of the borrower. A bill of sale transferred ownership of the property from one party to another if certain loan conditions were not met. The law required that these transactions were registered with the local municipality. Estimates indicate that in 1894 approximately 9400 bills of sale were registered in England, with most affiliated to professional moneylenders (Farrow 1896, p. 129). Data from forty moneylenders showed interest rates of 60 to 170 pcpa.[32] The vast majority of lending was in the form of unsecured or 'note-of-hand' promissory notes. The loan principal varied from just a few pounds to thousands. Like today's payday loans, a borrower promises to repay a loan based on future wages. These loans are inherently riskier than pawn or bills of sale and typically carry a higher interest rate.

Without official reporting requirements, interest rate data was relatively sparse. The Committee's witness pool provided what information they could. There was a general consensus that in East London the poor borrowed from professional moneylenders at a penny in the shilling a week (approximately 400 pcpa). Larger loans followed a pattern of £12 lent on a £18 promissory note with 30 shillings due in twelve monthly instalments.[33] Lesser valued promissory notes were priced at 1/2d in the shilling a pound a week or 216 pcpa.[34] The highest rate admitted during the proceedings approached 3000 pcpa.[35] Judge Francis Roxburgh of the Lord Mayor's Court of London suggested a common range of 60–600 pcpa.[36] George Lewis, a solicitor, testified that the usual rate was 60 pcpa, but admitted seeing rates exceeding 2000 pcpa.[37] Farrow estimated that the usual interest rate was 60 pcpa.[38] Isaac Samuel, a moneylender and principal-owner of Fieldings Limited, confirmed Farrow's estimate. Over seven years and six months, Samuel issued 34,344 loans, 99.2% of which were on promissory notes with an average rate of 60 pcpa.[39] While there was some consensus that the average rate hovered around 60 pcpa, lenders charged a variety of rates and loan amounts.

Moneylenders argued the rates reflected the expensive and risky nature of the business.[40] For them, it was a matter of risk and reward, with low-risk clients paying much lower rates in the 15–20 pcpa range, less than the legal pawnbroking rate of 25 pcpa.[41] Few witnesses appreciated the expense of lending small sums and many misunderstood the risk differential between collateralized pawn and promissory moneylending. Judge Stevenson Owen went so far as to declare that if a moneylender could not operate at the pawnbroker rate 25 pcpa, 'he should put his shutters up'.[42] Explaining their business model to a relatively hostile committee was an arduous affair.

As a percentage of the principal, and even more so, gross interest, moneylender loans were expensive to administer. Accountancy-certified income statements and witness testimony suggested expenses ran 15–22% of gross interest.[43] Moneylenders tried shifting the narrative away from percentages by comparing themselves to insurance underwriting and likening themselves to retailers of money.[44] Samuel explained, 'We sell £5 for £6 5s ... if a butcher sold 5s worth of meat and it cost him 4s that would be a shilling on the transaction; that is 20%. If that was multiplied as you multiply moneylenders' interest that would be 7,000 pcpa'.[45] Like in retailing, the principal is the product with an associated wholesale cost, whereas the interest charged is the product mark-up. Samuel further simplified saying that when he lent a shilling and earned a shilling one week later, his profit was but a shilling.[46] Whether it be pawnbrokers, moneylenders or their later payday loan counterparts, these businesses went to great lengths, though often with little success, explaining that small sums lending was expensive and risky.

Few outsiders appreciated that the interest rate charged had to cover expenses, default risk and provide a sufficient return on capital. The only thing that most people cared about appeared in shocking newspaper headlines quoting interest rates into the thousands. Overcoming the jury of public opinion portraying them as 'unscrupulous men who prey' and entrap borrowers with high interest rates that were 'a sore eating in the very life of the working-class' was insurmountable.[47] Some kind of regulation was an all but certain outcome of the Committee's findings.

Price Controls

On the cost side of the policy equation, price controls were the heavy-handed solution to high interest rates. Legal precedent and the Committee's continued comparison of moneylending to pawnbroking encouraged them to select a capped rate of 25 pcpa.[48] However, this rate barely exceeded some of the *lowest* unsecured rates for borrowers in good standing.[49] At that level, price caps would drive suppliers out of the market and shut down some of the industry. This was a clear signal that the market was better off with fewer lenders and such measures were needed to break an endless cycle of debt.[50] Moneylenders warned of a market contraction so severe that the smallest value and short-term loans, those typically used by the working poor, would cease existing, leaving vulnerable borrowers without loans to cover their basic needs.[51] No one debated the impact of price controls, the issue was whether small loans harmed consumers to the point that the government should force a market contraction.

Victorian policymakers rejected price controls. Foremost, there was an appeal to freedom of contract and a strong resistance to usury, an issue that many felt had been settled in 1854. The idea of regulating the price of money, as opposed to a pawned good, was impossible to overcome.[52]

Citing the liberal economic trinity of Bentham, Smith and Ricardo, Vicary Gibbs MP (Conservative) said that price controls were an attempt to 'knock ... against' natural law.[53] Despite the strongly held conviction that small loans made the conditions of poverty even worse, the benefits of free commerce and arguments against usury carried the day.[54] Trusting in market outcomes overrode any possibility of industry-wide price caps.

Policymakers also express concern over the practical difficulties of market distorting price controls.[55] They asked how the government could select, monitor and enforce a single interest rate across the entire moneylending industry that both protected borrowers and yet incentivized market activity. They wondered how a government committee could draw the line: what rate was 'too high':

> that no limit of interest can be prescribed which would be adapted to the widely different conditions under which these loans are contracted, and further, that if a maximum rate were fixed by statute, the interest would tend in all cases to rise to that maximum.[56]

The Committee's secondary concern over price clustering indicated a further reluctance to interfere in the market's pricing mechanism. Perhaps counterintuitively, it was argued that a price control measure would de facto operate as a floor in that pricing would gravitate towards the ceiling irrespective of risk profiles. Other borrowers would be left paying for those segmented out of the market.

Ruling out price controls did not solve the problem of high costs or abusive lending practices. If price controls could not mitigate situations when working men making their 30–40 shillings a week needed quick cash, what regulation would?[57] According to the chairman, '[E]verybody who has heard the evidence must feel that when people are hard pressed for money, and must get it, they will give anything for it. It is very hard for the law to protect people in that position'.[58] What the Committee wanted was a solution that improved an individual borrower's disadvantaged position without any hard-and-fast rule on market-wide loan pricing.

Price Controls Light

If not for the considerable amount of thought and engagement of the price control issue, accusing the Committee of lacking imagination might well be justified. They concluded that the only effective 'remedy for the evils in the system of moneylending by professionals is to give the courts absolute and unfettered discretion in dealing with these transactions'.[59] The Committee affirmed the revisionist judicial approach. A solution they believed relieved borrowers of abusive terms without distorting market-wide pricing. If Parliament adopted the measure, judges would have officially sanctioned revisionary powers over moneylending contracts.

The proposal was not without its complications and detractors. A case-by-case approach relied on the opinion of individual judges. This type of legal process jeopardized the consistency of the legal system.[60] Ironically, the system could actually increase borrowing costs to compensate lender's for increased legal risk. It was also feared that if sufficient judges rewrote contracts based solely on interest rates, they would, in effect, create an interest rate cap.[61] The Committee struggled with addressing these very real concerns. While there was little political will to reinstate usury, most of the problem with these loans stemmed from their cost. Reformers found themselves in a tight spot—how could they help judges determine if a transaction was extortionate without setting a price rule? From every which angle, the line between useful and harmful credit depended on the interest rate.[62] The Committee was sure it had to provide some kind of price guidance to the judiciary without crossing into the realm of a usury law.

Their goal was to select a 'guidance' interest rate that, if met or exceeded, allowed a judge to review an individual moneylending transaction without indirectly capping the interest rate charged across the entire market. This was no easy task. Among the witnesses and within the Committee there was no agreement on what the threshold rate should be. But there was some agreement on how the process could work. A transaction could not be reviewed unless the interest rate exceeded a guidance rate *and* the judge believed that the transaction was harsh and unconscionable.[63] The moneylender was not breaking the law by contracting at an interest rate that exceeded the guidance rate. An interest rate above the review level was not to be considered prima facie exorbitant. The guidance rate acted as a trigger, which, if exceeded, provided a legal basis for a judicial review of the transaction. Judges could consider a whole host of factors in their decision. If the lender charged a rate above the guidance rate, and the transaction was considered fair, the lender could expect to recover the debt. But if a lender charged a rate higher than the guidance rate and the transaction was found to be harsh and unconscionable, a judge had absolute discretion to deal with the transaction.[64]

The Committee members proposed a variety of guidance rates. One believed that 20 pcpa would suffice.[65] Samuel found the rate far too low and Gordon claimed that if the review rate was set below 30 pcpa, he would immediately close up shop.[66] Other moneylenders argued against any sort of government guidance or interference. Alfred Moore said that when 'two sane men enter into a contract' it would be 'unfair for anyone to interfere between them'.[67] John Kirkwood argued that such powers would be 'ruinous' to the market and interest rates charged would 'have to be enormous' to cover losses due to judicial interference. The passage of these powers would be a 'gross interference with the liberty of British subjects'.[68] Given the money at stake, Kirkwood's appeal to liberty is understandable, but his other point was lost on the Committee.[69] In so far as the cost of regulation had to be paid for, the lender had to experience either lower returns or charge higher rates. In the latter case, borrowers who had been approved bore the cost of regulation. Again, approved borrowers would pay for the cost of protecting those segmented out of the market.

The first draft parliamentary bill offered a range of guidance rates scaled down from the pawnbroking rate of 25 pcpa (Table 3.1).

A minority of voices denounced the guidance as 'an absurdly small and unreasonable' charge to be made for profitably administrating a small loan.[70] Birrell and Sydney Gedge MP (Conservative) argued that the judicial review process would burden the industry and reduce the supply of small loans to the poor.[71] Terrance Russell MP (Liberal) believed moneylenders were being targeted unfairly and questioned why bargains from every branch of trade should not be reviewed. He suggested that the laws dealing with fraud offered sufficient borrower protection. Opponents of the 'price control light' guidance rate asserted that it was too

Table 3.1 Schedule of guidance interest rate

In respect of a loan (whether made by one or more advances)	
Not exceeding 40 shillings	25 pcpa
Exceeding 40 shillings, but not exceeding £10	20 pcpa
Exceeding £10	15 pcpa

Source 1899 Bill 215 Money-lending (HL)

close to usury and kept the proposal from advancing. Arthur Balfour (Conservative, Leader of the Commons, Prime Minister 1902–1905) stated:

> Where we differ is as to whether the particular machinery which the Bill provides for dealing with harsh and unconscionable bargains is of a kind which interferes illegitimately with freedom of contract between adult human beings ... we have no desire to revive the usury laws in any disguise whatever.[72]

For its part, the Committee came up with a solution that interfered in transactions only after the market had priced risk and reward. To them, it seemed the best of both worlds, offering both price freedom and borrower protection. Too many of their colleagues disagreed. So strong was their resistance that once the guidance rate schedule was removed, opposition to the rest of bill collapsed. The enacted MLA 1900 officially granted judicial powers to reopen and revise moneylending contracts but did so without providing any interest rate guidance. Offensively high interest rates were not necessarily harsh and unconscionable. The overarching concern for freedom of contract outweighed state intervention aimed at stronger forms of price controls and forced market contraction. The Committee's preference for a guidance rate was overruled by MPs when the bill was debated in Parliament. In doing so, the MLA 1900 failed to address the key question: When was an interest too highrate?

Fraudulent Advertisement and Disclosure Terms

Interest rates were not the only hope for reform. There was a widespread belief that moneylenders frequently withheld critical information from borrowers. Farrow testified that 'These evils would not be, perhaps, so great if they were accompanied by a lower interest rate; but accompanied as they are by a minimum of 60 per cent they do become evils'.[73] In a more subdued fashion, the Attorney-General, Robert Finlay, who was one of the nation's leading lawyers, agreed that misleading advertisements had to be tackled.[74] Even ardent supporters of laissez-faire principles believed regulation was necessary to combat fraudulent advertisements and misleading contract terms.

Advertising was essential to the moneylending business. So strong was this relationship that James Dodwell denied being a moneylender because he did not advertise.[75] To measure the relationship between loan demand and advertising effectiveness, Farrow placed two advertisement as experiments. In one, he offered money to lend at 10% in four London daily newspapers, to which he received 283 replies in a single day. In the second, he placed three advertisements in a London weekly, for which he received 450 replies from across the spectrum of the working class.[76] While Farrow's experiment confirmed the effectiveness of advertising, it also demonstrated the fact that small loans were in great demand, a fact lost on the industry's detractors.

Farrow argued that newspaper advertisements were 'framed chiefly with the purpose of deceiving the ... poor and ignorant'.[77] Newspaper advertisements targeted low- to middle-end borrowers, while London's wealthy West End lenders sought high-end borrowers in circulars sent by post. Critics were especially incensed by advertised teaser rates offering money at 5% with most borrowers assumed this was an annual rate, however, the actual contracted interest rate was 5% a month, annualizing at 60 pcpa.[78] Apparently, borrowers often signed the contract without confirming the rate's time component.

A few sceptical MP's felt little obliged to protect 'foolish' borrowers who failed to confirm such basics as the interest rate and repayment terms.[79] Unfortunately, the economic realities of the working classes place the cost and terms of a loan as secondary to securing the cash. Both then and now, this is why advertising is so critical to the moneylending business model. Borrowers needed quick cash and advertising helped them locate the various providers. While there was consensus on the importance of advertising to generate new business, there was disagreement about how unambiguous the information was. Some held that disingenuous teaser rates were just the first step in a chain of predatory practices.

Having mislead borrowers through advertisements, lenders were also accused of failing to disclose critical loan features, including the interest rate stated in percentage form, amortization schedules and default terms.[80] The Committee heard wide-ranging evidence on all three topics. Moneylenders retorted that borrowers were welcome to request a copy of loan contracts and that nothing was ever hidden from them. John Faux, one of four borrowers interviewed by the Select Committee, disagreed, arguing that many of the details were concealed and that he did not understand the terms to which he had agreed.[81] This raised the question: What types of information should be disclosed to borrowingencourage informed?

Policymakers accused lenders of deception owing to their practice of quoting the interest rate in currency terms; for example, a £7 loan would carry a £3 interest charge. With this method lenders informed the borrower of 'exactly what [they had] to pay'.[82] The Committee received almost unanimous advice that the interest rate should be stated on the contract and disclosed in percentage terms.[83] As short-term retailers of money, lenders strongly opposed the APR measure.[84] Since retailers of other commodities were not required to state their costs in percentage terms, they should not be either. There were more practical reasons too. Two lenders admitted that they were unable to work out the interest rate.[85]

One lender argued that any legal requirement forcing percentage disclosure would require two more clerks in each office.[86] To this one Committee member responded, 'You could surely afford that expense at 179 per cent interest'. The moneylender reminded the Committee that his net profit margin was 11% and additional regulatory burdens would only decrease that already low rate. Expense aside, moneylenders believed that it made no sense to annualize a short-term loan and that the borrowers themselves preferred knowing the amount owed in pounds and pence.[87] The APR debate—that is, whether it was suitable for small loans issued on a short-term basis—resurfaced throughout this book. In fact, it was not until almost two decades into the twenty-first century that policymakers admitted that short-term borrowers do not consider percentages costs in their decisions. During this period, however, the word of moneylenders was not enough and almost all parties pushed for some sort of annual percentage disclosure.

Policymakers also expressed concern over deceiving interest-only terms, which stacked the repayment schedule against borrowers, encouraged default and incentivized loan rollovers.[88] Refusing a rollover then defaulting threatened public exposure and potential for a lawsuit, pressures most borrowers avoided at all costs. Exposure threats were particularly effective with public sector clerks, whose contract of employment forbade recourse to a moneylender and loss of employment.[89] Several references were made to the instant dismissal terms of clerks employed by the Bank of England.[90] On one occasion, Robert Linnell, a moneylender, took his collection efforts too far, having written to the senior managers of Messrs Pulham and Cooke, clerks at the Inland Revenue and the Ministry of Health, respectively.[91] Linnell complained of Pulham and Cooke's failure to repay. Refusing to succumb to 'blackmail', the Inland

Revenue pursued legal resource against the lender. Linnell was later found guilty by a London magistrate calling him a 'blood-sucking usurer'. The magistrate's language was no accident. Despite no longer having any legal basis, morals concept of usury found expression within the court system (O'Connell 2009, p. 133).

From advertisements through to the signing of the contract, policymakers pushed for increased transparency and accurate information disclosure. Though few borrower voices were heard during the deliberations, the 5% teaser rates and confusing terms were well documented. Borrowers deserved a much clearer picture of the contract than moneylenders typically offered. While later truth in lending regulation assumed that such improved information enhanced market efficiencies through better informed borrower decisions, at this point policymakers more simply sought less decreased fraudulent activity.

Trade Names

Policymakers of every stripe held the traditional banking profession in the highest regard and every effort was made to ensure that it was not to be confused with moneylending. William Anson MP (Liberal) declared that 'no one ever talks of a banker as a moneylender' and Lewis added that mistaking a professional moneylender for a banker was all but impossible.[92] During the Select Committee, not a single banker had been accused of charging an exorbitant interest rate or engaging in extortionate and predatory behaviour.[93] Whereas bankers loans were productive and societally useful, moneylenders issued predatory and harmful loans.[94] The debate raises an important point: Where is the boundary between a banker that lends money and a moneylender that does the same? Should the classification of a lender be determined by the income of its clients or the heights of their interest charges? What made a lender of money, a moneylender? Without an appropriate definition and boundary, enforcing moneylending regulation would be impossible.

Moneylenders holding themselves out as bankers irked the select committee to no end. Portraying oneself as a banker gave the public a false sense of security.[95] A few of the largest moneylending operations owned multiple offices, traded under different identifies and even some of the smallest lenders used the terms 'bank', 'finance' or 'trust company' as part of their company name. One moneylender admitted to trading under nine names, none of which was his own. Another conducted business using seven bank names.[96] Trading under assumed names with multiple identifies facilitated business transactions, the practice also stemmed from anti-Semitism and xenophobia (Orchard and May 1933, pp. 60–1, 84). Better to trade under a long-standing British name than risk prejudicial behaviour against foreigners. Lenders, much like borrowers, preferred anonymity.

The Committee was especially critical of loan consolidations issued by a single moneylender under different company names.[97] This could happen when a borrower took out a new loan to pay back an existing loan from what the borrower believed to be two separate companies. The Committee heard of one relatively well-off woman who had trouble repaying £50 owed to a Chester-based lender. In order to pay this lender, she secured a £70 loan from a Liverpool concern. Further troubles caused her to default on that loan too. In Birmingham, she acquired a third loan of £100 to repay the Liverpool-based lender. All three offices were owned by Gordon. When asked if this was an appropriate practice, he replied, 'I risk my money … and I have a perfect right to make any bargain I see fit … and give to that lady [under] forty names … I can do it'.[98] His cavalier attitude towards the debt cycle found little favour with the Committee. The interaction layers in yet another complicating factor: How many renewal loans were too many? Should the law limit the number of loans that a borrower could transact?

The MLA 1900 Concerning Fraud and Transparency

There was no agreement on remedies for fraud and transparency. Proposals included banning advertisements, licensing schemes for controlling market-entry and a requirement that all transactions be filed with a local authority. Banning advertising was an especially harsh measure, and a back-door way to curtail or even effectively eliminate the entire industry.[99] Like many of the reforms under consideration, the power to ban advertisements was supported by legal precedent. Proponents were extending the logic of clause 2 of the Betting and Loans (Infants) Act, which forbade advertising to those persons under the age of twenty-one.[100] Apparently, 'foolish and childish' borrowers needed protection as much as 'legal infants'.[101] Categorizing borrowers in such light facilitated a need for regulation, especially against a moneylending 'financial wolf and rapacious shark'.[102]

Committed economic liberals and moneylenders pointed out that criminal law already had the power to prosecute false statements.[103] While the imagery of childlike behaviour resonated, moneylending contracts were executed by able-minded adults. Parliament was not prepared to restrict free commerce on behalf of borrowers who misunderstood advertised terms. An outright ban on advertising was viewed as too harsh. If fraud or deception was proved in court, then judges could review and nullify the contract. Resistance to interfering in businesses is also evident in the MLA 1900s near silence concerning other disclosure issues including stating the interest rate in percentage terms, amortization schedules, default terms and renewal loans.[104]

Agreement was found concerning the use of trade names and the identity of moneylenders. Many policymakers saw value in the government knowing who moneylenders were. A government registry of moneylenders received widespread support. Henry Hawkins, a judge sitting in the High Court of Justice, declared that if moneylenders fought the proposal, it only showed how ashamed they were of their business.[105] The enacted registry required that each moneylender registers with the Inland Revenue under a single name and file each location of their business.[106] Only registered offices could transact legally. Economic liberals slipped in a strange quirk allow for a moneylender to file under a single name without specifying whether that name was given or assumed. This concession avoided damaging already well-known moneylending concerns whose business might suffer if forced to change its name.

Parliament still had to define what constituted a moneylender. They began with what they knew—banking. Bankers were defined as people who engaged in the activity of banking.[107] This definition did not get them very far, so one witness identified that the source of capital distinguished bankers from moneylenders as the former acquired deposits while the latter did not.[108] Others considered the entire exercise as unnecessary since moneylending was so readily understood.[109] The Committee disagreed and, working from the legal phraseology assigned to bankers, defined moneylenders as, 'every person whose business is that of moneylending'.[110] But, practically speaking, how did that differ from the function of a banker?

Parliament refined the definition by exclusion. The MLA 1900 cited four industries as not being moneylenders. These were pawnbrokers, friendly societies, any group granted special powers by Parliament to lend money and 'any person *bona fide* carrying on the business of banking or insurance'. In retrospect, Parliament utterly failed to provide a working definition of moneylenders. This was one of many mistakes rendering the registry ineffective. If the goal of a registry is controlling entry by placing certain requirements onto applications, then the 1900 Act seriously missed the mark. It did not require a moneylender to operate under his given name nor could the Inland Revenue deny an applicant or remove a moneylender from the registry. Even a lender with a criminal conviction could apply and later not be removed. Even after a 1911 amendment clarified that a moneylender whose registration name implied that it was banking concern could be removed and subject to a fine and imprisonment, the registry's entry and control requirements were minimal.

Notably stricter controls, such as a licensing scheme, were excluded from the MLA 1900. During the MLSC 1897 several witnesses, including moneylenders, asked for licensing and proposed enhanced regulation, including a supervisory authority to deny or revoke a licence, audit financial statements and required moneylenders to post bond and maintain capital reserves.[111] Samuel supported licensing and argued that '£500–£1000 should be deposited in Consols to prove' that they had money to lend.[112] Support for enhanced licensing regulation stemmed from an expectation that government screening rooted out ill-capitalized lenders and banning poorly behaving lenders providing legitimacy and offering a much-needed status boost to the industry. In that respect both gadfly reformers and moneylenders saw aspects of regulation as beneficial.

Prima facie registration and licensing might seem secondary to interest rates and disclosure terms, and the difference between a registry and licensing might seem trivial. However, the fact that the MLA 1900 adopted a registry rather than a licensing scheme proved crucial to the development of the market. The registry was a non-discriminatory administrative task. It required a moneylender to file his or her name and office location(s) and nothing more. The Inland Revenue had no supervisory role. The Committee's rejection of a licensing scheme reflected Parliament's unwillingness to legitimize moneylenders. It was recognized that a government licence implied implicit approval of the applicant and by extension the industry. Since a licensed business was 'approved', applicants who failed the process were unfit. The association of government-sanctioned suitability persuaded the judiciary and Committee against a licensing scheme. Years later, Ernley Blackwell, Assistant Under Secretary at the Home Office, admitted that it was rejected because 'it [gave the] impression that moneylenders had a sort of guarantee by the Government'.[113] Tellingly, for all of the 'evil' rhetoric, the government had rejected forms of strict regulation such as banning advertisements, price controls and licensing.

Aftermath

Based on trade group data and government estimates, during the first quarter of the 1900s, it is likely that professional moneylenders numbered between 4000 and 6000 operating in some 8000 offices.[114] Unfortunately, the reality is that no one knows how many moneylenders existed nor who those lenders actually were. The registry process never developed, the list was never released publicly, and the First World War furthered interrupted the Inland Revenue's administrative function. Not long after its passage other aspects of the Act's shortcomings also became apparent. In 1901, Horace Mansfield MP (Liberal) asked why the Inland Revenue had not prosecuted a single moneylender for failing to register.[115] This reveals how misunderstood and ill-crafted the Act was. The Inland Revenue was charged with registering moneylenders but had no power to prosecute failure to do so. In 1907, the Metropolitan Police brought to the attention of the Inland Revenue a Bethnal Green resident who, while legally registered as a moneylender, had been imprisoned twice and was under arrest for receiving stolen goods.[116] In 1910, Rufus Isaacs and John Simon, lawyers with the Board of Trade, expressed frustration that the MLA 1900 usual trade name clause allowed many to register under a pseudonym. Later that same year, the Board of Trade did not know whether it should prosecute Yorkshire Discount Bank and Cardiff Advance Bank for calling themselves a bank.[117]

Parliament sought legislation that balanced the fine line between preserving the freedom of two adults to engage in commerce, while offering meaningful borrower recourse against abusive lending. Freedom of contract was of paramount concern—that is, the ability to negotiate the price of money and conditions of contract. They found their answer in the court system and the activities of revisionist judges. In practice, judicial review process and the 1900 Act failed and did little to alter the business of moneylending or protect consumers (Matthews 1906; Collard 1912).[118] Asked how he had arrived at a decision regarding a moneylending case, Justice Scrutton replied that 'he did not propose to give a reason ... [it would] only be reported and used against him and other judges' (Collard 1912, p. 172). Without much guidance from the Act, judges were left to determine whether a borrower had fully understood the transaction, whether the lender had fulfilled the burden of proof and what constituted excessive interest. On top of that, few poor borrowers actually used the courts.

Oversights such as that are predictable since the Committee spent far more time deliberating about the working class than the lowest rung borrowers. Still, and notwithstanding its relatively ineffectiveness, one of the results of their efforts concerning the poor was the influx of small-time, mostly female, lenders onto the registry in the years immediately following the Act's passage. Registering gave them access to the court system and enhanced visibility within the lending community. Those benefits brought along increased scrutiny, and the behaviour of these 'slum lenders' and 'she-usurers' encouraged campaigners towards further reform in the 1920s (O'Connell 2009, pp. 132–7). Soon concerns over small loan 'scraps from the banker's plate' again challenged Parliament's willingness to intervene in markets on behalf of poor and vulnerable borrowers (Orchard and May, p. 31).

Reining in Small-Value Loans 1925–27

> *The world at large has recently had plenty of advertisements so far as the higher branches of blackmail are concerned. And presumably it is these revelations that prompted a Parliamentary effort to check the widespread and insidious evil... moneylenders are callous, bloodsucking parasites, without moral sense... lurking about in search of innocent victims.*
>
> "Upon usury," *Hull Daily Mail*, 27 March 1925

> *On all hands there appears to be a substantial measure of agreement that the Act of 1900 has hopelessly broken down, and that more drastic legislation is necessary in order to curb the machinations of sharks ... who wax fat on the misfortunes of others.*
>
> *Aberdeen Journal*, 18 March 1925

During the 1920s moneylending was growing rapidly. Between 1922 and 1924, 4647 new moneylending concerns had registered with the Inland Revenue.[119] This expansion did not go unnoticed. Newspaper headlines and articles called moneylenders evil, Shylocks, satanic and loan sharks. Many parliamentarians were frustrated by the incessant 'siren' and 'plague' of moneylending circulars they received in the post.[120] Edward Carson, Lord Carson (Ulster Unionist Party) bemoaned how a single moneylender had sent 190,000 circulars in just six months' time.[121] Reformers feared for 'the shark's prey' and claimed that the 1900 Act was not an 'effective curb on the social evil'.[122] Judges themselves believed that their powers were 'utterly useless' to control moneylenders.[123]

Carson's campaign was sparked by the plight of civil servants such as Fred Webb, who had filed for bankruptcy after borrowing from a moneylender, and a naval commander who paid exorbitant interest over three years before the loan was paid.[124] No doubt spiralling debt burdens encroached upon their ability to carry out their work and fears over bankruptcy could ruin their careers.[125] After investigating many cases of 'hardship and poverty', Carson doubted that moneylenders benefitted society and sought urgent action to curtail their practice.[126] By 1925 two moneylending bills, one proposed by Richard Wells MP (Conservative) and the other by Carson himself, attracted enough parliamentary interest to warrant a joint select committee (MLSC 1925). Although Carson was worried that the committee was a 'shelving procedure', the Home Secretary, William Joynson-Hicks MP (Conservative), affirmed the government's commitment towards meaningful reform.[127]

More far reaching than its 1897 predecessor, the MLSC 1925 heard testimony from a range of interested parties, including moneylending trade associations and charitable organizations.[128] Though expansive, the additional witnesses offered moneylenders little support. Hostility and contempt surfaced early and often, 'moneylenders ... are the scum of the earth' and that 'to look into the face of a moneylender ... is to see the picture of the devil incarnate'.[129] Erratic employment, causal labour, daily budget shortfalls and emergency needs drove the demand for cash loans. Gendered networks of female lenders offering small sums primarily to female clients while males tended towards work-place loans, both found lenders operating within and outside of the MLA 1900 (O'Connell 2009; Tebbutt 1983; Johnson 1985a, b). Across Britain, but especially in the industrial north, charity workers raised the alarm over an uptick in small-value lending which sparked the initial efforts towards conveying the MLSC 1925.

For the most part, this episode avoided harsh ideological debates between social reformers and free-market hardlines. Few Conservatives advocated for complete deregulation and only a handful of lone voices cautioned against too much of a 'grandmotherly' approach (Dorey 2011;

Taylor 2005; Ball 2013; Daunton 2007).[130] With the failure of the MLA 1900, moneylending was a specific problem that required an immediate and practical response. Taming moneylenders came more naturally to this generation of Parliamentarians. Policymakers argued that the pressing demands of borrowers created a 'peculiar' market dynamic, one that necessitated government oversight to level the scales away from predatory lenders.[131] Under consideration were critical issues such as price controls, judicial review, advertising and the role of moneylending in the wider financial system.

High Interest Rates, Price Controls and Judicial Review

Policymakers and society writ large focused on the 'misery' caused by moneylenders.[132] The first step was figuring out why the MLA 1900 had failed to ease abusive lending.[133] Moneylenders and their opponents agreed that the 1900 Act was inconsistently applied and that judicial rulings concerning harsh and unconscionable transactions varied widely.[134] MPs were highly critical of the way in which the system had developed and claimed that the men who had framed the MLA 1900 'never intended to give such wide powers to county courts'.[135] While these frustrations were reasonable, the MLA 1900 case-by-case system was operating as designed. The 1900 Act relied on a decentralized judicial mechanism for borrower recourse in order to avoid blanket, market-wide price restrictions.

Since the high costs of loans garnered such considerable attention, price caps quite naturally entered the conversation. Politicians cited loans such as a woman who borrowed 30 shillings and owed £5 17s in return.[136] Another had borrowed £2 to pay for medical expenses for a sick child. Over twelve months she paid 4 shillings a week, totalling £12. These were exactly the kinds of transaction that bothered policymakers twenty-five years earlier, when price controls were considered and rejected. This time the ghost of Bentham was no longer raised, nor were there many objections based on personal freedom in commerce. Instead, administrative concerns kept price controls off the debate floor. The Home Office argued that implementing a single rate that would compensate for the wide range of risks was impractical, if not impossible.[137] Judge Mackenzie Chalmers, a Permanent Secretary at the Home Office, believed that usury did not work as it was easy to evade, failed to compensate moneylenders for the risk of lending on a promissory note and encouraged credit rationing.[138] Richard Haldane, Lord Haldane (Labour) recounted that, in the past, usury had been avoided by creating similar financial products that fell outside regulatory restriction.[139] By the 1920s, theoretical debates over the merits and drawbacks of government-mandated price caps had developed into practical concerns over solving the immediate problem of high interest rates. For this generation of lawmakers, the messy business of price controls was not the answer.

The idea of a guidance rate resurfaced and proved popular as it provided a reference point for judges without totally capping the entire market. The trick, of course, with price controls and guidance rates, is figuring out the point at which loans become extortionate and abusive. Moneylenders highlighted bad debts and the expense of processing weekly repayments as justification for their interest rates.[140] Table 3.2

Table 3.2 Financial data on fifteen moneylenders

	% of charged interest		*%*
Lender	*Bad debts*	*Expenses*	*Return*
1	47.5	30.0	25.1
2	34.8	45.0	15.5
3	38.1	36.8	14.4
4	6.3	81.2	7.9
5	55.0	25.3	19.1
6	14.6	66.3	9.3
7	45.2	35.1	23.5
8	58.3	31.6	11.4
9	30.4	59.3	7.5
10	35.0	23.0	19.8
11	17.5	39.3	16.7
12	24.5	33.3	17.1
13	18.2	47.4	18.6
14	17.7	54.4	14.8
15	25.4	54.8	8.9
Average	31.2	44.2	15.3

Source MLSC 1925, 263–5, 274–5. The Committee report and testifying witness claimed that the sample above represented typical moneylending concerns and the data was selected at random without discrimination or elimination. Note that the return data excluded salary for the principal-owner and in some cases family members working for the firm. The evidence does not explain why lender 4 experienced relatively low levels of bad debt and a high expense ratio. Higher levels of due diligence expense could lead to less bad debt shows data on fifteen moneylending firms over a five-year period revealed an average loan interest rate of 60 pcpa and a 15.3% return on invested capital.[141] The return did not include a salary for the principal-owner and thus overstates their profitability. Within that, returns varied widely from moneylender to moneylender.[142] The sample average was less than the returned earned by banks and discount houses.[143] At the 60 pcpa average loan rate, there is little indication that industry-wide profits were excessive.

Sources from outside the moneylending industry endorsed the threshold 60 pcpa rate as the lowest rate at which an adequate return could be earned.[144] Dorothy Keeling, chairwoman of a Liverpool-based charitable loan fund, itself operating at a loss from charging too low a rate, testified that '60 per cent for unsecured loans would protect a fair but not exorbitant profit'.[145] At the very least such a limitation should trickle down to the lower classes where pricing typically followed a penny a week for each shilling, annualizing somewhere in the neighbourhood of 433%.[146] Knowing that the demand for loans would likely always exist, Keeling and others advocated for a regulated, respectable and profitable moneylending industry.[147] Keeling's platform came from studying the Russell Sage Foundation's small-loan reform efforts in America. Arthur Ham of the Sage Foundation led an intensive lobbying campaign focused on creating a legitimate, regulated, licensed and economically viable small-loan industry (Lisle 1912; Clemens 1997).[148] Keeling and Ham believed that mitigating the worst elements of small-value loans required a vibrant private sector competing within a tightly bound and regularly enforced regulatory framework. This Anglo-American approach differed from a municipal and non-profit model found in some European countries (O'Connell 2009; Tebbutt 1983). Britain never seriously considered a fully backed public option.

The profitable but not too profitable 60% guidance rate met some resistance. Mark Wilson, a Brighton moneylender, reminded the Committee that the money obtained by borrowers was 'not buried in the garden', but spent in the community.[149] He stressed the reality that regulation could leave borrowers without access to any money, a result that then ripples through their local economies. It was not until the twenty-first century that policymakers engaged the complexities of an alternative supply channel for poor borrowers. For now, the belief was that a judiciary operating with a guidance rate offered an immediate solution to predatory loans and high-cost credit.

The Committee accomplished their goal in two ways. First, they set the judicial review guidance rate at 4% a month (which in their view equated to 48 pcpa). Though various accounts exist as to the origin behind the 48% rate, according to Ronald Barnes, Lord Gorell (Liberal), the figure was arrived at by subtracting advertising circular costs (which the Act would ban) from the 60% average rate.[150] In setting the guidance Parliament hoped to constrict, but not totally eliminate, moneylending. Although Carson privately lobbied to reduce the guidance rate, he also admitted the inadequacies of his 15% opening gambit.[151] Second, they shifted the burden of proof by putting the onus on the moneylender to demonstrate that his rates were not excessive. In other words, moneylenders were guilty until proven innocent. By shifting the burden of proof, legislators hoped that borrowers would more readily exercise their legal rights. Neither of these developments were seen as an affront to freedom of contract or a violation of British values, but a practical response to a social issue that their predecessors had failed to address.

Advertising

Wells sought a back-door way of ending the industry through an all-out advertising prohibition, even personal letters to former clients would be banned.[152] The Moneylenders Association and the Yorkshire Moneylenders' Association reminded the Committee that equally controversial alcohol and gambling advertised freely without restriction.[153] The trade argued that if the public prosecutor enforced fraud laws, additional regulation would duplicitous and unnecessary.[154] Several moneylending associations instead pushed for limiting advertising to factual information such as name, address and the foundation year of the business.[155] Likely wanting to curry favour with wealthy MPs, and perpetuating anti-Semitism, much of the low-end business suggested banning circulars geared towards wealthy borrowers (O'Connell 2009, p. 142).[156]

The Committee's final proposal banned circulars and limited newspaper advertisements to basic information including registered names, address, statement of occupation and the date of establishment. So important were these restrictions that Robert Dennison MP (Labour) remarked, 'This is the most important clause in the Bill'.[157] Although Kenworthy protested that it was 'ridiculous' and 'perfectly absurd' to prevent people from sending circulars, both the ban and pared-down advertisement restrictions received little pushback.[158] These limitations struck at the heart of the industry's business model and Parliament knew it—curtailing the moneylending machine was a stated goal and they hoped this measure would do just that.

Terms and Conditions

The APR debate is particularly revealing as policymakers and moneylenders were at odds over its value and importance to borrowers. Policymakers stressed that borrowers were being deceived by quoting the amount due in cash terms as opposed to a percentage. Moneylenders offered policymakers various reasons why the monetary method made sense. Many claimed that they were incapable of calculating an APR, or if they could, it would be prohibitively expensive to do so.[159] In one exchange a moneylender admitted that he was rather 'bad at percentages' and could not do the calculation.[160] As the APR debate spilled into the public forum, proving how difficult it was to calculate the interest rate, one academic journal invited chartered accountants to calculate the interest on a small loan. Ten accountants responded, each with a different answer. Their answers ranged from 234 pcpa to 1564 pcpa.[161] Moneylenders were not deceiving Parliament, the instalment nature of differing amounts with various methods of amortization made calculating the interest rate difficult.

More compelling, moneylenders argued that their clients were not at all interested in percentage rates. One moneylender of forty years' standing pointed out that customers wanted to know 'how much they will owe in pounds and pennies'.[162] The qualitative data supports this.[163] It is understandable that the borrower would want to know how much it would cost, allowing for an easy comparison with wages. The Committee's insistence on expressing the cost of funds as a percentage projected an upper and commercial class mentality onto small-loan borrowers. It was assumed that if customers knew the percentage, they would forgo the high-cost loan or seek other sources of funds. In reality access to cash and simple cost calculations overrode other considerations. Though policymakers insisted on the importance of percentage disclosure, there was scant evidence that borrowers found the information particularly helpful.

The MLA 1927 departed from past practices requiring a standard contract stating the transaction date, the principal lent and the APR as calculated by a statutory formula. A copy of the contract had to be provided within seven days of execution. Contracts that failed to comply were null and void. At the borrower's request, and at a cost of a shilling, lenders were required to provide statements detailing the payments received and balances owed. Policymakers hoped that these would reduce fraud and encourage borrowers to more fully negotiate transactions.

Registration and Licensing

The MLA 1900 registry was ineffective. The paltry £1 registry listing fee failed to keep unwanted providers out of the industry. As a market-entry deterrent against undercapitalized lenders, the Yorkshire Moneylenders' Association argued for a £25 registry fee.[164] Policymakers and lenders debated the merits of strengthening the registry requirements. In pursuit of a 'respectable trade', the Yorkshire group supported Wells' proposal requiring a pre-registration police check.[165] Police certification informed the Inland Revenue whether the applicant was a person of good moral character and free from suspected or convicted criminal behaviour. It was hoped that the local police would be aware of an applicant's history and standing in the community. Enhancing the registry and devolving part of the application process should help combat lenders such as Mersey Financial, a company convicted of issuing illegal loans.[166] Despite their offence, they were operating 'quite cheerfully' as there was no government authority to prevent them from doing so.

A few lone voices opposed government involvement. Echoing liberal values of self-reliance and individualism of, Josiah Wedgwood MP (Labour), questioned whether the Home Office would ask, 'Who was your father? What school did you study [at]?' Cautioning against the registration process as an affront to free trade and commerce, he added that Parliament should not make it 'more difficult for a man to take risks. Safety first never made England' (Mulvey 2010).[167] He believed that a lender was only getting back what was legally his and claimed that moneylenders were acting no differently from other creditors. Reminiscent of the Victorian poverty debates, Wedgwood concluded that 'he hates [it when] superior people try to make workers moral'.[168] The liberal position gained little traction. The MLA 1900 had failed, and the way forward was for more state intervention.

Some even pushed for greater government oversight than a registry alone. Enhanced licensing schemes, such as capital requirements and posted bonds, received considerable attention.[169] These proposed requirements required a lender to prove that a balance of liquid funds from which to lend and, in the event of a fine, the monies in escrow ensured payment. A licence could be denied or revoked if someone failed to post bond or capital requirements were breached. In their ongoing push for legitimacy, moneylenders supported these provisions as a way to reduce ill-capitalized firms and 'dud' loan broker agencies.[170]

Another line of thinking sought industry-led self-regulation.[171] It was argued that self-regulation was in the interest of respectable lenders and that industry participants could better limit criminal activity than government supervisors would. The proposal expected that Parliament would determine the operational rules and standards, and a control board headed by a national moneylending association would ensure their implementation and monitor the membership.[172] Despite the support of numerous parties, an industry control board was not seriously considered. Self-regulation required societal support and trust, currency severely lacking in the moneylending trade.[173] Even if they could muster external support, moneylending was a localized affair and few trade associations existed. Even the largest trade association based in London, with its developed moneylending market and large borrowing population, had fewer than 300 members. No association was strong enough to bring the industry together under a national umbrella.[174] Lacking both internal and external support, self-regulation was a non-starter.

While certainly more robust than the 1900 Act, the MLA 1927 registration requirements were minimal. The MLA 1927 required moneylenders obtain an annual excise licence costing £15 for each location.[175] The excise licence required only that the government be aware of the actual and trade name(s), and the location of the lender.[176] Registering required a certificate granted by a petty sessional court. While court certificates addressed the government's prior inability to deny an application, the terminology was vague and provided few standards. The certificate did little more than ensure that the applicant was not a convicted criminal and forbade any implication that a moneylender operated as a bank.[177]

Conclusion

In the 1900s and again in the 1920s, high interest rates fuelled a strong anti-moneylending sentiment. In both decades, calls for an inquiry were based on an increase in moneylending and prolific advertising. High interest rates gave rise to sensational newspaper headlines. Moneylenders had few allies. The parliamentary mandate authorizing the MLSC 1897 targeted an 'evil' industry which encouraged gambling and fraud. Turn-of-the-century MPs associated moneylenders so strongly with crime that they stated as much in their summary findings. Later, in 1927, Wedgwood asserted that moneylenders were so vilified that he received more letters against his opposition to Carson's bill than in the whole of his political career.[178]

As Wedgwood's letterbox attested, these lenders invoked fierce debates. People focused on the high cost of these loans assuming that lenders profited excessively from an urgent demand for cash. Almost as immediate, the extreme option of price controls entered the debate. That Parliament twice rejected price controls in 1900 and again in 1927 is telling. For theoretical and practical reasons, policymakers were unwilling to regulate the price of money. Whatever the flaws of these small-time capitalists, price controls were considered an inappropriate remedy for the ills of the borrowing poor and the wealthier classes.

The 1900s price controls measures were rejected as many considered usury an affront to British values; controls would be difficult to implement and infringe competition. Policymakers simply could not imagine placing a limit on the freedom of two adults to agree on the price of a cash loan. The debates focused on how far the judiciary should intervene in private financial contracts executed by able-minded adults. Liberal theorists held contracts to be sacrosanct and argued against government intervention unless a crime was committed. Revisionists and reformers were willing to protect poor borrowers by rewriting contracts that were deemed extortionate, or to use the term of that time—harsh and unconscionable. This was a clash between rival theories and the participants happened to find themselves on the moneylending battlefield.

By the 1920s, the industry was growing, and the failures of the MLA 1900 became intolerable for Lord Carson and other politicians. Although these policymakers debated issues similar to those of their forebears, few offered opposition or support based on ideologies. Parliament felt free to restrict what many viewed as an unsavoury business and pernicious product. It sought to correct failed regulation and provide practical solutions for the moneylending problem. In fact, practical concerns ended a short-lived quest for price controls—they were difficult to implement, easily evaded and would segment the market.

Instead, the price control light guidance rate received broad support and was passed in the MLA 1927. Policymakers believed that the guidance rate would mitigate the damaging effects of a high interest rate and provide the precision needed for the judiciary to adjust harsh and unconscionable transactions. Borrowers would receive justice from the institution most suited to dispense it—the courts. That the once rejected guidance rate was adopted in 1927 can be considered a pragmatic response to the ineffectiveness of the MLA 1900.

This also presented in the overarching issue of information disclosure. By the late 1920s, policymakers paid little attention to why borrowers needed cash, and instead focused on how to limit the supply of funds flowing through the moneylending sector. Parliament's willingness to intervene evolved from quite little in the 1900s to the 1927 Act's ban on circulars and a limitation on newspaper advertisements. Fewer advertisements made accessing funds more difficult, an outcome that policymakers viewed positively. The uniformed APR disclosure discouraged borrowers from taking out high-cost loans, at least, that was the intent. Almost everyone, save moneylenders themselves, advocated for APR disclosure. The problem is that borrowers were little concerned with percentages and annual costs. For them, the amount owed in cash terms proved far more useful, as it could easily be compared to wages and stacked against other financial obligations.

There was also divergence concerning the legitimacy of moneylenders within the financial system. Some moneylenders wanted more stringent regulation than Parliament. Many of these small businessmen believed weeding out of the worst behaviour would add respectability to their disparaged industry; regulation was an avenue to legitimization. By that measure, by any measure really, neither the 1900 nor 1927 Act provided much in the way of respectability for lenders or success for its political framers. Their quest for respectability pushed against policymakers insistency that moneylenders remained far from the boundaries of legitimate banking. Whatever moneylenders were, they were not bankers. The boundary deserved far more attention than Parliament devoted to it. In the decades that followed Parliament's failure to define precisely what constituted a moneylender caused major and unforeseen consequences in what later became a vast consumer credit market. Many moneylenders sought regulation as an avenue to legitimization. By that measure, by any measure really, neither the 1900 nor 1927 Act provided much in the way of respectability for lenders or success for its political framers.

While the 1927 Act was more severe than its predecessor, it too was ineffective. Both Acts relied too heavily on the courts, which most borrowers avoided. The toothless 1900 and 1927 legislation did not significantly alter the course of the market's development or offer much borrower protection.

Notes

1. "Alleged Legal Abuse," *Liverpool Mercury*, 3 January 1895; "The Moneylending Business," *Pall Mall Gazette*, 9 January 1895.
2. "Moneylenders," *Cheshire Observer*, 15 May 1897.
3. "Interest at 400 Per cent," *Lloyd's Weekly*, 1 July 1900; "Ruined by Exorbitant Interest," *Leicester Chronicle and Mercury*, 20 February 1897.
4. "Alleged Legal Abuse," *Liverpool Mercury*, 3 January 1895.
5. See the British Banking History Society entry concerning "Farrow's Bank." Ironically, in 1921, Farrow was convicted of fraud, having lost approximately £2.8 million (£119 million in 2018 terms) of investor funds.
6. "The Usury Laws," *Northern Echo*, 18 June 1895.
7. "Money-Lending Revelations, 350 Per cent Interest," *Sheffield Evening Telegraph*, 27 February 1896.
8. MLSC 1897, 1914.
9. MLSC 1897, 1914.
10. MLSC 1897, 4522–3.
11. MLSC 1898, 1440–1450.
12. MLSC 1897, 3660.
13. MLSC 1897, 4431.
14. MLSC 1898, 7–8, 241–2; *Nevill v. Snelling* (1880) LR 15 CH D 679.
15. MLSC 1897, 3659–60, 4432–6.
16. MLSC 1898, 228.
17. MLSC 1897, 826, 931.
18. MLSC 1897, 4659; MLSC 1898, 1440.
19. MLSC 1897, 4493, 4542.
20. MLSC 1897, 3450–1.
21. "Literary Notes Review," *Birmingham Daily Post*, 15 February 1895.
22. HC deb. 21 June 1900, vol. 84.
23. MLSC 1898, 303–4.
24. "The Bill Against Moneylenders," *The Spectator*, 25 February 1899.
25. HC deb. 10 May 1894, vol. 24; HC deb. 1 April 1895, vol. 32.
26. "Money-Lenders," *Western Mail*, 2 April 1895.
27. HC deb. 8 June 1896, vol. 41; HC deb. 6 April 1897, vol. 48; MLSC 1897, Introduction.
28. MLSC 1898, i–v.
29. HL deb. 16 March, vol. 68.
30. MLSC 1897, 1292.
31. HC deb. 26 June 1900, vol. 84.
32. MLSC 1897, 110.
33. "Moneylenders," *Marlborough Express*, vol. XLI: 213, 1907.

34. MLSC 1897, 110.
35. MLSC 1898, iii–v.
36. MLSC 1898, 3556.
37. MLSC 1898, 6.
38. MLSC 1897, 110.
39. MLSC 1897, 1868–92.
40. MLSC 1897, 3369.
41. MLSC 1897, 2204.
42. MLSC 1897, 583, 4007.
43. HC deb. 21 June 1900, vol. 84. Moneylenders referred to 'gross interest,' and from that amount subtracted expenses and bad debts. Samuel reported that over six years his gross interest was approximately 33%, from which he subtracted 11% in expenses and 11% in bad debt, which left 11% in profit; MLSC 1897, 1901.
44. MLSC 1897, 2173, 2841.
45. MLSC 1897, 2080.
46. MLSC 1897, 2089, 4000.
47. HC deb. 21 June 1900, vol. 84.
48. MLSC 1898, 3516.
49. MLSC 1897, 2204.
50. MLSC 1897, 4587–8.
51. MLSC 1897, 3094, 4586.
52. MLSC 1897, 4425.
53. HC deb. 21 June 1900, vol. 84.
54. MLSC 1898, 249; HL deb. 20 February 1899, vol. 66; HC deb. 21 June 1900, vol. 84. Charles Geisst (2013), a financial historian, suggested that pressure to repeal usury in Britain was based on Bentham's essays on the subject.
55. MLSC 1897, 1525.
56. MLSC 1898, v–vi.
57. MLSC 1897, 1106, 3493, 1645, 4665.
58. MLSC 1897, 2481.
59. MLSC 1897, 4659; MLSC 1898, vi, 228.
60. MLSC 1898, 303.
61. MLSC 1897, 3492.
62. MLSC 1898, 1525–32.
63. HC deb. 21 June 1900, vol. 84.
64. HC deb. 21 June 1900, vol. 84.
65. 1899 Bill 215 Money-lending (HL). A Bill Instituted an Act to Amend the Law with Respect to Persons Carrying on Business As Moneylenders; MLSC 1897, 1936–43.
66. MLSC 1897, 1936–43, 3091.
67. MLSC 1898, 2634.

68. MLSC 1897, 4492–4.
69. On 21 June 1900, Terrance Russell MP (Liberal) argued the same in a House debate: 'The result must depend upon the Court in which the case may happen to be tried and the idiosyncrasies of the Judge who happens to preside. The risk which the money-lender will run of having his bargains upset will have to be paid for by those who borrow; in other words, instead of lightening the burden of the borrower the money-lender will require to exact a higher rate of interest for the money he lends in order to cover this additional risk.'
70. HL deb. 16 March 1899, vol. 68 and 21 June 1900, vol. 84.
71. HC deb. 21 June 1900, vol. 84.
72. HC deb. 21 June 1900, vol. 84.
73. MLSC 1897, 160–1.
74. HC deb. 21 June 1900, vol. 84.
75. MLSC 1898, 335–404.
76. MLSC 1897, 150–1.
77. "Shylock's Methods," *Yorkshire Evening Post*, 20 May 1897.
78. MLSC 1898, 4, 140–2, 293. *The Liverpool Daily Post* had twenty such offers in a single weekday edition; HC deb. 21 June 1900, vol. 84; MLSC 1898, 422.
79. MLSC 1897, 1135, 4573.
80. MLSC 1897, 121–2, 134–5, 917–18, 925, 1004, 1100–1, 3855–68.
81. MLSC 1897, 301–5, 635–6, 2177, 2718–26, 3854–8; MLSC 1898, iii–v, 1488, 1846.
82. MLSC 1897, 1765.
83. MLSC 1897, 1458; MLSC 1898, 1839.
84. MLSC 1897, 1765, 2002–8, 2170–3, 2287, 3346–52.
85. MLSC 1897, 1836, 3345–8.
86. MLSC 1897, 2002–5.
87. MLSC 1897, 2002–5; MLSC 1898, 300–1.
88. MLSC 1897, 1099–100, 1553–4, 3020, 3536, 4569; MLSC 1898, iv–v, 1441, 1559, 3429
89. MLSC 1898, 3610–11.
90. See MLSC 1898, Appendix "Bank of England."
91. CUST 49/2069 (Customs and Excise) "Civil Servant Case and Moneylender," 24 September 1936, 6 November 1936, The National Archives (TNA). This example is indicative of the pressure placed on public sector clerks by moneylenders.
92. HC deb. 21 June 1900, vol. 84; MLSC 1897, 3731; MLSC 1898, 162.
93. HC deb. 21 June 1900, vol. 84; MLSC 1897, 1548–51, 4494.
94. MLSC 1897, 1525–31.
95. MLSC 1897, 4420; MLSC 1898, 1–2.
96. MLSC 1898, 46.

97. MLSC 1897, 194, 2874–7.
98. MLSC 1898, 2874–7.
99. MLSC 1898, 4, 140–2, 3614; HC deb. 21 June 1900, vol. 84; HC deb. 31 July 1900, vol. 87.
100. MLSC 1898, 3620.
101. MLSC 1898, 3632.
102. MLSC 1898, 1436.
103. HC deb. 21 June 1900, vol. 84; MLSC 1897, 3980.
104. Though clause 4 of the MLA addresses fraudulent behaviour, the wording was vague and relied on pre-existing law.
105. MLSC 1898, 427.
106. MLSC 1897, 1302, 1356, 1552; MLSC 1898, iii–xi, 1503, 1524; MLA 1900 2(1)(a).
107. MLSC 1898, 165.
108. MLSC 1897, 1734–7.
109. MLSC 1897, 1357.
110. MLA 1900, clause 6.
111. MLSC 1897, 2101; MLSC 1898, 184–5, 429.
112. MLSC 1897, 2101.
113. MLSC 1925, 1185–90.
114. "The Moneylenders' Federation Manual and Directory For The Year 1913," General Collection PP2501, The British Library; IR 40/2736 (Inland Revenue), "Chief Inspector of Taxes Internal Memorandum, Registrations under the MLA 1900," 15–31 January 1908, 14 January 1921, 3 March 1922, 1923, TNA; IR 40/3555 (Inland Revenue), "Registration of Moneylenders and Evasions of Tax, Mr Pool, Office of the Chief Inspector of Taxes," 8 November 1929, 28 November 1929, 30 November 1929, 26 September 1931, TNA.
115. HC deb. 18 June 1901, vol. 11.
116. MEPO 2/814 (Records of the Metropolitan Police Office), "Memorandum on MLA 1900, The Commissioner of Metropolitan Police, Executive Branch," 2 August 1907, TNA.
117. BT 103/28 (Board of Trade Solicitor's Department), "Letter Rufus Isaacs, John Simon, MLA 1900–1911," 29 December 1910, TNA.
118. *Samuel v. Bukton* (1903), *CAE-Bingtons v. Smith* (1905); *Wilton v. Osborne* (1901) and *Barnett v. Corunna* (1902) ruled that the interest rate alone without further evidence could deem a transaction harsh and unconscionable, whereas *Re a debtor, ex parte The Debtor* 1 Kings Bench 705, 1903 ruled the opposite.
119. HC deb. 23 April 1926, vol. 194.
120. "Moneylending Evils," *The Times*, 18 March 1925; "Plague of Moneylenders; MPs Swamped With Circulars," *Western Daily Press*, 3 July 1924.

121. "Letter 21 December 1925," Edward Carson Papers Non-Irish 1921–1926, D1507/B/43 1–28, Public Records Office of Northern Ireland.
122. "The Shark's Prey," *Edinburgh Evening News*, 26 September 1924.
123. HL deb. 1 December 1925, vol. 62.
124. HL deb. 1 December 1925, vol. 62; "Moneylenders' Methods," *Lancashire Evening Post*, 13 December 1924.
125. "Civil Servant Affair," *Gloucester Journal*, 14 March 1925; "Moneylending Evils," *The Times*, 18 March 1925; HL deb. 11 February 1926, vol. 63.
126. MLSC 1925, 5; HL deb. 1 December 1925, vol. 62.
127. "Letter 14 March 1925," Edward Carson Papers Non-Irish 1921–1926, D1507/B/43 1–28, Public Records Office of Northern Ireland; HL deb. 1 December 1925, vol. 62.
128. MLSC 1925, 9; HC deb. 23 April 1926, vol. 194.
129. HC deb. 4 March 1927, vol. 203.
130. HL deb. 4 March 1927, vol. 203; HC deb. 23 April 1926, vol. 194.
131. HL deb. 3 February 1926, vol. 63.
132. HC deb. 23 April 1926, vol. 194.
133. "Letter 14 March 1925," Edward Carson Papers Non-Irish 1921–1926, D1507/B/43 1–28, Public Records Office of Northern Ireland.
134. MLSC 1925, 3.
135. HC deb. 4 March 1927, vol. 203; HL deb. 3 January 1926, vol. 63.
136. HC deb. 23 April 1926, vol. 194.
137. MLSC 1925, 1174–7; HC deb. 23 April 1926, vol. 194.
138. MLSC 1925, 1246, 1279, 1291–2, 1309, 1325. It was estimated that 95% of the market were promissory notes. See MLSC 1925, 64.
139. HL deb. 11 February 1926, vol. 63.
140. MLSC 1925, 500, 1477.
141. MLSC 1925, 263–5, 274–5.
142. MLSC 1925, 1996.
143. MLSC 1925, 280. Cited bank and discount house dividend rates included Midland (18%), Lloyds (16.6%), National Provincial (16%), Westminster (20%), Barclays (14%), Alexanders (25%), the Union (25%) and the National (28%).
144. MLSC 1925, 76, 281–3, 1722.
145. MLSC 1925, 905; HC deb. 23 April 1926, vol. 194.
146. See the MLSC 1925 testimony of Dorothy Keeling.
147. MLSC 1925, 900–1; HC deb. 23 April 1926, vol. 194.
148. Arthur Ham, "Opening Address," AAPFC 1921 convention, The United States Library of Congress (LOC) Russell Sage Foundation Archives (RSFA) Box 88; Arthur Ham, "Letter to Hedwig Weiss," 9 November 1914, LOC RSFA Box 25; Fredic Haskin, "Loan Sharks," *The Missonlian*, 3 February 1911, LOC RSFA Box 1; Ansley Wilcox,

"Remedial Legislation, its Possibilities and its Limitations," *The Legal Aid Review*, October 1911, LOC RSFA Box 38.
149. MLSC 1925, 1511–15.
150. HC deb. 26 November 1925, vol. 62.
151. "Letter 21 April 1926," Edward Carson Papers Non-Irish 1921–1926, D1507/B/43 1–28, Public Records Office of Northern Ireland; HL deb. 26 November 1925, vol. 62.
152. 1924–25 (88) Moneylenders (Amendment). A Bill to Amend the Law With Respect to Persons Carrying On Business as Moneylenders [Wells]; MLSC 1925, 9, 153–4.
153. MLSC 1925, 1546. Though medical and legal trade associations prohibited members from advertising, it was not required by law.
154. MLSC 1925, 4, 29–30, 915, 1544–6; HC deb. 4 March 1927, vol. 203.
155. MLSC 1925, 4, 197–201, 2255.
156. MLSC 1925, 491, 1437–8, 1598.
157. HC deb. 4 March 1927, vol. 203.
158. HC deb. 23 April 1926, vol. 194.
159. MLSC 1925, 14, 831.
160. MLSC 1925, 13, 1479–89.
161. MLSC 1925, 235–9.
162. MLSC 1925, 250, 519–23, 1789, 1898, 1958–62.
163. Even after the MLA 1927, certain transactions were agreed to in monetary terms and only after were calculations made for documentation purposes. For example, CUST 49/2942 (Custom & Excise), "Moneylender Case," 4 October 1948, TNA.
164. MLSC 1925, 44–8, 122–9
165. MLSC 1925, 68–70.
166. MLSC 1925, 905.
167. HC deb. 4 March 1927, vol. 203.
168. HC deb. 23 April 1926, vol. 194.
169. MLSC 1925, 632–42.
170. HC deb. 23 April 1926, vol. 194.
171. MLSC 1925, 584.
172. MLSC 1925, 972.
173. MLSC 1925, 1191–2.
174. MLSC 1925, 159, 1839.
175. £15 was a compromise figure. Some policymakers wanted to license every partner in a firm and every location, for a maximum of £100 annually.
176. MLA 1927, 1(1–2).
177. MLA 1927, 2(1–2, 6), 3 (3).
178. HC deb. 4 March 1927, vol. 203.

Bibliography

Archives

The British Library, London.
PP2501 The Moneylenders' Federation Manual and Directory, 1913.
The National Archives, London.
BT 103 Board of Trade Solicitor's Department.
BT103/28 Correspondence and Papers, MLA 1900–1911.
UST 49 Customs & Excise.
CUST49/2069 Linnell Moneylending Case.
CUST49/2942 Moneylender Case.
IR40 Board of Inland Revenue: Stamps and Taxes Division.
IR40/2736 Registrations under the MLA 1900.
IR40/3555 Registrations of Moneylenders and Evasion of Tax.
EPO2 Records of the Metropolitan Police Office.
MEPO2/814 Special Report no. 282 ref 459818 'MLA 1900'.
The United States Library of Congress.
The Russell Sage Foundation.
Box 1 Fredic Haskin, "Loan Sharks," *The Missonlian*, 3 February 1911.
Box 25 Arthur Ham, "Letter to Hedwig Weiss." 9 November 1914.
Box 38 Ansley Wilcox, "Remedial Legislation, its Possibilities and its Limitations," The Legal Aid Review, October 1911.
Box 88 Arthur Ham, "Opening address," AAPFC convention, 1921.
Public Records Office of Northern Ireland.
D1507 Edward Carson Non-Irish Papers.
D1507/B/43/1–28 Letters, 1925–26.
Official Publications.
Report from the Joint Select Committee of the House of Lords and the House of Commons on the Moneylenders Bill 1925 (153).
Report from the Select Committee on Moneylending 1897 (364).
Report from the Select Committee on Moneylenders 1898 (260).
The House of Commons Debate Sessions.
The House of Lords Debate Sessions.
The Moneylenders Act 1900: 63 & 64 Vic. c. 51.
The Moneylenders Act 1911: 1 & 2 Geo. 5 c. 51.
The Moneylenders Act 1927: 17 & 18 Geo. 5 c. 21.

Sources

Aberdeen Journal. 1925, 18 March.
"Alleged Legal Abuse." 1895. *Liverpool Mercury*, 3 January.

Ball, Stuart. 2013. *Portrait of a Party: The Conservative Party in Britain 1918–1945*. Oxford: Oxford University Press, 2013.

"Civil Servant Affair." 1925. *Gloucester Journal*, 14 March.

Church, Roy. 2000. "Advertising Consumer Goods in Nineteenth-Century Britain: Reinterpretations." *Economic History Review* 53 (4):621–45.

Clemens, Elisabeth Stephanie. 1997. *The People's Lobby: Organizational Innovation and the Rise of Interest Group Politics in the United States, 1890–1925*. Chicago: University of Chicago Press.

Collard, Charles. 1912. *The Money-Lenders Acts, 1900–1911*. London: Butterworth.

Daunton, Martin. 2007. *Wealth and Welfare: An Economic and Social History of Britain, 1851–1951*. Oxford: Oxford University Press.

Dorey, Peter. 2011. *British Conservatism: The Politics and Philosophy of Inequality*. London: I.B. Tauris.

Farrow, Thomas. 1896. *In the Money Lender's Clutches*. London: Yeoman Company.

———. 1895. *The Moneylender Unmasked*. London: Roxburghe Press.

Finn, Margot. 2003. *The Character of Credit: Personal Debt in English Culture, 1740–1914*. Cambridge: Cambridge University Press.

Fraser, Derek. 2009. *The Evolution of the British Welfare State: A History of Social Policy Since the Industrial Revolution*. London: Palgrave Macmillan.

Geisst, Charles. 2013. *Beggar Thy Neighbour: A History of Usury and Debt*. Philadelphia: University of Pennsylvania Press.

"Interest at 400 Per cent." 1900. *Lloyd's Weekly*, 1 July.

Johnson, Paul. 1985a. *Savings and Spending: The Working-Class Economy in Britain, 1870–1939*. Oxford: Clarendon Press.

———. 1985b. "Credit and Thrift and the British Working Class, 1870–1939." In *The Working Class in Modern British History*, edited by J. M. Winter, 147–70. Cambridge: Cambridge University Press.

"Literary Notes Review." 1895. *Birmingham Daily Post*, 15 February.

Lisle, John. 1912. "A Widespread Form of Usury: The Loan Shark." *Journal of the American Institute of Criminal Law and Criminology* 3 (2):167–71.

Matthews, Joseph. 1906. *The Law of Money-Lending, Past and Present*. London: Sweet & Maxwell.

"Moneylenders." 1897. *Cheshire Observer*, 15 May.

"Moneylenders." 1907. *Marlborough Express*. XLI:213.

"Money-lenders." 1895. *Western Mail*, 2 April.

"Moneylending Evils." 1925. *The Times*, 18 March.

"Moneylenders' Methods." 1924. *Lancashire Evening Post*, 13 December.

"Money-lending Revelations, 350 Per cent Interest." 1896. *Sheffield Evening Telegraph*, 27 February.

Mulvey, Paul. 2010. *The Political Life of Josiah C. Wedgwood: Land, Liberty and Empire, 1872–1943*. Woodbridge: Boydell & Brewer.
O'Connell, Sean. 2009. *Credit and Community: Working-Class Debt in the UK Since 1880*. Oxford: Oxford University Press.
Orchard, Dorothy, and Geoffrey May. 1933. *Moneylending in Great Britain*. New York: Russell Sage Foundation.
"Plague of Moneylenders; MPs Swamped with Circulars." 1924. *Western Daily Press*, 3 July.
"Ruined by Exorbitant Interest." 1895. *Leicester Chronicle and Mercury*, 20 February.
"Shylock's Methods." 1897. *Yorkshire Evening Post*, 20 May.
Taylor, Andrew. 2005. "Stanley Baldwin, Heresthetics and the Realignment of British Politics." *British Journal of Political Sciences* 35 (3): 429–63.
Tebbutt, Melanie. 1983. *Making Ends Meet: Pawnbroking & Working-Class Credit*. Leicester: Leicester University Press.
"The Bill Against Moneylenders." 1899. *The Spectator*, 25 February.
"The Evils of the Usury System: The Prospect of Legislation." 1898. *St James's Gazette*, 12 October.
"The Moneylending Business." 1895. *Pall Mall Gazette*, 9 January.
"The Shark's Prey." 1924. *Edinburgh Evening News*, 26 September.
"The Usury Laws." 1895. *Northern Echo*, 18 June.
"Upon Usury." 1925. *Hull Daily Mail*, 27 March.

CHAPTER 4

Legitimate Bankers: Pawnbrokers and Moneylenders Join the Premier League

By the 1970s the small-loan industry was a shadow of its former self. Pawning volume had steadily declined since its peak in 1914 and moneylenders fared little better (Minkes 1953). The welfare state had brought an end to 'real poverty' and with it the need for small loans.[1] While historically moneylenders performed a useful function as a 'child could die or a family be put out on the street for the want of a few shillings', by the 1970s the state provided for those basic necessities.[2] Higher wages, regular employment, the welfare state, and more credit options had lessened the need for pawnbroking and moneylending.

In the meantime, the rest of the credit market had grown into a vital component of the national economy. Industry and policymakers were concerned that a web of regulation hampered the flow of consumer and business credit. The significance and growth of consumer credit to the economy encouraged a review of the relevant laws.[3] Ironically, while the MLA 1927 had little disturbed moneylenders, by the 1960s its vague wording impacted lenders having nothing to do with small loans. Reforming the credit market found its way into Prime Minister Edward Heath's bureaucratic modernization drive. Parliament convened the Crowther Committee to consolidate multiple consumer credit acts into a unified regulatory framework.[4]

Financial regulation was seen as one way to enhance market efficiency, improve competition and to lower borrowing costs. Whereas previous

© The Author(s), under exclusive license to Springer Nature Switzerland AG 2021

C. McMahon, *Taming the Fringe*, Palgrave Studies in the History of Finance, https://doi.org/10.1007/978-3-030-70615-9_4

regulation sought limitations on the size and scope of the credit markets, and especially small loans, for Crowther and the Consumer Credit Act 1974 (CCA 1974), competition enhanced by a streamlined regulatory structure provided far better consumer protection than punitive credit market restrictions. Policymakers wanted a single licence and a uniform set of rules allowing lenders to issue a variety of credit products across the full spectrum of borrowers. Small loans were no exception. Under the CCA 1974, small-loan lenders and borrowers were treated in the same way as other market participants. For the first time in British history, moneylending and pawnbroking were legitimized. One cannot be a fringe credit provider if the fringe does not exist in the first place.

Perhaps small lenders were of less concern because the industry contributed marginally to overall credit volume. Some expected the pawn industry to disappear, and others believed mainstream banks would outcompete moneylenders in providing short-term credit. What is clear is that Crowther et al. were unwilling to regulate small loans on behalf of the few who might suffer from credit use. Credit access and a well-functioning market override social policy concerns, so much so that pawnbroking price caps were eliminated. Centuries of legislation requiring pawn price caps were jettisoned in favour of levelling the playing field between lenders.

That is not to say that Crowther was unconcerned with the relationship between poverty, financial regulation and capitalism. Nor did Crowther espouse a complete laissez-faire attitude—after all, they were designing new regulation. The first point is that for most people, even the poor, well-functioning markets provided ample protection. The second point, which has echoed since the 1870s, was a belief that it is extremely difficult, if not impossible, to devise adequate regulation in response to the unique borrowing needs of the poor most in need. Encouraging competition between providers was the best regulation could do, which contrasts with previous efforts of restricting the small-loan 'evil' and government's paternalistic attitude towards 'child-like' borrowers.

Market and Political Developments

Market Background

In the 1970s consumer credit statistics were lacking and unreliable. Information concerning the small-loan market proved no exception. Under the Finance Act 1949, the power to license had devolved to the local authorities, making it difficult to collect information. Even before 1949 very little data was made available and what is available is of little value as it fails to distinguish between professional moneylenders and individuals who issued loans from time to time. In 1927, there were 28,236 registered moneylenders; but, only an estimated 4,000 were considered professionals.[5] By 1969, that number had declined to 2,500 licences outstanding, of which 500 or so were professional full-time lenders.[6]

Decimated as they were, moneylenders fared far better than pawnbroking. Table 4.1 shows the distribution of pawnbroking and moneylending licences issued in 1969 and Fig. 4.1 combines a variety of sources to demonstrate the post-First World War decline in the pawnbroking market.

By 1970 the pawn market was at levels not seen since the early 1800s. Not only were there fewer pawnbrokers, but overall loan volumes had collapsed. According to a Crowther-commissioned report, 50% of pawnbrokers issued fewer than 9,000 loans annually.[7] At the beginning of the twentieth century, many pawnbrokers would have issued that number monthly. In 1969, the NPA estimated that a busy shop transacted 20–30 pawns a day.[8] The magnitude of this decrease can be appreciated by recalling that, on 2 May 1870, Mr Barnett of Lambeth took in 725

Table 4.1 Pawnbroking and moneylending licensing, 1969

	PB	*ML*
Greater London	108	730
Rest of South East	26	122
North West	64	461
Yorkshire	38	403
Northern	29	124
West Midlands	24	117
East Midlands	16	85
South West	11	78
East Anglia	6	13
Scotland	74	152
Wales	6	180
Total	402	2,468

Source BT 250/93 (Councils on Moneylending and Pawnbroking), 'Licensing Data, Board of Trade Letter from Robin Gray to Peter Dewey', 12 March 1970, TNA. The geographic boundaries were determined by the Board of Trade

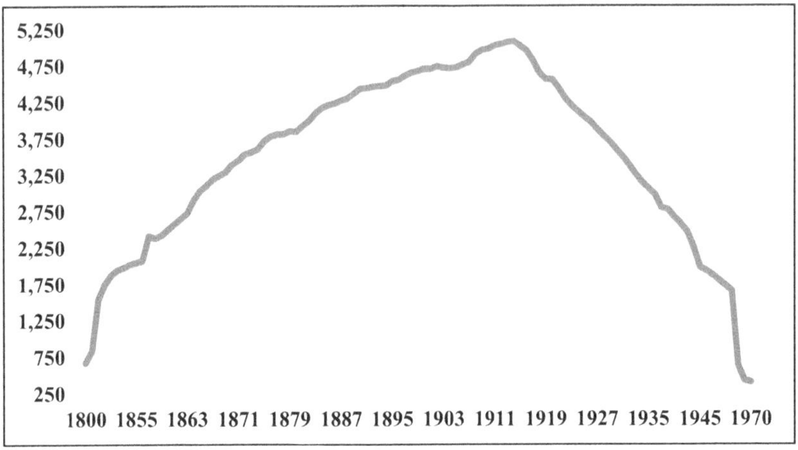

Fig. 4.1 Pawnbroking licences, 1800–1970 (*Source* Annual report of the Commissioners of HM Inland Revenue and HM Customs & Excise, 1870–1970; Crowther testimony; National Pawnbrokers Association; and the PBSC 1870)

pledges and delivered 249. On Saturday of that week he delivered 1,899 and took in 225.

In 1969, it was estimated that the 402 licensed pawnbrokers had issued approximately £6.3 million in loans on 1.4 million pledges, with an average pledge of £4.33. A century earlier, thirty pawnbrokers in Liverpool issued 1.4 million pledges valued at £300,000. Adjusted for inflation the £300,000 in 1869 was worth approximately £2.2 million in 1969.[9] The average pledge in the 1869 Liverpool sample was 4s 7.5d, which in 1969 terms was approximately £1.80. The NPA estimated that for a typical shop in London the average pledge was £5.[10] The increase in average pledge size corresponded to an increase in the value of pledged items. No longer did pawnbrokers participate in a low-value weekly pledge cycle, but took in items such as radios, cameras, tape recorders, typewriters and jewellery. The NPA claimed that 'only one firm in London will take clothes at all, and then only brand new … You have to auction them … and you'll likely only get a £3 for a £40 suit … they took so long to parcel up, and then they're so bulky to store'.[11]

The increase in average pawn loans supported the NPA's qualitative narrative. Tables 4.2 and 4.3 show the breakdown and average value of low, auction and contract pledges. While low pledges comprised the

Table 4.2 Pawnbroking market estimates, 1970

	Volume	*Market Value*		*Avg. pledge*
Pledge type	*as a %*	*£m*	*as a %*	*range*
Low	48	0.89	14	20–35s
Auction	30	1.84	29	£2–£4
Contract	21	3.61	57	£10–£20
	100	6.34	100	–

Source NOP Research

Table 4.3 Pledge analysis, 1970

Avg. value Low	*Number of PBs*	*Avg. value Auction*	*Number of PBs*	*Avg. value Contract*	*Number of PBs*
10s	2	£2	1	£5	8
15s	4	£2 10s	13	£10	29
£1	24	£3	16	£15	13
25s	22	£3 10s	24	£20	7
30s	15	£4	13	£25–£30	4
35s	3	£4 10s	0	£31–£40	3
£2	4	£5	4	£41–£50	1
NR	10	No response	14	No response	21
	85		85		85

Source NOP Research

highest volume, contract pledges were the most valuable. The trend for fewer, but high-value pledges contributing the most to market value were little changed from the 1870s.[12] Less consistent are redemption rates which had fallen by the 1970s to 75–95%, compared to early results suggesting a uniform 90–98%.[13] The wider spread and higher rate of default may indicate that pawnbrokers issued more risky loans to compensate for lower loan volumes and perhaps it was more difficult for low-income borrowers to raise the cash for redeeming higher-value goods.

Moneylending trends are more difficult to track than pawnbrokers. The considerable number of new market entrants after the MLA 1927 licensing requirement resulted from previously non-professional lenders joining the legal system. Within a few years, companies saw little value in registering as the local authorities failed to enforce the 1927 Act.

The moneylending market bottomed in the early 1940s but by 1946 started rebounding. Figure 4.2 demonstrates this trend. The growth corresponded to a sharp decline in pawnbroking. From 1946 to 1969, the pawn industry had *contracted* by 79%, compared to a 74% *increase* in moneylending. This dynamic coincided with the New Towns Act 1946, which relocated low-income families from urban to newly constructed population centres. It is difficult to demonstrate that moneylenders definitely benefited from the decline in pawnbroking, however, Table 4.4 shows that in 1946 the moneylending industry began to expand, and at the same time the pawn market experienced an increase in the rate of its decline. It is likely that a general trend towards unsecured lending benefited moneylenders and also suggests a type of substitutability between small-loan products.

After the 1960s the moneylending industry attracted a considerable number of new entrants. Of the 276 sampled, 40% had been in business for less than five years, 66% for less than ten years and 76% for less than 16 years. Old and new lenders alike issued a government estimated £2.5 million annually.[14] The National Association of Moneylenders provided a higher estimate of £5 million annually.[15] Most of the concerns were relatively small affairs. Of the 276-lender sample, approximately 16% issued

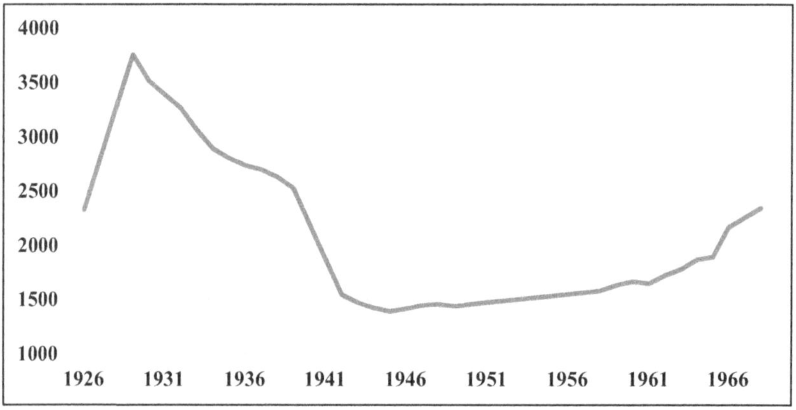

Fig. 4.2 Moneylending licences, 1925–1970 (*Source* [NOP Research; and author estimates using data from the MLSC 1925 and Customs & Excise, England and Wales])

Table 4.4 Pawnbroking and moneylending licences, 1942–1970

	Pawnbrokers	*Moneylenders*
1942	2,256	1,548
1943	–	1,472
1945	–	1,389
1946	1,932	1,414
1950	1,654	1,459
1964	632	1,869
1968	–	2,342
1969	402	2,468

Source NOP Research; Author estimates using data from the MLSC 1925; Customs & Excise, England and Wales (1929–1950); Crowther testimony; and the National Pawnbrokers Association

less than £2,000 annually, 40% issued less than £10,000 annually, 60% issued less than £20,000 annually and only 11% issued more than £50,000 annually. Few lenders occupied a middle ground (more than £20,000 but less than £50,000). Approximately 100 of the 276 lenders said that unsecured loans of less than £50 comprised more than 75% of their business. The market's structure was similar to its composition in 1927 when most lenders issued small loans, with a minority providing large loans to a wealthier clientele.

Table 4.5 shows the average interest rate on unsecured loans in the 276-lender sample, with 166 of the 276 lenders charging 10–50 pcpa. That 15% of lenders were unable to provide percentage information is not surprising, as most borrowers and lenders preferred monetary disclosure in pounds and pence. Table 4.6 summarizes data from 1969 provided by the National Association of Moneylenders. It supports average loan sizes of £20–£50 and that most loans were issued on a short-term basis.[16] The estimated average income of borrowers of between £18 and £35 a week is higher than the results provided by the John Hilton Bureau of £12–£13 a week. This is not surprising as the Bureau's data was provided by customers who had defaulted or found the loan terms and conditions difficult to comply with.

The pricing data lends support to the idea that the 48% guidance rate deterred lenders from competing on price and encouraged a gravitation towards an artificial price ceiling. A Consumer Council investigation also found a typical rate across the industry of 48 pcpa and a range of 20–90 pcpa.[17] The National Association of Moneylenders found a normal

Table 4.5 Average rates on unsecured loans

Average pcpa (%)	*Number of MLs*	*%*
10–20	69	25
21–30	33	12
31–40	25	9
41–50	39	14
51–60	8	3
61–70	3	1
71–80	0	0
81–90	6	2
91–100	3	1
100%+	0	0
No unsecured	50	18
Do not know	41	15
Total	276	100

Source NOP Research

Table 4.6 Unsecured loan profile

Range of duration	1–24 months
Common duration	6–18 months
Average duration	3–6 months
Range of loan size	£5–£1,000
Common range	£30–£150
Average range	£20–£50

Source BT 250/34 (National Association of Moneylenders), 'Letter from RB Selig, Chairman, to Mr Gray, Board of Trade, Committee on Consumer Credit', 23 April 1970, TNA

rate range of 20–100 pcpa, which is not far off the Consumer Council, but higher than the Crowther's 276-lender sample.[18] The Islington Consumer Group found a £20 loan was repayable in eleven weekly instalments of 50s or approximately 54 pcpa. A second Consumer Council study found typical loan patterns of £100 repayable by instalments of £5 weekly over seven months gave a rate of approximately 145 pcpa, a rate, they argued, was far too high.[19] They, however, incorrectly stated that 'it is extremely unlikely that the moneylender could enforce this interest in court, as he has to prove that a rate of 48 per cent is reasonable'.[20] It is impossible to state what a court would have decided as each judges considered both the price and risk in determining extortion. What is clear, as they always have, moneylenders issued a variety of loan sizes and charged different rates dependent on the risks involved.

Moving from rates to expenses, the National Association of Moneylenders suggested that 'the average cost of administering any loan was £9 and with the current rate of inflation it was necessary to charge 18 per cent interest even to stand still on a below average risk loan'.[21] The Lancashire and Cheshire Moneylenders Association estimated that its average member a 15.2% return on capital employed.[22] This result is remarkably similar to data from 1925, as shown in Table 3.2. These returns and profits were distributed to the owner-principals, and like pawnbrokers, moneylenders were funded primarily from their owner capital.[23] This capital structure had changed little since the Victorian era. It wasn't until the turn of the twenty-first century that meaningful amounts of external capital and bank debt entered the small-loan market.

After the Second World War the pawnbroking and moneylending markets underwent significant changes. Developments in the welfare state, rising wages, urban redevelopment and an increase in credit products led to fewer providers and smaller loan volumes. By the time of Crowther, only 400 or so pawnbrokers remained active compared to a peak of 5,087 in 1914. Comparing details from the PBSC 1870 with data almost one hundred years later reveals not just fewer lenders, but a changed business model from a weekly low-value cycle towards higher end less frequent pledging. But, as before, only the highest value items pushed pawnbrokers towards profitability. Population shifts and more credit options had taken their toll on pawnbrokers. Still, for people in need, pawnbrokers remained an important source of cash.[24]

Crowther similarly positioned moneylenders, saying that they were 'at the end of the credit line ... and his clients could usually not secure accommodation elsewhere'.[25] Moneylending had grown, and likely did so at the expense of pawnbroking, but, as the next chapter documents, the industry had not yet transitioned into its modern multi-billion pound payday lending form. In the 1970s, the amounts lent were relatively inconsequential and the trade drew far less media attention than during previous reform.

Political Background

Strangely enough, while the MLA 1927 failed to tame moneylending, by the 1960s its rules and regulations hamstrung major consumer credit providers. Legally, lenders-of-money not exempted by the MLA 1927 needed a licence. With so few credit options in the 1920s, exempting financial institutions was easy enough. As the markets diversified, it was unclear whether the likes of finance houses, hire-purchase companies and instalment lenders required a moneylending licence. Since unlicensed lenders-of-money had no legal recourse against borrower default, at risk were billions in credit contracts having nothing to do with small loans.[26] Though Parliament had patched through temporary fixes, such as section 123 of the 1967 Companies Act, a long-term solution was needed.

This market evolution took place between two periods of economic and social change. In the 1940s and 1950s Britain saw the extension of the welfare state (the Education Act, The Beveridge Report, the NHS, etc.) while towards the end of the 1970s the mantra of deregulation had taken root.[27] The once dominant narrative, suggesting that the financial regulation could correct market failure, was, by the late 1970s, in question (Balleisen and Moss 2010). Social scientists and policymakers argued that government intervention made matters worse. The prevailing mantra was that the government's role in the economy was modernizing and supportive of markets rather than restrictive and coercive (Tomlinson 2007).

A groundswell of support rallied behind a regulatory structure allowing financial institutions to issue any and all forms of consumer credit.[28] Demonstrating the breadth of support for credit market reform, Crowther was appointed by a Labour government led by Harold Wilson and completed under Edward Heath's Conservative government. The CCA 1974 itself was enacted during Wilson's second premiership. Heath was committed to organizational reform, streamlining and the modernization of government and industry (Seldon 2013). Crowther identified similar goals before Heath's administration took office (Sloman 2016). No one political group guided Crowther. This is perhaps why the Crowther process continued alongside changes in government and was well received across the political spectrum. Nor was Crowther influenced by the 'rediscovery of poverty' in the 1960s (Banting 1979; Pinker 1974; Abel-Smith and Townsend 1965; Gazeley 2017). Poverty was not on trial as in the 1870s pawn reform, but instead Crowther was a technocratic process whereby a group of experts sought to solve the problem assigned to it.

The Crowther Committee 1968–1971

Crowther was Britain's first systematic study of the consumer credit market.[29] With Geoffrey Crowther as chairman, the committee was appointed by the Treasury and the Board of Trade in September 1968.[30] Its parliamentary mandate was to investigate the consumer credit regulatory structure, explore possible alternatives and consider amending the Moneylenders Act.[31] The committee held thirty-four days of formal meetings and an unspecified number of informal meetings. Forty-two organizations presented oral evidence and eighty individuals and organizations submitted written evidence. Organizational testimony included groups as diverse as the Federation of British Carpet Manufacturers, the Leeds Junior Chamber of Commerce, the Law Society of Scotland, the Finance Houses Association, the clearing banks, the National Association of Moneylenders and the National Pawnbrokers Association. Government departments providing evidence included the Treasury, the Board of Trade, the Bank of England and local councils. Seemingly the breadth of potential evidence raised alarm bells with Treasury mandarins, with an internal memo stating:

> I think it would be unwise to give the impression that we are positively inviting Crowther to solve these particular problems for us, since we might then find it more difficult at a later stage to disregard any of the Committee's findings which were embarrassing to us.[32]

Lord Crowther rebuked such behaviour warning there would be 'consequences' if facts were 'concealed'.[33] Tensions aside never before had the consumer credit market been investigated in such detail. Since the PBA 1872, only eight committees had analysed any aspect of the market.

Managing an investigation into such a complex industry chimed well with Lord Crowther's 'tremendous capacity for work'.[34] When integrating their findings proved difficult, Lord Crowther convened a weekend retreat of senior committee members held at a hotel outside London, where the members discussed, debated and synthesized their policy recommendations.[35] Crowther found that existing consumer credit legislation was defective, legally ambiguous and unnecessarily restricted lending activities (Goode 1979, p. 6). The ill-equipped 1927 Act demonstrated the inefficiencies and deficiencies in regulating by credit product type. 1970s policymakers saw little value in segmenting the market by credit provider or 'form of lender', that is pawnbrokers, moneylenders, finance houses, etc. that kind of legal construct failed to perform and evolve with real-world business conditions.[36]

The MLA 1927 epitomized the failures of the existing system. Vague wording and the framer's failures to define moneylending had unduly restricted other forms of credit (Megrah 1967). Since the 1927 Act made no distinction between a minor breach and a grave infringement, both of which voided a contract, considerable amounts of credit issued by major lenders were at risk of borrower default. On the flip side, the Act's failure to protect small-loan borrowers was an issue of concern for a budding generation of non-profits and legal advice services.[37] Concerned that a moneylender executed a contract in violation of the 1927 Act, the National Citizens Advice Bureau Council was dismayed to learn that no government agency enforced its provisions.[38] In 1901, Horace Mansfield MP was similarly disconcerted upon learning that the Inland Revenue lacked powers of prosecution under the MLA 1900.[39]

For almost seventy-five years, government, advocacy and lenders had expressed frustration that moneylending laws lacked an enforcement mechanism. There are no records of any major police force having systematically dedicated resources to enforcing the MLA 1927. There were few if any suspensions of licences. Of 170 licensing authorities surveyed by Crowther, only one had suspended a licence between 1958 and 1968 (Goode 1979, p. 103). Judges and the much-vaunted guidance rate fared little better. For reasons of privacy, legal costs, time away from work and unfamiliarity with the law, consumers were unwilling and unable to utilize the court system. Even when borrowers used the courts, the 48% guidance rate offered little protection (Goode 1979, pp. 103, 204–20).[40] The Islington Consumer Group suggested that moneylenders rarely had to justify their rates, even those exceeding 145 pcpa.[41] While rich in legal theory, in practice the MLA 1927 failed to relieve borrowers from problematic loans and high interest rates.[42]

Moneylending laws symbolized the old method of regulation by credit product, which was now deemed fragmented, ineffective and restrictive. The MLA 1927's market effects served as a warning of the systematic failure to demarcate the consumer credit industry by credit product and form of lender. The entire system required a complete overhaul and less government interference in the credit markets (Goode 1979). Crowther reported:

> the existing legal tangle is badly overdue, and that liberation of the consumer credit industry from the antiquated provisions, and from the official restrictions, that hobble it will enable it to make an increasing contribution to the efficiency of the national economy and to the standard of living of the public.[43]

The state was to interfere as little as possible with consumer choice and it remained 'a basic tenet of a free society that people themselves must be the judge of what contributes to their material welfare'.[44] By the middle of the twentieth century consumer debt became a sanctioned and acceptable part of daily life (Finlay 2009, p. 7; Burton 2008, pp. 1–3). Such thinking was different from the days when credit use was morally stigmatized and even more so regulators sought to restrict 'evil' small loans. It was believed that credit enabled poor and rich families to maintain a high standard of living.[45]

According to Crowther, '*Our principal concern* is that this [market] mechanism should operate as efficiently as possible, by enabling the transfer of funds to be completed with the minimal use of real resources'.[46] For its part, government would unify regulation and simplify disclosure terms.[47] Armed with accurate and reliable information, consumer protection occurred naturally in an increasingly competitive market that would price credit appropriately without yielding excessive profits.[48]

Deficient regulation led to an examination of the history of pawnbroking and moneylending. The Treasury and the Board of Trade found that 'the evil which the [historic] Acts aimed to control was the exploitation of borrowers who were in extremis'.[49] Since abject poverty had long vanished, the reasoning went that small-loan regulation was now irrelevant.[50] Since moneylenders were no longer regarded as 'vultures from whom poor and feckless required protection', there was no valid reason to impose heavy restrictions on them or pawnbrokers.[51]

If lenders were no longer seen as evil and borrowers were not teetering on the brink of destitution, the existing regulation was ill suited to the needs of consumers in the 1970s. Even if they were rarely enforced, the detailed requirements of the MLA 1927, patchwork exemptions, restrictions on advertising and price controls in the pawnbroking market were flawed measures. This is a clear shift in policy from the PBA 1872 and MLA 1900–1927. Now, moneylenders and pawnbrokers were to be considered as legitimate participants in the financial system. Section 7.2.5 Crowther states:

> Since we recommend that the Moneylenders and Pawnbrokers Acts should be repealed, these categories of lenders would, for the purpose of licensing, *be treated on an equal footing to all others*. Our reasons for this are partly to avoid the practical difficulties have arisen over the problem of defining certain categories of institutions that are exempted from the Moneylenders Act, especially banks, and partly because of our belief that the general principle that all lenders, and all forms of lending, should be treated as nearly as possible alike.

The regulatory agenda sought market efficiency, reduced costs and an easier transfer of resources from savers to borrowers. Crowther believed that regulation should allow the market and the lenders competing in it the 'maximum freedom to develop'.[52] This begs the question: If lenders were to be treated uniformly, what was Crowther's opinion of borrowers of small sums?

The Borrower

The Consumers Association (Which?) found that small-loan borrowers lacked assets and bank accounts, and earned incomes well below the national average.[53] Long-held assumptions found data supporting that most of the working poor managed unpredictable budgets and utilized credit to avoid disaster when 'as little as ten shillings on the wrong side' was of great consequence.[54] Far from over-indebted, the working poor have little ability to deal with unpredictable income streams and yet to a 'striking degree' managed without incurring 'excessive debt'. The once typical charges of crime, gambling and immorality also fell by the wayside, with Crowther finding that small sums were borrowed to purchase food, pay heating bills and care for a sick relative.

Much like pawnbrokers a century before, Crowther suggested that the demand for cash was driven primarily by 'insufficient income ... illness of the wage-earner ... or loss through fraud'. Data suggests that 56% of pawn and 43% of moneylending loans were issued to pay immediately due bills.[55] Small-loan lender, the Beneficial Financial Company, concurred saying that its loans went towards 'the needs of the necessitous borrower confronted by bills, personal and family needs and emergencies'.[56] The Standing Conference on Organisation of Social Workers suggested that small-loan borrowing occurred as a result of 'difficulties which arise in a family due to a sudden change in circumstances, perhaps from death, illness or unemployment'.[57] Across the board, once anecdotal claims found support from modern research—most borrowers used small loans to manage difficult life circumstances and using high-cost credit was better than the alternative such as missing bill payments (Goode 1979, p. 339). Borrowed monies primarily went towards immediate and unavoidable cash needs.

For all of its affirmation of market behaviour certain borrower routines puzzled Crowther. Since poor borrowers failed to shop around for the lowest price credit option too many lenders earned returns in excess of the assumed risk. Crowther reported that 'the less-educated and poorer members of the community, through their ignorance of the credit market and of the protection of legislation, combined with their unwillingness to shop around, are frequently paying higher rates than is justified by their relative credit-worthiness'.[58] They joined a long line of policymakers failing to make sense of why borrowers valued convenience and maintaining their existing line of credit at least, if not more than, the total cost of that credit. Borrowing decisions were driven by non-price factors such as ease of applying, speed of cash delivery, product diversity, welcoming employees and convenient operating hours. Though it came at a cost, no other financial institution met the needs of low-income borrowers as did moneylenders.

If in the past small-loan usage was thought suspect, if not a moral failing, a failure to repay was worse. By the 1970s this was no longer the case. Crowther even went as far as to categorize certain kinds of default as honest. Honest default was associated with conditions of unavoidable poverty resulting from illness and unemployment.[59] One such case recounted the debts of a father of four owed to a moneylender. The small loan was issued to consolidate hire purchase (HP) debts which he could not repay because his wife had become ill and, without adequate savings and suffering a loss of income, he diverted spending towards medical expenses and necessities. Wanting to avoid repossession of the HP goods, he borrowed £20 from a moneylender. Owing to several late payments, he incurred total charges of £60.[60] Often these kind of defaults involved people earning between £12 and £13 a week, which was far less than the average for full-time manual workers of £28 weekly.[61] These defaulters demonstrate a type of sympathy, encouraging society writ large to understand certain situations went beyond the borrower's control. Reformers of yesteryear likely could never imagine associating honesty and default.

For Crowther, borrowers were perfectly able to decide whether the benefits of a small loan outweighed the costs.[62] Rich or poor, every consumer had or could learn about competing credit products.[63] This stands in contrast to Lucas Stubbs, a Liverpool magistrate, who during the PBSC 1870 had said, 'On the same principle that we shelter children who cannot take care of themselves, we ought to protect weak and ignorant men'.[64] From appropriate credit usage to credit product evaluation, a case was building that borrowers in the 1970s required less protection than in prior decades.

Turning yet one more regulatory motivation upside down, Crowther recognized that most poor borrowers avoided the courts.[65] Of 1,238 consumer-related county court cases heard in Leeds, Bolton, Leicester, Cambridge, Guildford and Worcester (including but not limited to credit), only 9% were initiated by individuals.[66] Fear of publicity, cost and a lack of knowledge concerning legal protection kept debtors from the courts.[67] Over a century of evidence suggests that the court system is not the preferred mechanism for small-loan borrowers struggling within indebtedness. What's different is that the main policymakers actually recognized the reality and sought a solution.

While the need for small loans has changed little over the decades, the perceived need for regulation had evolved. Gone were the days when poor borrowers were considered immoral, irrational and incapable of managing their own affairs. Some policymakers in the 1970s even marvelled at their capacity to stretch thin budgets during normal times, much less when tragedy or emergencies struck. With these changes, the building blocks for streamlined regulation that would lower costs and expanded credit access were falling into place. Policymakers were not, however, advocating for a small-loan free-for-all. The goal was designing both an efficient and protective regulatory structure. Exploring the latter placed Crowther front and centre in the by now long debate concerning the troublesome high cost of small loans.[68]

Price Controls, the Harsh and Unconscionable Test and the Guidance Rate

From one perspective the market was operating perfectly fine such that borrowers valued certain loan features more than others and the price incorporated a lender's assessment of the risks involved. That does not mean that high loan prices went unchallenged. For all of its market-oriented leanings, Crowther suggested a 'socially desirable' interest rate existed which was often lower than the market's pricing mechanism.[69] Despite their mathematical models, an army of researchers, and a preference for market-based capitalism, much like regulators before, Crowther claimed that high rates simply 'felt wrong'. A duelling tension manifest that while on the one hand small loans should be treated no differently than other forms of credit, yet on the other hand excessive loan prices caused social harm.

To most observers the costs felt too high and a similar intuition opened discussions around price controls. Given Crowther's disposition for a minimal disruption of markets, implementing price controls was a long shot. Government-limitations on profits ran contrary to the very core of Crowther's modern regulatory system. As with previous naysayers, Crowther questioned how the government could select and apply a single maximum rate across an entire market sector. Given the diversity of borrower needs, a single rate could never account for the variety of loan sizes, risks and duration.

Even more problematic, since not all high-priced loans were extortionate, a blanket market-wide price cap would needlessly restrict market activity. Crowther explained that while a £10 loan repayable with £1 charges in twenty weekly instalments of 11s seemed reasonable it carried with it an effective interest rate of 61 pcpa. While the £1 repayment was not particularly burdensome, the percentage rate cost could be considered high.[70] A government-mandated price cap would distort far too many loans that that did not warrant such an intervention.[71] The reinstatement of price controls was not the answer and they were, once again, rejected.[72]

Crowther did recognize that a small percentage of the population would get into trouble through their use of credit. It suggested that if it could be demonstrated that a meaningful number of borrowers suffered from hardship, then there would be a case on social grounds to implement price controls and other harsh restrictions, but until that point, credit should be freely available.[73] Protecting certain borrowers through government-mandated pricing necessitated market interference that would deny large numbers of consumers from the benefits of credit.[74] For most people access to credit was cited as beneficial which meant that price control-induced rationing harmed borrowers. Credit access overrode social policy obligations to protect the minority of users who struggled with indebtedness.

As if on a historic playback loop, with price controls binned the debate focused on the guidance rate and testing for extortionate terms.[75] Effectively testing for extortionate terms had vexed policymakers since their implementation in the early 1900s, and Crowther was no different. It was unclear how to determine whether a transaction was, in fact, extortionate. While an age of consent and diminished mental capacity were relatively straightforward, determining the influence of other factors was ambiguous. Goode suggested that a small-loan borrower experienced 'conditions which make him particularly vulnerable to acceptance of a harsh agreement; but on the other hand, it is these self-same conditions that may generate an urgent need for financial assistance, while making it difficult for the debtor to obtain credit because of his poor income prospects' (Goode 1979, p. 339). The reality is that most low-income borrowers were in dire straits before seeking a loan, making it almost impossible for a judge to untangle the complexity of borrowing costs and risk factors.

A written exchange between Mr Hyde of the DTI's policy division and Mr Holmes of the Lord Chancellor's Office highlighted the limitations of testing for extortion. In January 1973 Holmes wrote to Hyde, 'How, for example, can the lender know about the circumstances of the borrower at the time of transaction ... is the enforceability of the contract to depend, for example, on the number of children the borrower has ...?'[76] Holmes pondered how the entire system would operate if identical transactions were to be treated differently based on the personal circumstances of the borrower, where a contract between 'A and X is valid', but between 'A and Y is void' owing to Y's personal circumstances.[77] In 1897, Judge Collier of Liverpool had voiced similar concerns. He questioned the wisdom of providing county court judges such discretion which would breed untold confusion in the system.[78] The practicality of testing for extortion was no less erroneous in the 1970s than in the 1900s.

The National Association of Moneylenders argued against carrying forward the 'baseless' 48% guidance rate.[79] The Association instead suggested thirty-three factors, which were the typical elements considered by loan offices.[80] Moneylenders widened the test to include the size of the loan, its duration, repayment schedule, flexibility in default, the age, sex, marital status, income, stability of employment, owner or rental status, and educational background of the borrower and the lender's overheads and percentage return on capital. The lender's logic is compelling. They believed that a judge should review the same evaluative factors on which the loan was issued. If the judge found that the price of the loan grossly exceeded the risk assessment based on those thirty-three factors, then the contract should be rewritten. For them, carrying forward the failed guidance rate made little sense. History demonstrates that the policy did not protect borrowers and was too narrow a criterion to pass fair and consistent judgement on extortionate transactions.

Crowther disagreed and fell back on the same idea that drove support for the guidance rate in 1897. Reviewing individual transactions was a midway point between absolute price controls and providing no guidance whatsoever. So confident was Crowther it suggested applying the guidance rate across all forms of consumer credit—not just small loans.[81] Mitigating borrower's avoidance of the courts, it devised a new government department under the authority of a Consumer Credit Commissioner supervise the entire credit industry. Lenders that consistently charged above the guidance rate would be required to submit quarterly returns and the Commissioner could initiate proceedings if a loan was deemed extortionate.[82]

For the same reasons that they had been twice rejected, Crowther believed that price controls distorted market operations beyond the benefits of protecting the small minority of users in need of debt relief. This makes Crowther's updated guidance rate scheme all the more interesting, not only because it proposed expanding its application, but for the fact that it, like so many policymakers before, felt that at some point the market price of borrowed money could do more harm than good. Again, the intent was for the lighter touch towards market operations without sacrificing wider social protections.

Disclosure Terms

Policymakers focused on advertising, loan contracts and were especially concerned with protecting the public from misleading fees and charges.[83] Consensus was reached that uniform cost disclosure reduced misleading advertising and improved market competitiveness.[84] Advocates believed 'true interest rate' disclosure encouraged comparison between competing credit options, which in the end drove down pricing.[85] The APR was a central component of Crowther's information disclosure program.[86]

While small loan providers largely supported standardized APR calculations, they once again contended that borrowers did not want such information.[87] Unlike before consumer advocates, banks and cheque traders, to name a few, agreed. The National Citizens Advice Bureau Council believed that no matter what the quoted interest rate was, consumers were 'more concerned with whether or not they can afford what is being asked'.[88] Midland Bank believed that 'most people appeared to be interested only in the amount they had to repay and over what period'.[89] A frustrated Crowther found the situation circular—consumers did not want the information because the information was not available. And, the information was not available because consumers did not demand it.[90] Almost as a force of nature then, APR disclosure encouraged rational consumer credit decisions. A long list of policymakers have put great faith in the merits of a percentage disclosure, and with similar conviction, held that borrowers should value the information more than they actually do.

Whatever its benefits, calculating an APR remained a complicated affair. In 1897, a moneylender estimated that percentage disclosures would require two more clerks in each office.[91] Moneylenders and pawnbrokers of the day expressed similar anxieties. That small-loan lenders bemoaned certain mathematical complexities aligns them with their historical counterparts. That government and outside bodies agreed was a significant break from the past. The Home and Social Affairs Committee recognized the difficulties involved and noted that there was no foolproof formula.[92] For example, the APR on a £100 loan due in one month's time at 5% interest with a £10 application fee can be expressed without the fee as approximately 80% and with the fee as approximately 435%. Even today, the only accurate rate is found using an actuarial approach, which takes into consideration the ratio of interest to funds available to the borrower. The entire Crowther report and the 1974 legislation was delayed owing to the issue of a standardized and accurate formula (Goode 1979, p. 158).[93]

Without a uniformed APR calculation, there was little chance of the bill passing through Parliament.[94] In response the Government Actuary's Department provided seven pages of APR calculation guidance.

Secondary mandated disclosure terms included the size of the loan, a summary of fees and charges, the total amount repayment amount and the amount of each instalment and its due date.[95]

These measures were meant to increase market competitiveness through more accurate information. The idea that borrowers should have access to pricing information expressed in percentage terms was similar to 1900 and 1927. What had changed was policymaker's perspective on the borrower's capabilities and the role of disclosure. When once borrowers were incapable of managing their own affairs and disclosure requirements were meant to limit fraud and curtail lending, by the 1970s disclosure terms aimed at market efficiency and competitiveness.

Enforcement and Licensing

Unless borrowers pursued legal recourse, moneylenders operated without meaningful government oversight. As the years progressed, fewer lenders registered and fewer still were prosecuted for violations under the 1927 Act. Updating regulation necessitated a government ministry responsible for enforcing the law. Crowther argued for the creation of an independent agency that would be autonomous of current government departments. This idea found its roots in Britain's first independent regulator, dating back to 1954 with the creation of the Independent Television Authority (Baldwin 2011). It was believed that an independent agency was better suited to enforce and monitor the consumer credit markets.[96] Likely influenced by the 1968 Fulton Committee's findings, Crowther was concerned that the civil services narrowed expertise inhibited the recruitment of highly qualified financial experts.[97]

The plan was for a Consumer Credit Commissioner to administer the licensing scheme, regulate possible changing circumstances, enforce the Act, collect statistical data and educate the public about consumer credit.[98] Controlling market entry and punishing deviant behaviour through licensing was a critical consumer protection feature. Financial institutions issuing loans to an individual or partnership at a sum not exceeding £2,000 required a licence.[99] These loans were subdivided into connected and unconnected loans. Connected loans were issued by a seller to a consumer in order to purchase a specific good or service from a seller. Connected loans repayable in three or more instalments required a licence. Unconnected or 'straight money' loans carrying an interest rate of 2.5% above Bank rate also required a licence. The Bank rate test excluded certain socially oriented lenders including building societies, life assurers and loan societies. Focusing on the end-user and loan size, as opposed to the form or lender or credit product, eliminated the need for multiple types of consumer credit licences. Whether the lender was a pawnbroker, moneylender or a bank, mattered not. What mattered was the credit recipient and the principal amount. These well-defined boundaries eliminated much of the confusion and ambiguity of previous policy.

Unless the applicant demonstrated a history of inappropriate behaviour, the Consumer Credit Commission automatically granted a licence.[100] With the inclusion of 220 banks, an estimated 50,000–60,000 financial institutions required licensing.[101] After issuance the Commissioner could deny, revoke or refuse a licence renewal.[102] Simplified initial licensing was offset by a strict enforcement of the law. The concentration of power within the Commissioner's office drove Crowther's insistency that the agency's staff possess a deep expertise in the credit markets.

Many small-loan lenders had long viewed regulation as a route to legitimacy and have sought to quell deviant behaviour within the ranks. Their support for the Commissioner's licensing and enforcement powers was widespread. With similar consistency, moneylenders have proposed regulatory features beyond those which policymakers entertained. The 1970s proved no exception when the National Association of Moneylenders sought a more stringent procedure by licensing each branch manager and proprietor. Under their scheme an individual would be held accountable for unacceptable or illegal conduct. Though dismissive of their plan, small-loan lenders offered support for the Commissioner, hoping that they would find equitable treatment under the law.

Parts of government remain unconvinced and voiced strong opposition to the Commissioner's power. The DTI argued that there was no basis for an independent agency to adapt statutory provisions based on evolving market conditions without approval of a government minister.[103] The DTI advocated for licensing enforcement at the local level through the Weights and Measures authorities. Unsurprisingly, it felt that the British civil service possessed ample qualifications to monitor and control the consumer credit market and would do so more economically at that.[104] As the bill weaved through Parliament, their strong opposition shaped the CCA 1974's final outcome.

Final Remarks on the Crowther Committee (1968–1971)

Crowther's research found that consumer credit legislation had failed to define the market, encourage competition among lenders, stifled innovation and offered inadequate consumer protection. While the value of moneylending was of little consequence to the economy, the financial regulation governing it was the starting point of reform. Over the decades following the MLA 1927 various amendments and exclusions were enacted in response to its poor design and the evolving credit markets. Crowther sought to unify regulation and increase competition, which in turn protected borrowers and encouraged financial innovation. Borrowers armed with consistent and standardized information disclosure drove the markets towards efficient outcomes (Baldwin 2011; Hayek 1945).

Since Victorian times policymakers treated percentage disclosure of costs and fees as a lynchpin regulatory device. This, despite the fact that borrowers were more interested in monetary rather than percentage terms. As discussed in Chapter 4, it was not until 2015 that ample data confirmed what lenders have long argued: access to credit, the speed of approval and the quick delivery of funds are more important to borrowers than the cost of credit and its related APR. Nonetheless, Crowther argued that a uniform APR would increase competition and drive efficiencies absent from the British credit markets.

For poor borrowers, small loans offered a much-needed lifeline and allowed them to survive during periods of financial difficulties.[105] Since the market demand for small loans differed from, for example, purchasing a dishwasher on instalment credit, Crowther debated if targeted regulation might help low-income households. The difficulty, they found, is that consumer credit legislation could do little to protect those 'who through no fault of their own' have an insufficient income.[106] Reminiscent of the Victorian era, it was doubted that regulation could actually mitigate the unique demand features of small-loan borrowers. Instead, Crowther set out to regulate the suppliers of credit, whereas the need of the poor to borrow in the first place was considered as a social issue beyond the scope of their purview, if not the capabilities of credit legislation more generally.

This line of thinking echoes in Crowther's unwillingness to recommend a statutory price cap on the cost of small loans. It argued that a price cap would lead to market segmentation and price clustering—two features of uncompetitive markets which it found extremely problematic.

Crowther suggested that the lone remnant of statutory usury—the profit restrictions placed on pawnbrokers—be rescinded. Instead, it extended the 48% guidance rate and the harsh and unconscionable test to the entire field of consumer credit. This is a quite remarkable turn of events. What had originated as a regulatory protection mechanism in the small-loan market would be applied to all consumer credit products. As was the case in 1927, the guidance rate was seen as corrective of an individual contract that had deviated from the agreed 'trigger' norm of 48% interest. And, like their Edwardian predecessors, Crowther did not provide strict determinant criteria but felt lenders and borrowers would be better served by a flexible mechanism.

When and where individual lenders harmed consumers, Crowther advocated for a centralized office under a Credit Commissioner to control the licensing process and initiate enforcement proceedings. The use of licensing and punishment for violation are considered a 'micro-prudential' financial regulatory response that seeks to influence behaviour at the firm level (Moloney et al. 2015). By consolidating regulatory power in one agency, Crowther tried to make rules uniform and enforce them consistently, while granting enough flexibility to overcome the strict nature of regulation in the past, which had failed to account for the dynamic nature of the market.

Whether Parliament followed Crowther's recommendations pertaining to small-loan providers is explored in the next section.

The Consumer Credit Act 1974

The Crowther Report was published in March 1971. Consumer groups and the business community found its framework favourable.[107] The *Observer* remarked, 'Seldom has a report of such a complex subject been greeted with such a chorus of approval'.[108] While the Hire Purchase Association said, 'The Committee were given a task of truly herculean proportions; few we believe will disagree with the view that they have done it superbly well'.[109] In more muted terms, John Davies, Secretary of State for Trade and Industry, wrote to Prime Minister Heath that the Report 'as a whole has not had an unfriendly reception from commercial interests'.[110]

The government's White Paper response, 'Reform of the Law on Consumer Credit', found existing regulation deficient and charged the MLA 1927 with inhibiting the growth of consumer and commercial credit.[111] The government announced a bill that aligned with Crowther's offering of a unified yet flexible framework applicable across the entire consumer credit system. It was expected that legislation would modernize regulation, encourage competition and protect consumers.[112]

The government's bill was not uncontroversial. An unnamed employee at the DTI argued that Parliament would not engage in wholesale reform of the credit markets 'simply on the grounds that [the] existing law is untidy'.[113] F. J. Broomfield of the Board of Trade yet averred that reform efforts of Crowther's magnitude were unrealistic.[114] Ever practical, the Home and Social Affairs Committee suggested that any proposed bill longer than fifty clauses stood little chance in Parliament.[115] Even if that were true, while the draft bill was 84 pages long, it removed 126 pages of legislation, giving a net loss of 42 pages.[116] Others championed the 'considerable sex-appeal' in focusing attention on the protection benefits the CCA 1974 would bring to the poor.[117] Motives aside, they were not alone in expressing interest in protecting the poor. Harold Davies, Lord Davies of Leek (Labour), argued that it was the duty of legislation to keep an eye on 'the sharks and cheats'.[118]

The bill applied to cash loans or any other form of financial accommodation not exceeding £5,000 issued to individuals and non-corporate bodies. Certain requirements were lifted for small-loan agreements below £30 including mail-order, cheque trading, and running accounts such as a milk delivery. For similar agreements, the Act waived periodic account statements, cooling-off provisions and contract formalities. There were no significant exemptions for small cash loans, and many of the bill's provisions applied to all loans regardless of the principal amount. The lessons of the past encouraged great attention to definitions. Few sources of credit were granted exemptions nor were boundaries designed around the source of credit.

Concerning the pawn market, sections 114–122 of the Act dealt with pledged items. Again, the law dealt with pledged items and not pawnbrokers per se. Any financial institution with a credit licence could loan on pledged items. With price controls lifted, much of the section dealt with receipt issuance and the minimum six-month redemption process. An interesting change from prior legislation concerns the sale of forfeited goods. It was far less complicated than previous laws. For goods valued over £15, the proceeds of sale beyond the amount owed and reasonable expenses were payable to the pawner. And with that, those eight or so sections replaced voluminous pawnbroking regulation.

The following analyses the final developments concerning price controls, terms of disclosure, licensing and enforcement. It pays particular attention to areas where Crowther and the final bill differ as they relate to the small-loan market.

Price Controls

Debates concerning the interest rate followed a similar pattern to previous periods. There was limited support for usury and disagreement about a guidance interest rate; neither was implemented.[119] On two occasions then, the first being the MLSC 1897, and now Crowther, Parliament rejected the respective committee's preference for a guidance rate. The 1970s Parliament argued that a guidance rate failed to account for the diversity of credit products and would narrow the judicial review process. As in 1900, Parliament feared too much interest rate specificity would distort the credit market and limit the application of the law. Lord Pery of Limerick (Conservative, Under Secretary of State for Trade) believed that no single rate could cover a loan for the purchase of a car and a 'loan granted to someone in a very straitened circumstance to tide him over the weekend'.[120] The White Paper offered an example of a £10, two-day loan, carrying a charge of 10p, which few would consider excessive, yet it works out at 100 pcpa. Removing the guidance rate afforded the courts wider latitude to review and revise credit transactions.[121]

The CCA 1974 provided the court power to reopen a consumer credit transaction when the debtor alleged and provided evidence of extortion.[122] Any consumer credit transaction—large or small—could be reviewed. The court could revise, in part or whole, any obligation of the borrower. Lender had to prove a transaction was not extortionate based on loan size and duration, prevailing interest rates, collateral-backed versus unsecured loans and the credit profit of a borrower.[123] Mitigating risk factors included the age, experience, business acumen, financial position and the borrower's physical health. As Goode pointed out, to be considered extortionate the lender must have been aware of the borrower's specific situation when the loan was issued (Goode 1975). The courts could also review auxiliary bargains dealing with compulsory charges. Though rollovers loans were insufficient grounds to reopen a current transaction nothing precluded a borrower from presenting a past transaction as an additional grievance (Goode 1979, p. 334).

Where the CCA 1974 resembles past legislation was the definition of extortion. As contained in Section 138(1) a credit bargain was extortionate if,

a. it requires the debtor or a relative of his to make payments which are grossly exorbitant, or
b. otherwise grossly contravenes ordinary principles of fair dealing.

The CCA 1974 did not define 'grossly exorbitant' or 'grossly contravenes ordinary principles'. Fears of confining the courts with strict definitions had again found their way into the final bill. Since 1900, policymakers had debated the merits of providing the judiciary with specific criteria versus the use of general but accepted legal terminology. Time and again, the latitude argument won over appeals for legislative specificity.

Terms of Disclosure

The bill made provisions to ensure that the borrower was aware of the terms and conditions.[124] Disclosure requirements included the sum borrowed, the total owed, payment schedules, the date of execution, creditor information, debtor information, the type of credit offered and the duration. Prior to default penalties, for secured loans of more than £15 and all cash loans the lender had to issue a notice of default.[125] It was argued that clear information aided a rational choice among competing credit products.[126] Transparent and truthful disclosure enhanced consumer welfare and encouraged a more respectable industry, as only the 'sharks ... who bleed dry unsuspecting and naive' people will protest.[127]

Major difficulties remained, especially in calculating the rate of interest. Even the banking industry utilized various methods, as Table 4.7 shows the difference between advertised nominal and effective rates as calculated by each bank. Note that while Midland's actual rate was lower than Lloyds's, its effective rate was higher.[128] The proposed bill sought to standardized APR across the board, which was no easy task.

The motivation behind truth in lending was to increase competition. The government's position was made clear by Alan Williams MP (Labour), who on the floor of the Commons stated,

Table 4.7 Actual versus effective rates

	Interest Rate	
	Actual pcpa (%)	*Effective pcpa (%)*
NatWest	8.0	15.7
Midland	9.0	17.7
Lloyds	9.5	17.2

Source (Lindgren 1977)

> We want to give greater equality in bargaining between the debtor and the creditor, and we believe, as did the Conservative Government, that we can achieve this greater protection and this greater equality in bargaining only by establishing greater truth in lending. Through truth in lending, we hope that we shall have open disclosure of all the terms which are involved in an agreement. We hope that this will make for true competition and will avoid some of the grosser examples that we have had of interest rates in the last few years.[129]

Even when compared to the guidance rate mechanism, the government relied even more heavily on increased competition driven by information disclosure. This, despite the fact that, at least pertaining to small loans, most borrowers ranked the APR much lower in their decision process than consistent loan approval and speed of the cash delivery.

Enforcement and Licensing

The Government agreed that an independent Consumer Credit Commissioner be appointed with primary administrative responsibilities for the licensing system and for monitoring developments in the consumer credit industry. However, Crowther's vision was somewhat curtailed by making the appointment subject to the Secretary of State who in turn issued formal operational priorities to the Commissioner.[130] The Fair Trading Act and the Director General of Fair Trading were cited as precedents.[131] Weights and Measures handled local routine violations, leaving the Commissioner to deal with systemic issues.[132] Regulatory adjustments occurred through the Commissioner, but under the scrutiny of Parliament. The minister would be given power to set rules of conduct, and the Commissioner would issue, suspend or revoke a licence.[133]

Ongoing licensing provided a flexible regulatory tool responding to the ever-evolving credit markets.[134]

Unfit applicants were denied a licence based on past behaviour including a violation under the Act or similar consumer legislation, charging excessive interest, conduct unfair to the consumer or refusing credit based on the borrower's race, creed or gender.[135] An appeal process was provided. Oliver Kitson, Lord Airedale of Gledhow (Liberal) questioned whether the Director would have enough localized knowledge to make an informed decision.[136] His concerns echoed Josiah Wedgwood MP's (Labour), who, during the MLSC 1927, inquired whether the Home Office would send inspectors to ask 'Who was your father? What school did you study [in]?'[137] Though in the extreme minority, some lawmakers objected to the subjective concept of a 'fit' person. Conceptually, the idea of fit and suitable joins early attempts at refining the industry by improving the type of person engaged in lending small sums.

A licence enabled a lender to issue all forms of consumer credit. This provision substantially changed the moneylending and pawnbroking markets. Within a relatively short period small-loan lenders evolved from proprietor and partnerships into corporations offering multiple products, including payday, pawnbroking, cheque cashing, automobile title and similar loans. While policymakers had hoped that traditional financial institutions would move downstream, in fact, traditionally fringe providers expanded their product offerings with little to no competition from farther up the financial food chain. In hindsight, as did the repeal of usury in 1854, a significant regulatory overhaul unleashed a familiar but novel product, the payday loan.

Conclusion

In the decades following the 1927 Act, credit markets became increasingly important for Britain's economic prosperity. Outdated and restrictive regulation hindered the market's ability to allocate credit efficiently and policymakers sought wholesale reform. Crowther believed that fewer government restrictions encouraged more efficient market outcomes. The CCA 1974 sought competition across the entire spectrum of credit providers, resulting in lower pricing and fewer abusive contracts for the poor and the rich alike.[138]

Crowther had a strong preference for less government interference in the market not because it wanted to leave the poor high and dry, but because for most users' credit afforded them an opportunity to overcome financial hardship. Nor can one reasonably claim that their approach was an extreme form of traditional economic liberalism. Crowther devised a robust system of rules upheld by a sophisticated enforcement mechanism. Its hesitation in targeting small-loan lenders stems in part from its overall strategy seeking a uniformed regulatory system and also from a belief that by itself the law cannot overcome the shortfalls in personal finance (Goode 1979, p. 130). A sceptical Crowther doubted the effectiveness of regulation's ability to overcome the unique situation of low-income borrowers.

Price controls are a prime example. While some borrowers may benefit from lower pricing, higher risk borrowers are capped out of the market. Presumably, the capped-out poor still needed cash, yet had fewer options of securing funds. Price controls measures would not and could not overcome the reality that the poor needed cash. Intervening in the pricing mechanism had consequences and distorted markets in a way that most 1970s policymakers were uncomfortable with.

Whereas former regulation created barriers between credit providers and attempted to restrict the small-loan market, Crowther designed a system of competitive equality between lenders. Ideally, a single licence encouraged well-capitalized banks and major financial institutions to offer products tailored to low-income borrowers at more competitive rates than moneylenders and pawnbrokers could. As the next chapter recounts, that ideal never materialized. In many respects the opposite occurred because the single licence facilitated, if not incentivized, a dramatic expansion in the services provided by small-loan lenders.

Notes

1. BT 250/38 (National Pawnbrokers' Association), "Oral Evidence," 20 March 1970, The National Archives (hereafter TNA); BT 250/52 (Beneficial Finance Company), "Memorandum to Crowther," 26 September 1968, TNA; BT 250/66 (Provident Clothing and Supply Company), "Oral Evidence," 20 March 1969, TNA; FV 62/29 (Consumer Sale and Loan Group), "Department of Trade and Industry, Pawnbrokers Special Provisions Internal Report," 19 June 1972, TNA; BT 250/4 (Official Bodies), "Background Memorandum on the Scope of Enquiry, Board of Trade and HM Treasury," 1968, TNA.

2. BT 250/100–101 (Newspaper Advice Bureaux), "Letter from Mr Gray, Board of Trade, to Royston Goode, Crowther Committee," 3 July 1970, TNA.
3. BT 250/2 (Consumer Credit), "Summary Conclusions from the Department of Trade and Industry," March 1971 and BT 250/4 (Official Bodies), "Background Memorandum on the Scope of Enquiry, Board of Trade and HM Treasury," 1968, TNA; BT 250/2 (Consumer Credit), "Bank of England, Memorandum," July 1969, TNA. BT 250/2 (Consumer Credit), "Summary Conclusions from the Department of Trade and Industry," "Bank of England, Memorandum," "Bank of England, Oral Evidence," 1969, and BT 250/4 (Official Bodies), "Board of Trade, Committee on Consumer Credit, Minutes," 25 September 1968; "Letter from FW Glaves-Smith to RJ Painter," HM Treasury, TNA; "MPs Told of Credit Curbs," *Guardian*, 2 November 1968; HC written answers 2 July 1968, vol. 767.
4. Hereafter Crowther refers to the committee and the Consumer Credit: Report of the Committee 1971 (4596). References to the person will appear as Lord Crowther. The other committee members were Andrew Carnwath, George Clayton, Cyril Colton, Royston Goode, Desmond Hirshfield, Kenneth Mackenzie, Millie Miller and Douglas Steen. The CCA 1974 repealed the PBA 1872, MLA 1900, MLA 1927, PBA 1960, Hire-Purchase Act 1965 and Advertisement (Hire Purchase) Act 1967.
5. IR 40/3555 (Inland Revenue), "Office of Chief Inspector of Taxes, Letter from Mr Wilcox to Mr Pool," 28 November 1929, TNA.
6. BT 250/34 (National Association of Moneylenders), "Oral Evidence, R.B. Selig, Chairman, C.A. Yonwin, Secretary," 20 March 1969, TNA. Non-professionals were lenders who issued loans infrequently and/or loans of extremely low value.
7. The study sampled 373 moneylenders and 115 pawnbrokers of whom 276 moneylenders and 85 pawnbrokers responded. See "Pawnbrokers and Moneylenders," a report for the Department of Trade and Industry by NOP Market Research, 1971 (NOP Research).
8. BT 250/38 (National Pawnbrokers' Association), "The Pawnbroker" by Ruth Brandon of New Society, 16 June 1970, TNA.
9. The Bank of England inflation calculator.
10. BT 250/38 (National Pawnbrokers' Association), "Oral Evidence," 20 March 1970, TNA.
11. BT 250/38 (National Pawnbrokers' Association), "Oral Evidence," 20 March 1970, TNA.
12. After 1872, small parts of the PBA were amended. The last was the Pawnbrokers Act 1960: 8 & 9 Eliz.2. Ch.25. This Act increased allowable charges and the loan maximum from £10 to £50. Because the Act

is considered minor, was enacted with little debate and was rescinded by the CCA 1974, it is not covered by this research.

13. FV 62/34 (Moneylenders, Cheque Traders and Pawnbrokers trade associations), "National Pawnbrokers' Association," 21 November 1972, TNA.
14. BT 250/4 (Official Bodies), "Background Memorandum on the Scope of Enquiry, Board of Trade and HM Treasury," 1968, TNA.
15. BT 250/34 (National Association of Moneylenders), "Letter from RB Selig, Chairman, to Mr Gray, Board of Trade, Committee on Consumer Credit," 23 April 1970, TNA.
16. BT 250/34 (National Association of Moneylenders), "Letter from RB Selig, Chairman, to Mr Gray, Board of Trade, Committee on Consumer Credit," 23 April 1970, TNA.
17. BT 250/47 (Consumer Council), "Consumer Council: About Credit," Undated, TNA.
18. BT 250/34 (National Association of Moneylenders), "Oral Evidence, RB Selig, Chairman, CA Yonwin, Secretary," 20 March 1969, TNA.
19. BT 250/50 (National Federation of Consumer Groups), "The Islington Consumers' Group: Fair Deal," 1967, TNA.
20. BT 250/50 (National Federation of Consumer Groups), "The Islington Consumers' Group: Fair Deal," 1967, TNA.
21. FV 62/34 (Moneylenders, Cheque Traders and Pawnbrokers trade associations), "Board of Trade Meeting with the National Moneylenders Association," 19 April 1971, TNA.
22. BT 250/27 (Lancashire and Cheshire Moneylenders Association), "Letter from MH Watson, Secretary, to NH Nail, Secretary, Board of Trade, Committee on Consumer Credit," 12 June 1969, TNA.
23. Crowther, 2.4.21.
24. BT 250/38 (National Pawnbrokers' Association), "Oral Evidence," 20 March 1970, TNA.
25. Crowther, 2.4.15.
26. BT 250/2 (Consumer Credit), "Summary Conclusions from the Department of Trade and Industry," March 1971, TNA.
27. The Institute for Economic Affairs among others challenged the so-called Big Bang deregulation of financial services under the Thatcher government. See Larry Elliot, "Margaret Thatcher's Deregulation of the City a Myth, Says Think Tank," *Guardian*, 25 May 2015.
28. HC deb. 14 February 1967, 741; HC deb. 12 July 1967, vol. 650; HC deb. 19 July 1967, vol. 750; HL 22 November 1966, vol. 278; AJ 10/60 (Consumer Council), "Memorandum to the Committee on Consumer Credit," Undated, TNA. Ultimately, the CCA 1974 repealed the PBA 1872, MLA 1900, MLA 1927, PBA 1960, Hire-Purchase Act 1965 and Advertisement (Hire Purchase) Act 1967. For

example, George Darling MP (Labour, Minister of State at the Board of Trade), his predecessor, Niall Macpherson, Lord Drumalbyn of Whitesands (Conservative) and the Consumer Council pushed to overhaul the outdated and patchwork of legislation and Lord Chancellor Gerald Gardiner, Lord Gardiner of Kittisford (Labour) stated (incorrectly as this book demonstrates) that historically policymakers easily distinguished between a banker and a moneylender, he, along with Frank Soskice, Lord Stow Hill of Newport (former Home Secretary and Lord Privy Seal, Labour) and Thomas Jay MP (Labour, President Board of Trade).

29. Crowther's final report was segmented into a Lending and Security Act and A Consumer Sale and Loan Act. This research focuses on the latter.
30. On 19 October 1970, The Board of Trade was merged with the Ministry of Technology, creating a new cabinet post of Secretary of State for Trade and Industry. Hereafter the Department for Trade and Industry is abbreviated as DTI.
31. Crowther, iii. A portion of Crowther's work dealt with lending and securities, which falls outside the scope of this research, which focuses on consumer credit.
32. BT 250/4 (Official Bodies), "HM Treasury, Internal Letter RJ Painter to Mr Michelson," 29 October 1968, TNA.
33. BT 250/4 (Official Bodies), "Board of Trade, Internal Memorandum," 11 November 1968, TNA.
34. Royston Goode, Interview, 20 November 2015.
35. Royston Goode, Interview, 20 November 2015.
36. Crowther, 1.3.6; "High Cost of Credit to be Reviewed," *Guardian*, 3 July 1968; "Tighter Law on Loan Advertising," *Guardian*, 12 September 1968; Michael Blanden, "What Is the Cost of Credit?" *Guardian*, 5 October 1968.
37. Crowther, 7.4.1.
38. BT 250/49 (The National Citizens' Advice Bureau Council), "Oral Evidence," 16 May 1969, TNA.
39. HC deb. 18 June 1901, vol. 11.
40. Ibid., 103, 204–205.
41. BT 250/50 (National Federation of Consumer Groups), "Letter from RGA Youard, Chairman, to NH Nail, Secretary to the Committee on Consumer Credit," 29 May 1969, TNA.
42. BT 250/112 (Summary of Existing Legislation), "HM Treasury and Board of Trade, 'Equity in Consumer Credit'", 18 December 1968, TNA.
43. Crowther, 3.9.1.
44. Crowther, 3.9.1.
45. FV 62/10 (Inter-Departmental Consideration), "Department of Trade and Industry, Draft White Paper," 20 July 1973, TNA. Again, a distinction should be made between productive and consumptive credit.

46. Crowther, 3.3.2. Emphasis added.
47. Crowther, 3.3.2, 3.7.17, 3.9.5.
48. Crowther, 3.3.2.
49. BT 250/4 (Official Bodies), "Background Memorandum on the Scope of Enquiry, Board of Trade and HM Treasury," 1968, TNA.
50. FV 62/29 (Consumer Sale and Loan Group), "Department of Trade and Industry, Pawnbrokers Special Provision," 19 June 1972, TNA.
51. BT 250/75 (County of West Sussex), "Letter from GC Goldberg, Clerk of the County Council, to Mr Gray, Assistant Secretary to the Committee on Consumer Credit," 31 January 1969, TNA.
52. Crowther, 1.3.4.
53. BT 250/48 (Consumers Association), "Oral Evidence," 17 July 1969, TNA.
54. Crowther, 3.7.8, 3.7.16, 6.1.9–6.1.10.
55. NOP Research. Excludes essential living and household expenses.
56. BT 250/52 (Beneficial Finance Company), "Memorandum," 26 September 1968, TNA.
57. BT 250/46 (Association of Family Case Workers), "Memorandum," 1969, TNA.
58. Crowther, 3.3.5, 3.6.3–3.6.8.
59. Crowther, 3.7.16, 3.83–3.85, 6.1.8.
60. BT 250/100–101 (Newspaper Advice Bureaux), "Summary Report," 3 July 1970, TNA.
61. The sample set was composed of 70 borrowers who experienced problems with their loan and took the initiative to recount their troubles to the John Hilton Bureau; HC Deb 28 January 1971 vol 810.
62. Crowther, 3.2.6, 3.7.17.
63. Crowther, 3.7.13, 6.1.7.
64. PBSC 1870, 3138–48.
65. BT 250/100–101 (Newspaper Advice Bureaux), "Summary Report," 3 July 1970, TNA.
66. BT 250/47 (Consumer Council), "Is the Legal System Any Use to Consumers? By Susan Marsden-Smedley," 7 January 1969, TNA.
67. BT 250/100–101 (Newspaper Advice Bureaux), "Summary Report," 3 July 1970, TNA; BT 250/16 (Association of County Court Registrars), "Oral Evidence, JG Bryson, President," 2 December 1969, TNA. The implications of the borrower's failure to utilize the court system are analysed below.
68. Crowther, 6.6.5.
69. Crowther, 6.6.6–6.6.7.
70. Crowther, 6.6.8.
71. BT 250/28 (Law Society), "Oral Evidence," 15 May 1969, TNA.
72. Crowther, 1.3.33, 6.6.9.

73. Crowther, 1.3.64–66, 3.7.12, 3.7.16.
74. Crowther, 3.3.5.
75. The term 'extortionate' and 'harsh' and unconscionable are used interchangeably. According to Goode, Judge Perks established as much in *Castle Phillips Finance Co. v. Khan* (1978).
76. FV 62/60 (Regulation of the Cost of Credit: Recommendations), "Correspondence Lord's Chancellor's Office, House of Lords, RJ Holmes and DG Hyde," 30 January, 5–6 February 1973, TNA.
77. FV 62/60 (Regulation of the Cost of Credit: Recommendations), "Correspondence Lord's Chancellor's Office, House of Lords, RJ Holmes and DG Hyde," 30 January, 5–6 February 1973, TNA.
78. MLSC 1897, 303. See also Lawson Walton MP: HC deb. 21 June 1900, vol. 84.
79. FV 62/34 (Moneylenders, Cheque Traders and Pawnbrokers Trade Associations), "Pawnbroker Views," 21 November 1972, TNA.
80. FV 62/34 (Moneylenders, Cheque Traders and Pawnbrokers Trade Associations), "Pawnbroker Views," 21 November 1972, TNA.
81. Crowther, 6.6.9.
82. Crowther, 1.3.33, 6.1.12, 6.6.9. While Crowther believed that the Commissioner should be empowered to initiate civil proceedings, a measure found in some countries with no comparable provision in British law, it felt such a provision should be decided by Parliament.
83. BT 250/112 (Summary of Existing Legislation), "Inter-Departmental Meeting, Department of Trade and Industry, HM Treasury, Board of Trade," 18 December 1968, TNA.
84. FV 62/35, (Inter-Departmental Consideration and Submission to Ministers), "Department of Trade and Industry General Considerations," 13 January 1972, TNA.
85. BT 250/25 (Institute of Credit Management), "Memorandum," November 1968, TNA; BT 250/48 (Consumers Association), "Oral Evidence," 17 July 1969, TNA.
86. Crowther, 6.3.1.
87. FV 62/34 (Moneylenders, Cheque Traders and Pawnbrokers Trade Associations), "Meeting, Department of Trade and Industry, National Association Pawnbrokers' Association, Moneylenders Association," 19 April, 25 April, 21 November 1972, TNA.
88. BT 250/49 (National Citizens' Advice Bureau Council), "Written Evidence," 1969, TNA.
89. BT 250/61 (Midland Bank), "Oral Evidence," 22 April 1970, TNA.
90. Crowther, 3.3.13, 3.8.1–3.8.5.
91. MLSC 1897, 2002–2005.
92. FV 62/102 (Major Policy Papers on the Whole of Proposed Legislation), "Home and Social Affairs Committee," 1 June 1972, TNA.

93. BT 250/112 (Summary of Existing Legislation), "Equity in Consumer Credit," 18 December 1968, TNA.
94. FV 62/41 (Report of the Committee), "Submission to Ministers," 16 December 1971; FV 62/102 (Major Policy Papers on the Whole of Proposed Legislation), "Department of Trade and Industry, Correspondence D Simpson and RW Gray," 9 March 1972, TNA.
95. See Crowther, 6.5.11 for the complete listing.
96. Crowther, 7.1.6.
97. Report of the Committee on the Civil Service, vol. 1 1966–68, June 1968 (Cmnd 3638). Fulton had been set up by the Labour government led by Harold Wilson.
98. See Crowther, 7.1.4 for a complete listing.
99. See Crowther, 7.2.3 for the complete definition.
100. Crowther, 7.2.9; FV 62/102 (Major Policy Papers on the Whole of Proposed Legislation), "Home and Social Affairs Committee," 12 June 1972, TNA.
101. Crowther, 2.1.28, 7.2.8.
102. Crowther, 7.4.3.
103. FV 62/25 (Consideration by Administrative Group), "Department of Trade and Industry, Evaluation of Consumer Credit Commissioner," 7 November 1972, TNA.
104. FV 62/25 (Consideration by Administrative Group), "Department of Trade and Industry, Evaluation of Consumer Credit Commissioner," 7 November 1972, TNA; FV 62/104 (Major Policy Papers on the Whole of Proposed Legislation), "Minister for Trade and Consumer Affairs, Proposed Consumer Credit Bill," 16 March 1973, TNA.
105. BT 250/14 (HM Treasury), "Meeting of the Committee, HM Treasury, Board of Trade," 20 December 1968, TNA.
106. Crowther, 6.1.8–6.1.9.
107. There was a great deal of controversy surrounding Crowther's proposal to create a registry of securities. This and similar issues were dealt with by the Lending and Security Act, which falls outside the scope of this research, which focuses on the Consumer Sales and Loan Act.
108. "All for Crowther," *Observer*, 28 March 1971.
109. BT 250/23 (Hire Purchase Trade Association), "The Journal of the Hire Purchase Trade Association," Spring 1971, TNA.
110. FV 62/157 (Crowther Committee Report on Consumer Credit: Letter from Prime Minister's Secretary Suggesting Early Action), "Letter from John Davies, Secretary of State of the Department of Trade and Industry, to Prime Minister Edward Heath," 30 June 1971, TNA.
111. "Reform of the Law on Consumer Credit," Department for Trade and Industry (5427), 1973, 5–8 (White Paper).
112. White Paper, 5–8.

113. FV 62/27 (Consideration by Lending and Security Group), "Department of Trade and Industry, Memorandum," 20 November 1972, TNA.
114. BT 250/5 (Board of Trade Evidence Submitted), "Memorandum, FJ Broomfield," 2 January 1969, TNA.
115. FV 62/102–103 (Major Policy Papers on the Whole of Proposed Legislation), "Home and Social Affairs," 1 June 1972, TNA. Others were concerned about the length of the bill. See also BT 250/5 (Board of Trade Evidence Submitted), "NH Nail, Secretary," 2 May 1969.
116. FV 62/106 (Major Policy Papers on the Whole of Proposed Legislation), "Minister for Trade and Consumer Affairs," 7 September 1973, TNA. The enacted CCA 1974 repealed six Acts and overturned 232 sections and 22 schedules of legislation.
117. FV 62/103 (Major Policy Papers for the Whole of Proposed Legislation), "Department of Trade and Industry, Minutes," 24 July 1972, TNA; FV 62/104 (Major Policy Papers for the Whole of Proposed Legislation), "Minister for Trade and Consumer Affairs, RJ Meadway, Office Minute 993," 2 April 1973, TNA.
118. HL deb. 28 June 1972, vol. 332.
119. HL deb. 28 June 1972, vol. 332; HC deb. 14 November 1973, vol. 864; White Paper, 20.
120. HL deb. 28 June 1972, vol. 32.
121. HC deb. 14 November 1973, vol. 864.
122. A hirer is protected under s.132.
123. White Paper, 20; HC deb. 17 June 1974, vol. 875.
124. White Paper, 15.
125. White Paper, 18.
126. White Paper, 12; HC deb. 14 November 1973, vol. 864.
127. HC deb. 14 November 1973, vol. 864.
128. The raw data are not available. It is likely that fees, charges and the effects of period compounding contributed to the difference.
129. HC deb. 17 June 1974, vol. 875.
130. White Paper, 10.
131. White Paper, 8.
132. White Paper, 26–27.
133. White Paper, 25–26.
134. HL deb. 28 June 1972, vol. 332.
135. HL deb. 28 June 1972, vol. 332.
136. HL deb. 30 April 1974, vol. 351.
137. HC deb. 4 March 1927, vol. 203.
138. FV 62/35 (Inter-Departmental Consideration and Submission to Ministers), "Department of Trade and Industry General Considerations," 13 January 1972, TNA.

Bibliography

Archives

The National Archives, London.
AJ 10 Consumer Council.
AJ10/60 Submissions to Public Inquiries.
BT 250 Board of Trade Committee on Consumer Credit.
BT250/2 Consumer Credit: Summary of Conclusions.
BT250/4 Official Bodies.
BT250/5 BT Evidence Submitted.
BT250/14 HM Treasury.
BT250/16 Association of County Court Registrars.
BT250/23 Hire Purchase Trade Association.
BT250/24 HP Information Ltd.
BT250/25 Institute of Credit Management.
BT250/27 Lancashire and Cheshire Moneylenders Association.
BT250/28 Law Society.
BT250/34 National Association of Moneylenders.
BT250/38 National Pawnbrokers' Association.
BT250/46 Association of Family Case Workers.
BT250/47 Consumer Council.
BT250/48 Consumers' Association.
BT250/49 National Citizens Advice Bureaux Council.
BT250/50 National Federation of Consumer Groups.
BT250/52 Beneficial Finance Company.
BT250/61 Midland Bank.
BT250/66 Provident Clothing and Supply Company.
BT250/75 County of West Sussex.
BT250/93 Councils on Moneylending and Pawnbroking.
BT250/100–01 Newspaper Advice Bureaux.
BT250/112 Summary of Existing Legislation on Consumer (Credit) Protection.
FV 62 Department of Trade and Industry: Industrial and Commercial Policy D2.
FV62/10 Inter-departmental Consideration.
FV62/25 Consideration by Administration Group.
FV62/27 Consideration by Lending and Security Group.
FV62/29 Consumer Sale and Loan Group.
FV62/34 National Association of Moneylenders, Cheque Traders Federation and National Pawnbrokers Association.
FV62/35 Inter-departmental Consideration and Submission to Ministers.
FV62/41 Consumer Credit: Report of the Committee; Submission to Ministers.
FV62/52 Consideration of Pawnbrokers: Recommendation 197.
FV62/60 Regulation of the Cost of Credit: Recommendations 237–241, 244.

FV62/102–06 Major Policy Papers on the Whole of Proposed Legislation.
FV62/157 Crowther Committee Report on Consumer Credit: Letter from Prime Minister's Secretary Suggesting Early Action.
IR40 Board of Inland Revenue: Stamps and Taxes Division.
IR40/3555 Registrations of Moneylenders and Evasion of Tax.
T326 Treasury: Finance, Home and General Division.
T326/805 Setting up of Crowther Committee on Consumer Credit: Composition and Terms of Reference.

Interview

Sir Royston Goode, CBE, QC, DCL, FBA, 20 November 2015.
Member of the Crowther Committee.

Official Publications

The Consumer Credit Act 1974, c. 39.
Consumer Credit, Report of the Committee 1971 (4596).
The House of Commons Debate Sessions.
The House of Lords Debate Sessions.
The Pawnbrokers Select Committee 1870 (377).
Report of the Committee on the Civil Service, vol. 1. 1966–68 (3638).
Report of the Commissioners of HM Inland Revenue. 1870–1909.
Report of the Commissioners of HM Customs & Excise. 1910–70.

Sources

Abel-Smith, Brian, and Peter Townsend. 1965. *The Poor and the Poorest: A New Analysis of the Ministry of Labour's Family Expenditure Surveys for 1953 54 and 1960*. London. G. Bell & Sons.
Baldwin, Robert. 2011. "Introduction." In *Understanding Regulation: Theory, Strategy and Practice*, edited by Robert Baldwin, Martin Cave, and Martin Lodge, 1–11. Oxford: Oxford University Press.
Balleisen, Edward, and David Moss. 2010. "Introduction." In *Government and Markets: Toward a New Theory of Regulation*, edited by Edward Balleisen and David Moss, 1–10. New York: Cambridge University Press.
Banting, Keith. 1979. *Poverty, Politics and Policy: Britain in the 1960s*. London: Macmillan.
Blanden, Michael. 1968. "What Is the Cost of Credit?" *Guardian*, October 5.
Burton, Dawn. 2008. *Credit and Consumer Society*. Oxford: Routledge.
Elliot, Larry. 2015. "Margaret Thatcher's Deregulation of the City a Myth, Says Thinktank." *Guardian*, May 25.

Finlay, Steven. 2009. *Consumer Credit Fundamentals*. Basingstoke: Palgrave Macmillan.
Gazeley, Ian. 2017. "The Poor and the Poorest, 50 Years On: Evidence from British Household Expenditure Surveys of the 1950s and 1960s." *Journal of the Royal Statistical Society* A 180: 455–75.
Goode, Royston. 1975. "The Consumer Credit Act 1974." *The Cambridge Law Journal* 34 (1): 79–130.
———. 1979. *The Consumer Credit Act: A Student's Guide*. London: Butterworth.
Hayek, Friedrich. 1945. "The Use of Knowledge in Society." *The American Economic Review* XXXV (4): 519–30.
"High Cost of Credit to be Reviewed." 1968. *Guardian*, July 3.
Lindgren, Kevin. 1977. "The Consumer Credit Act 1974: Its Scope." *The Modern Law Review* 40:159–73.
Megrah, Maurice. 1967. "Banks and Moneylenders." *Modern Law Review* 13 (1): 86–9.
Minkes, Aron. 1953. "The Decline of Pawnbroking." *Economica* 20: 10–23.
"MPs Told of Credit Curbs." 1968. *Guardian*, November 2.
Moloney, Niamh, Eilis Ferran, and Jennifer Payne. 2015. "Introduction." In *The Handbook of Financial Regulation*, edited by Niamh Moloney, Eilis Ferran, and Jennifer Payne, 1–12. Oxford: Oxford University Press.
"Pawnbrokers and Moneylenders." 1971. A Report for the Department of Trade and Industry on Behalf of the Crowther Committee by NOP Market Research.
Pinker, Robert. 1974. "Social Policy and Social Justice." *Journal of Social Policy* 3 (1): 1–19.
Reform of the Law on Consumer Credit. 1973. Department for Trade and Industry 5427.
Seldon, Anthony. 2013. "The Heath Government in History." In *The Heath Government 1970–74: A Reprisal*, edited by Stuart Ball and Anthony Seldon, 1–20. London: Routledge.
Sloman, Peter. 2016. "The Pragmatist's Solution to Poverty: The Heath Government Tax's Credit Scheme and the Politics of Social Policy in the 1970s." *Twentieth Century British History* 27 (2): 220–41.
Study on Interest Rate Restrictions in the EU, Final Report for the EU Commission DG Internal Market and Services, Project ETD/2009/IM/H3/87, Brussels/Hamburg/Mannheim.
"Tighter Law on Loan Advertising." 1968. *Guardian*, September 12.
Tomlinson, Jim. 2007. "Managing the Economy, Managing the People." In *20th-Century Britain, Economic, Cultural and Social Change*, edited by Francesca Carnevali and Julie-Marie Strange, 234–46. London: Pearson Longman.

CHAPTER 5

Small-Loan Providers: Sent Back to the Fringe

By the early twenty-first century, the financial sector had grown dramatically. Oddly enough, this expansion left some poor households more excluded than ever. Those outside traditional banking still paid high rates for credit, but on top of that it became more expensive to pay bills and save money without a bank account. As traditional banks retreated from poor neighbourhoods, payday lenders, pawnbrokers, and rent-to-own stores filled the void (Leyshon and Thrift 1993, 2005). Crowther-era predictions of the demise of small-loan companies had missed the mark.

Both rich and poor households borrowed heavily during this period. By 2004, for the first time, British personal debt exceeded £1 trillion.[1] As debts mounted, Parliament was especially concerned with protecting poor borrowers. Policymakers blamed a proliferation of 'irresponsible' lenders for issuing expensive loans that entrapped borrowers in a cycle of debt. The Consumer Credit Act 2006 (CCA 2006) broke with Crowther and required stringent licensing of high-risk lenders, and with that, small-loan providers were sent back the fringe. Efforts at financial inclusion drove much of the thinking behind the CCA 2006 and the segmentation of high-cost credit. Policymakers hoped that inclusive mainstream banking would offer basic accounts and issue affordable credit to low-income households. Ideally, these 'responsible' lenders would compete the worst offending high-cost lenders out of the market and the remaining

© The Author(s), under exclusive license to Springer Nature Switzerland AG 2021

C. McMahon, *Taming the Fringe*, Palgrave Studies in the History of Finance, https://doi.org/10.1007/978-3-030-70615-9_5

survivors would operate under strict regulation. While separating high-cost providers from mainstream finance broke from Crowther's uniform licensing, the underlying belief that market and competitive-led process offered ample consumer protection and appropriately priced credit went mostly unchallenged.

The Global Financial Crises pushed policymakers towards more extreme measures. What started as a targeted policy against irresponsible lenders in 2006 had evolved towards a campaign against all payday lending. In the post-crash world, policymakers viewed the entire sector as predatory. Many believed that high-cost payday loans made the problems of poverty worse.[2] Solving the issue became a matter of social justice. The minority and distant solution of price controls soon gained majority backing. What once kept price controls from being seriously entertained, that is segmenting the poorest borrowers from the market, was now viewed positively.

In 2015 policymakers implemented price controls on payday loans, the leading small-value credit of its day. Social justice concerns over economic fairness guided the implementation of price controls on payday loans—a major and monumental reversal of government policy. Although today's borrower needs are remarkably similar to those found in the nineteenth century, what has changed is how policymakers understand poverty and how the state protects the working poor from certain kinds of finance. The verdict was clear: payday loans were harmful and marginal borrowers were better off without one. Price controls pushed lenders from the lowest and riskiest end of the market.

Political and Market Developments

Political Developments

Beginning in the 1980s, globalization and the deregulation of the financial system influenced British banking. Both were associated for increasing market competitiveness and product diversity (Kempson et al. 2000; Berthoud and Kempson 1992; Davies and Richardson 2010). The credit markets responded in dramatic fashion. Adjusted for inflation, the amount of unsecured credit more than doubled between 1994 and 2001 (Kempson 2002, pp. i–iv). In 1974, the credit card system was in its infancy, with one provider, Barclays, issuing £32 million. By 2003, there were over 1,300 credit card products with £49 billion outstanding.[3] In 2004–2005, the Office of Fair Trading (OFT) had issued 16,568 consumer credit licences.[4] It was believed that consumer credit had contributed to economic growth and rising real incomes. The government argued that a competitive and innovative financial system was vital for continued economic growth and consumer spending (Offer 2007).[5] The government's position assumed that as affluence rises society develops an increased capacity for rational (or less fallible) decision making. A distinction should be made between credit use to secure consumer wants versus credit use to satisfy an immediate need, such as rent or a utility bill. Whether it is 'prudent' or 'rational' to use high-cost small loans for an emergency payment remains debated.

Not all debt was considered beneficial. In an almost omniscient fashion, three years before the onset of the Global Financial Crises, the Bank of England feared that unsecured debts would prove problematic during an economic downturn (Nickell 2003). The Bank was not alone, between 2001 and 2004, the DTI published three reports on over-indebtedness and pushed for 'responsible' lending.[6] Ideas of responsible and irresponsible lenders soon challenged Crowther's keystone premises of equal treatment of lenders. Support for 'appropriate' financial institutions and lending activities coalesced around New Labour's social and financial inclusion agenda.

By 1997 the Labour government inclusionary platforms targeted low-income households. Access to mainstream banks for low-income households was a critical element of financial inclusion.[7] Financial inclusion, they argued, provided well-being and consumer freedom in an increasingly competitive and globalized world (Marron 2013; Rose 1999).[8] Participation in the mainstream financial system helped alleviate some of the conditions of poverty, or so the logic went. Any reduction in poverty also left the government with decreasing welfare spend, a result that critiques suggested was a back-door route for governmental shirking certain social obligations onto the private financial system (Marron 2013). A relationship does exist between the financial access and welfare. In 2003 and 2004, the majority of households lacking access to basic banking facilities were also supported by the government: 64% received council tax benefit, 62% received housing benefit and 48% received income support.[9]

By extending affordable banking products and credit options to low-income households, the government's agenda encouraged a kind of normative market participation akin to the Victorian era poverty debates which treated friendly societies as institutions assisting the working classes to obtain a middle-class life. The goal was shifting towards the 'right' kind of financial market, that is one offering affordable credit and affordable banking options, into the lower end of the market.

Strangely enough, banks already served more of society than ever. In 1975, only 45% of adults held a current account; by 1998 that figure had risen to approximately 85% (Kempson et al. 2000, p. 11; Kempson and Whyley 1999; Maron 2013, pp. 789–90). Once a reserve for the wealthy few, financial services had become mainstream. The paradox is that while mainstream banking expanded it also quit the lowest (and least profitable) end of the market, both physically by closing branches in low-income neighbourhoods and by raising account minimums. The alternative lending industry quickly filled the unmet demand. The government desired further movement down the income ladder to squeeze out these 'irresponsible' lenders.[10]

Like its 1974 predecessor, the CCA 2006 reform sought competitive and innovative markets without sacrificing consumer protections. However, evolving concepts including over-indebtedness and social justice guided policymakers to separate risk lenders from mainstream providers.[11] The government prioritized eliminating predatory finance and helping borrowers 'on the brink' owing to a 'change of circumstances'. Implementing more widespread financial inclusion offered a concrete solution to achieve both ends.

Economic Conditions and Developments in the Small-Loan Market, 1970s–2006

If the post-Second World War era initiated a relatively benign environment for the small-loan market, the post-Crowther world ushered in a period of impressive expansion. An influx of investment led to the rise of multi-location providers and increased loan volumes in a growing market. Demand for small-loan products was driven by stagnate wages and economic inequality. While average real incomes rose by approximately 40% between 1979 and 1995, they were not distributed evenly. The income of the bottom 10% grew by 10%, whereas the top 10% grew by 60–68%. Between 1979 and 1988 the bottom 10% gained a 'mere half of one per cent of the increase in national disposable income' (Berthoud and Kempson 1992, p. 9). If housing costs are taken into consideration, the poorest 10% experienced an 8% decrease in real income (Kempson et al. 2000, p. 11). From 1979 to 2005 the Gini coefficient increased from 0.25 to 0.35 (Cribb 2013).

This income inequality can be partly explained by changes in the labour market conditions, including a higher premium on skilled labour, the contraction of some trade unions, an increase in part-time labour and a widening of the pay gap between senior managers and employees (Kempson et al. 2000). Tax, welfare and trade policy also contributed to greater inequality (Cribb 2013). Various studies confirmed that half of working-age adults living in poverty could be found in households with at least one adult in paid work (Palmer et al. 2006). These results support the reality of the often-used term—the working poor.

Those experiencing insecure and low incomes were at high risk of financial exclusion. In 1998, approximately 20% of adults were without a current account, 31–37% had no savings and 29% had no access to credit from a mainstream provider.[12] Those with low incomes were most likely to be without a mainstream bank account to manage weekly budgets (Berthoud and Kempson 1992). In 2002, 25% of households reported having been in financial difficulties in the last twelve months, with 18% on at least one occasion in arrears on household bills (Kempson 2002). Another study found that 7.7 million people were in debt to utility companies and that more than 1 million had their telephone service disconnected owing to late payments (Rossiter and Cooper 2005, p. 7).

More often than not, poor households used credit to overcome poverty rather than to raise their standard of living by acquiring consumer goods. Those on low incomes used credit differently from higher-income families (Berthoud and Kempson, p. 56). Unlike wealthy households, households living in hardship scored low on a consumerism index designed to measure the value of durable goods purchased in the previous twelve months. Nor was their credit usage a result of lifecycle borrowing, when people use credit to establish themselves in early adulthood. Not only do the poor borrow for different reasons, they have far fewer options than wealthier households. Households with low incomes accessed half as many credit sources as higher-income families and many of the available products were far more expensive than bank loans.

It's no surprise that the poor pay more for credit, but despite decades of policymakers arguing otherwise, borrowers were well aware that small-loan providers charged high rates. Borrowers demanded convenient, speedy and easily understood repayment options. Alternative credit providers are conveniently located and offer extended trading hours.

Lenders provide a fast service as the application process is simple and there is a high level of confidence that the loan application will be approved. Borrowers also find that contract terms are transparent as the principle and amount owed are stated clearly. This harkens back to the 'pounds and pennies' argument a century earlier. For most borrowers, percentages are irrelevant, what matters is the total cash price. Alternative providers tailored their products to meet the needs of low-income borrowers in a way that banks, credit unions and the Social Fund failed to.[13] Most borrowers were relatively happy with the service and the product that they received. Lenders had designed a product that borrowers needed, and the market grew as a result.

No definitive data exist on the total market size of the alternative credit sector or small lenders within it. Estimates suggest that in 2005 there were approximately 800 pawnshops in the UK, or double the number in the early 1970s, but far smaller than its 1914 peak of 5,087 (Collard and Kempson 2005, pp. 3–6). Pawnbrokers earned an estimated £130 million in revenues in 2006, and it was expected to reach £165 million by 2008. Typical charges ranged from 5 to 12% a month; based on a loan of £100, this equates to an APR of some 70–200%.[14] The pawn market had grown significantly since Crowther, and all signs pointed to continued expansion into the first decade of the twenty-first century.

The basics of pawnbroking had hardly changed over the centuries. Though the Internet has altered the competitive dynamic, mostly, borrowers visit pawnshops that are conveniently located. In 2005, one owner of a multi-location pawnshop business claimed that 90% of his customers lived within two miles of his outlets (Kempson and Whyley 1999, p. 18). Only the largest of pawnbrokers bothered much with promotional materials.[15] T. M. Sutton, founded in 1800, and George Attenborough Company, advertised in the London Yellow Pages, but few others followed suit. From 1975 to 1990, London Yellow Pages listings averaged less than twenty pawnshop locations annually.[16] The importance of conveniently located shops has remained remarkably stable. What has changed is the market structure and breadth of product offerings.

By 2006 demand for small loans was being fulfilled by multi-location 'supermarket' providers. Many pawnbrokers now offered cheque cashing, prepaid debit cards, payday and unsecured loans. Pawnbrokers adopted modern retailing methods including updated floor plans, sophisticated accounting software, high-end security systems and e-commerce.[17] Their high-street locations and storefront windows attracted pawners and shoppers alike. These upgrades coincided with a shift from loaning on clothing and home goods towards jewellery, gold and watches. These items were easily appraised and stored, generally held their value and could be sold quickly on the second-hand market. While financial exclusion and inequality have contributed towards the industry's growth, likewise capital investment, extensive rebranding and innovative retail management helped to satisfy unmet consumer demand (Burton 2008; Leyshon and Thrift 1993, 2005). When coupled with the recession of the early 1990s, the pawning market was quite active (Boggan 2016; Jenkins 2010).

Much of the growth leading up to the Global Financial Crises was led by two of the industry's largest players, H&T Group and Albemarle & Bond. In 2006, publicly traded H&T operated sixty-nine outlets, up from twenty-seven in 1992. In 1992, H&T was acquired by North American-based, Cash America Inc. Shortly thereafter it transformed into a multi-channel provider of small loans. In 2004, Rutland Partners, a private equity fund, led a management buyout. From 2001 to 2005, net revenue and cash flow grew at an annualized compound rate of 14.1 and 14.9%, respectively. Between 2003 and 2005 revenue increased from £16.4 million to £20.1 million and cash flow from £5 million to £7.4 million. Over 70% of the business was from pawn services, and its pledge book grew from £21.3 million to £24.4 million, 98% of which was secured by gold or jewellery.[18]

In 2005, H&T charged between 7 and 9% per month, with an average of 7.1%. For the three months ending 31 March 2005, by value, approximately 22% of pledges were forfeited after an average of 8.7 months in pawn.[19] This forfeiture level was higher than most in the Victorian era and in line with the Crowther study. In Crowther's pawnbroker sample set, and for H&T, approximately 50% of items were redeemed within three months. Both results are lower than in the Victorian and Edwardian eras, when they were approximately 80–85%. This could be because there was a greater likelihood of redemption of lower-value goods in the weekly pawn cycle than higher valued, less frequent pawns. The infrequency is demonstrated by the 15% of H&T's customers that had not pawned in the last twelve months. H&T's 2005 non-pawn revenue included £27 million in cheque cashing, with an average value of £356 at an average fee of £23. Their typical payday loan was £365, carrying with it an average fee of

£47.[20] This compares with an industry-wide average of £75 for a £300 loan.

In 2005–2006, H&T's closest competitor, Albemarle & Bond, had a pledge book of £11 million, up from £496,000 in 1988.[21] In 2005–2006, it acquired eleven shops and increased its pre-tax profit by 18% year on year to £6.7 million. It averaged £96 per pawn loan on a total of 135,000 loans across its entire network. By comparison, a single shop in nineteenth-century Liverpool issued almost as many loans annually. Albemarle & Bond offered a range of services, including cheque cashing, payday loans and retail sales. Over the previous twelve months, secured, unsecured and cheque cashing services had grown. It operated 62 of the estimated 550 cheque cashing outlets in the UK.

Unlike in the past, and unlike their customers, larger pawnbrokers had access to a wide variety of capital sources. A borrower could walk into a shop backed by American private equity and chose from a variety of loan products. Many of the shops employed modern retailing techniques and had invested heavily in information technology. Once hidden alleyway shops had transformed into fixtures on many a high street. Multilocation providers backed by global capital—in many ways, Crowther's vision of a single licence facilitating the provision of credit had come true. The vision blurs when considering that these supermarket credit providers operated completely within the 'fringe'; mainstream financial institutions did not dip into the lowest end of the credit market.

Pawnbrokers were not alone. The moneylending market underwent dramatic change too. By the late 1990s, the term 'payday lending' had gained in usage over the traditional form of moneylender. The main loan features and the typical borrower profile of moneylenders and payday lenders are similar. Both lend small-value, short-term unsecured credit. The essential loan product is identical as is the primary borrower profile. Since the 1890s, a typical borrower will have struggled to cover basic expenses and was without savings to cover an emergency expenditure (Kempson and Whyley 1999, pp. 13–15). Though payday lenders rely on sophisticated software, the criterion is similar to that of decades past, including an applicant's financial, personal and borrowing history.

There are differences between the two businesses. Though certain payday lenders provide 'cash on site' in retail locations, many issue loans and collect repayment by electronically accessing a borrower's current account. Payday loans are repaid in a single instalment inclusive of the loan principal and interest. The payday namesake derives from the single instalment falling due on the borrowers 'pay day'. This bullet structure differs from earlier when repayment occurred through a series of small weekly payments. As seen in pawnbroking, and beginning in the 1990s, multi-location loan providers offering a wide range of credit products had, for the most, replaced single shop proprietorships. International and domestic corporations had emerged, bringing with them capital market and bank financing. These corporations deployed expansion capital and had invested in e-commerce platforms. Still, the key loan features and the typical borrower profile are consistent overtime, payday lenders are not terribly different from moneylenders.

Since the 1970s, the overall consumer credit market had grown in volume and in the range of offered products. Small-loan lenders grew in response to growing inequality, financial exclusion and a generally overlooked market niche.[22] As with previous episodes, rapid market expansion prompted a policy response and the Office of Fair Trading investigated the effectiveness of the CCA 1974 to regulate small-loan providers (Kempson and Whyley 1999).[23] These initial government findings were the first steps of the CCA 2006 process.

Financial Inclusion and the Consumer Credit Act 2006

Rising debts brought attention onto the small-loan sector and higher volumes invited vilification and regulatory scrutiny. More and more policymakers believed small loans made poverty worse. A 2003 government white paper, 'Fair, Clear and Competitive: The Consumer Credit Market in the 21st Century' was especially critical of alternative fringe credit providers.[24] Two years later, the House of Commons Treasury Committee stated that financial inclusion would lower the cost of credit and 'make a substantial contribution to the fight against poverty'.[25] Issues related to over-indebtedness and payday lending required a new regulatory approach.[26]

What's somewhat confusing then, is that in many respects the government's vision for improved regulation echoed that of policymakers in the 1970s. The goal was to create a framework that encouraged innovation, improved competition and provided ample consumer protection. The 2006 reform efforts focused on improving information disclosure which was expected to enhance the competitive environment. In 2003, the DTI found that 56% of borrowers did not understand the terms used in credit agreements and 77% found credit advertisements confusing.[27] It was argued that more transparency enabled consumers to make better decisions. In turn, better-informed consumers would drive the market towards 'fairer deals' for consumers. Heightened competition among lenders, and especially banks, would also lower pricing. So too, consistently applied regulation would 'level the playing field' for lenders.[28] The 2006 reform was driven by a belief that under the right regulatory conditions the market would efficiently and fairly allocate credit. The concepts, if not the very language, are remarkable similar to Crowther and the CCA 1974.

Price Controls

There was very little support for implementing price controls. As seen in 1900, 1927 and in 1974, government caps on credit costs was viewed as too complex and unlikely to reduce borrowing costs. It was too easy for lenders to offer products and charge fees that fell outside of regulatory control. Once again accessing credit and the freedom to choose from among a variety of products were more important than capping the cost to the benefit of the few. Consumer groups including the Consumers Association, Citizens Advice Bureaux and the National Consumer Council, alongside academics such as Kempson and Collard, argued against price controls (Collard and Kempson 2005, p. 30). There was concern that poor households would be harmed by a decrease in credit supply, leaving illegal lenders to fill the gap. These fears were not without merit, as evidence from several EU countries and the United States suggest that interest caps led to a less diverse credit market and more illegal lending.[29]

Though they lost the day, the voices of dissent demonstrate a distinct break from Crowther, and more readily resemble early episodes from the late 1800s and early 1900s. Price control advocates framed the issue in moral tones. David Chaytor MP (Labour) and Edward Vaizey MP (Conservative) believed there was 'no moral case' to allow excessive rates of interest.[30] Vaizey suggested that lenders 'enslaved' people in debt. He went on to argue that even in a free market 1,000% rates could not be justified. Stephen Hepburn MP (Labour) argued for caps and likened them to limits on speeding. He added that when drivers were caught speeding, they paid severely for their indiscretion; so too lenders should be 'hammered' for excessive charges. Ethical and moral concerns within the context of regulating the cost of small-value credit appeared far more frequently than in the 1970s. While Crowther also suggested that a line existed when the market price of credit shifted from acceptable to unacceptable, now, ensuring that line was not crossed was a matter of social justice.

Cracks in Crowther's assessment of borrower capabilities also emerged. Some policymakers considered low-income borrowers as always and everywhere vulnerable persons. It wasn't just about savings and spending, but educational and other social factors that disadvantaged poor borrowers in the credit markets. While the inertia for tighter regulation was gaining, the government never seriously considered price controls. Instead, the 'old reliable' methods of enhanced licensing and improved disclosure requirements received widespread support. The push for expanded mainstream banking offered the system a new tool in the ongoing quest for competitive markets and consumer protection. Regulation supporting an enhanced competitive environment that reduced costs and increased access to credit issued by responsible bankers eliminated the need for the invasive and blunt method of price controls.

APR Disclosure

Policymakers again sought the holy grail of credit policy—a transparent and easily understood system for controlling advertising and comparing pricing. Contemporary policymakers believed that past efforts had failed because the disclosure rules were too technical, ambiguous and confusing.[31] Similar charges were made against the MLA 1900 and 1927. Now with Crowther added to the list, apparently, all of the twentieth-century efforts had failed. Twenty first century policymakers set out to simplify disclosure requirements making them easier to understand and had promised a reduction in the fine print.

Even so and somewhat begrudgingly, policymakers admitted that the APR was not borrowers' primary concern, and that it often 'distorted the apparent' cost of small loans. As the next chapter documents, many policymakers and academics began questioning the usefulness of financial disclosure, and yet, as was the case for over a century, there was an expectation that if only borrowers would pit lenders against each other, the price of credit would fall. APR seemed like the right answer, but in real life borrowers seemed not to care. The problem was that few suggested suitable alternatives (Kempson and Whyley 1999, pp. 21–22).

Worse still, the calculation of an APR had long baffled many an expert and this period proved no exception. Failure meant that there could not be an informed consumer or competitive markets.[32] Likely without knowing the long historical debate between cash and percentage terms, one MP even suggested that the cost of credit should be disclosed in pounds and pence, so that consumers could see what they had to pay.[33] In the end, the CCA 2006 was more evolutionary than revolutionary. It updated the requirements for mandatory annual statements, and it tweaked the APR calculation.[34]

From Extortionate Lending to Unfair Relationships

In the twentieth century the court system provided the only real mechanism for borrower relief from extortionate transactions. Few would argue it a successful endeavour. Since 1974, a mere twenty-six to thirty extortionate cases had reached the courts, with ten finding in favour of the borrower.[35] The legal process was expensive, complicated and risky. Decade after decade, poor borrowers avoided the courts. A point that a few lone voices such as John Battle MP (Labour) in the 1970s and Walter Wormersley MP (Conservative) in the 1920s argued to no avail.[36]

It is not that Battle, Wormersley and others were considered incorrect, but that each generation of policymakers believed they had devised a way to entice more borrowers to seek legal recourse. The decades-old debate on whether the judicial test should be detailed and narrowed or vaguer had scarcely evolved. If a definition or rule was written too narrowly, policymakers believed lenders would evade the law. If a definition or rule was too broad, the judiciary was left with little guidance and tended to focus almost exclusively on the interest rate.

The CCA 2006 provided judges with considerable and expansive flexibility. What started as harsh and unconscionable in 1900, then extortionate in 1970s, had evolved towards unfair bargains in 2006. Along with traditional consideration of cost and payment terms, the relationship test empowered judges to consider the lender's tactics, late-fees and history of interactions with the borrower. Whereas previous extortionate tests were seen to be too narrow, the 'unfairness relationship' would take full account of the borrower's circumstances. The DTI white paper made clear that transaction costs were not 'high or low in the abstract' but had to be evaluated in the context in which they were agreed.

As with all of the previous iterations, some MPs pushed back against the vague concept of an unfair transaction. Hendry argued that 'There is no guidance in this whatsoever. It is a bit like a minister coming in and saying "We have introduced a new punishment, which is a fine of £3,000" and when we ask, "What is it for?" he replies, "Well, I haven't actually thought of that yet, but I am sure it must be for something"'.[37] Concerns of listing factors and narrowed criteria that lenders could 'hide' behind overrode Hendry's push for more specific guidance. The key was drawing more borrowers into the court system and expanding the powers of judicial relief was thought the best method of doing so.

Though similar in their basic assumption and goal, each generation added their own special feature to 'the test'. Since many borrowers avoided the court system, the CCA 2006 introduced an Alternative Dispute Resolution (ADR) scheme administered by the Financial Ombudsman Service. Because the scheme was free to consumers and required no legal representation, it was hoped that more consumers would challenge burdensome credit agreements. While on the one hand the ADR was a novel development, the CCA 2006 still relied on a case-by-case approach of handling consumer credit complaints. The ADR evolution was more a lurch forward than a definitive break from the historical norm.

Licensing and Enforcement

The licensing and enforcement system broke from the past. As was the case in 1900 and in 1927, under the CCA 1974 only a serious offence called for a licence suspension or revocation.[38] Since only the worst offenders found themselves penalized out of the market, many infractions went unpunished. The CCA 2006 granted the OFT power to place penalties on lenders without a full-on licence suspension. A penalty-condition required a lender to address an identified problem. Failure to comply could lead to civil penalties and eventually a licence being suspended or revoked.

In even more dramatic fashion, risk-based monitoring was a major departure from the 1970s. Lenders offering high-risk products and targeting vulnerable persons would be subject to 'fitness' tests, on-site visits, and compliance and accounts reviews. Lenders operating in a high-risk category were required to submit a credit competence plan demonstrating their suitability as a lender. The OFT would consider whether a business had a history of irresponsible lending, it stated:

> lenders should always take reasonable care in making loans or advancing lines of credit and should take full account of the interests of consumers in doing so. Lenders should undertake proper and appropriate checks on the potential borrower's creditworthiness and ability to repay the loan and to meet the terms of the agreement.[39]

These new policies were a major break from Crowther's equal treatment of lenders. The government's focus on financial exclusion, poverty reduction and sense of economic fairness facilitated these changes. Proponents claimed that systemic over-indebtedness was the result of 'irresponsible' lending. This belief argued that it should be the prerogative of lenders to ensure that borrowers incurred debts appropriate to their income. Leading political figures such as Battle, Ian Wright MP (Labour), Lamb and the DTI white paper believed that the concept of 'responsible lending' should be incorporated into the unfair bargain and licensing fitness test.[40] Battle reminded the Commons that the concept of responsible lending was incorporated in mortgages and believed it should be extended to other credit products.[41] While not embraced as fully as Battle hoped, these ideas opened the possibility that the entire payday loan sector was predatory in its practices. At this stage though the policy targeted individual lenders thought to be operating outside the evolving concept of responsible lending. Writ large the entire sector was not yet thought of as entirely destructive for borrowers. For now, the answer to 'how big was the problem' was limited to certain fringe elements within the small-loan industry.

Conclusion to Financial Inclusion and the Consumer Credit Act 2006

While Crowther put all lenders on an equal footing, by 2006 certain high-risk lenders had been singled out. Small-loan providers were targeted because their clientele was vulnerable and got by on low incomes. The mere state of seeking small-value credit indicated a serious vulnerability. A low income, financial exclusion and resorting to payday lenders made people vulnerable.[42] This expansive understanding of vulnerability was influenced by the sheer magnitude of the debt burden. The Bank of

England indicated that the lowest income group's average debt as a percentage of income had risen from 17% in 1995 to 36% in 2000.[43]

Regulating high-risk lenders was one aspect of the government's poverty reduction and financial inclusion strategy. Other areas included financial education, cultivating alternative supply channels and the Social Fund. It was precisely that agenda that facilitated a demonstrable shift in how policymakers understood small sum lending and, in turn, their intervention strategy. The goal was to increase the availability of 'proper' and 'responsible' credit. Regulation was intended to form the 'right' kind of market.

While it was understood that many lenders acted responsibly, negative terms such as 'predatory', 'loan sharks' and 'rogue' crept back into common usage. This coincided with certain MPs advocated regulation based on moral and ethical reasons, which less prevalent during Crowther. Financial exclusion, inequality and poverty shifted the policy response towards a social justice mandate not witnessed in the 1970s. Putting lenders in risk categories, intermediate sanctions and the ADR expanded regulation. The price control debate related to these factors. It was viewed as a direct response to relieve the pressure on low-income borrowers by some. To most elected officials, academics and charities it was a blunt instrument that would fail to solve the high cost of short-term credit. Either lenders would allocate costs not captured in the cap, or worse, a cap would segment the market and encourage illegal lending. Much of the rationale echoed past concerns. Price controls and interest rate capping was not seen as an effective way to reduce the cost of small loans.

The financial crisis of 2007–2008 encouraged a substantial increase in loan volumes and sharpened regulators focus on small-value loans. Did this growth encourage a response similar to that seen in 1900 and 1927 when regulators sought to restrict the market? Were the goals of the financial inclusion agenda considered during the Global Financial Crisis and its aftermath? The next section analyses the development of policy and the small-loan market during the crisis, with a focus on price controls and the APR debate.

The Global Financial Crisis and Market Expansion

By 2013, an estimated 1,800 retail outlets were offering payday loans, more than the approximate 1,200 McDonalds and 764 Starbucks outlets operating in the UK.[44] From 2008 to 2014, at least 2–5 new payday lenders entered quarterly.[45] While in 2010, estimates suggest that 1,300 pawnshops were lending £192 million annually, as compared to 800 in 2003.[46] From 2007 to 2010, NPA membership rose from 530 to 1,080 outlets, and by 2015, pawnbrokers were lending almost a billion pounds a year.[47] One independent pawnbroker with four shops competed with thirteen others in his vicinity. Another claimed that 10–12 pawnshops operated in his local area.[48] A main shopping street in the borough of Rochdale was reported to have at least ten payday lenders.[49] Although a far cry from the late 1920s, in Manchester, where forty-seven pawnbrokers competed within six miles of each other, pawnbrokers and payday lenders expanded rapidly between 2006 and 2013 (Tebbutt 1983, p. 142). Table 5.1 demonstrates the growth of payday loans from 2008 to 2013. In 2013–2015, pawn and payday lenders issued approximately £3.5 billion annually, an approximate threefold increase over 2008. Table 5.2 supports the expansion narrative, demonstrating that from 2006 market entry and acquisition activity had increased.

Payday lending grew in response to financial exclusion, economic inequality, stagnant wages and the rising cost of living, conditions which were exacerbated by the Global Financial Crises. In 2011, the Institute for Fiscal Studies expected that household disposable income would experience its largest fall since 1981.[50] StepChange, Consumer Focus and the Money Advice Trust saw increased arrears across priority debt categories, including telephone, energy, water, rent and council tax.[51] It was argued that up to 6.2 million low-income people could not meet modest expenditure without borrowing (Edmonds 2014). The CMA found that over 70% of payday loans were taken out to cover living, household and vehicle expenses.[52] This is up dramatically from the 1970s, when 43% of loans were used for immediately due bills.[53] Clive Hollick, Lord Hollick of Notting Hill (Labour), argued that,

Table 5.1 Payday loan market growth

	2008	*2011*	*2012*	*2013*
Estimated				
Value of loans	£700–£800 m	£1.9 bn	£2.8 bn	£2.5 bn
Number of loans	2.3–3.0 m	7.4 m	10.2 m	10.0 m

Source CMA (2015), NPA (2015), and the Bristol Report (2013)

Table 5.2 M&A and market expansion

Lender (owned by)	*Market Entry*	*Acquired*
Cheque Centres (CNG Financial)	1996	2006
The Money Shop (DFC)	1998	1999
Payday Express (DFC)	1999	2009
H&T	2003	–
PaydayUK (DFC)	2006	2011
WageDayAdvance (Speedy Group)	2007	2013
Wonga	2007	–
CashEuroNet (Cash America)	2008	–
CFO Lending	2008	–
Global Analytics	2009	–
MYJAR	2009	–
Ariste (EZCORP)	2009	2012
The Cash Store	2010	–
Speedy Cash (Speedy Group)	2010	–

Source CMA (2015, Table 7.1)

> The demand for short-term payday loans and longer-term high-interest loans is being driven by the crushing impact that the very tough economic climate is having on personal and family budgets. The fall in real incomes and the above-inflation increases in the price of essentials such as utilities and food are leaving many people short of the money they need to make ends meet, so they turn to the payday lenders.[54]

The working poor used payday loans to avoid having to choose between 'putting the heating on and putting food on the table'.[55] This is similar to Mabel Robinson's findings in 1888 when the use of small loans was driven by insufficient wages that were 'barely enough to keep body and soul together'.[56] Both then and now, many believed lenders targeted vulnerable borrowers. While the CCA 1974 sought to small-loan providers equally, and the CCA 2006 reversed that process somewhat, by 2010 the industry was understood to be largely predatory. Yvonne Fovargue MP (Labour) sought to regulate payday lenders and ease 'the pressure on their [borrowers'] squeezed living standards and ... ever-rising bills'.[57] The Global Financial Crisis had amplified concerns demonstrated during the 2006 episode.

In the wake of the Financial Crisis, payday lenders found themselves on the fringe and had re-joined the loan sharks of yesteryear (Aldohni

2013).[58] Pawnbrokers had not escaped notice either. Using language straight out of the Victorian era, Tom Blenkinsop MP (Labour) argued that they facilitated 'criminal activities', including 'hiding fenced goods, drugs and weapons'.[59] Ethical arguments were found across party lines. Susan Jones MP (Labour), Duncan Hames MP (Liberal Democrat), Neil Parish MP (Conservative) and Andrew Percy MP (Conservative) sought to reform, and even shut down, the immoral and evil industry.[60] Such moralizing had not systematically been heard since the nineteenth century.

The media paid considerable attention to the high cost of borrowing small sums (Osborne 2013).[61] And, for the first time, in any meaningful way, politicians had heard the plight of borrowers' experiences. MPs and peers, among them Stella Creasy, Rachel Reeves (Labour), Justin Tomlison (Conservative), Yvonne Fovargue, Sheila Gilmore (Labour), Rebecca Harris (Conservative), Lorely Burt (Liberal Democrat), Parry Mitchell, Lord Mitchell of Hampstead (Labour) and Maurice Glasman, Lord Glasman of Stoke Newington and Stamford Hill (Labour) had directly encountered many of the issues involved in their surgeries, and by consulting charities and lenders.[62] This groundswell of activity encouraged research into the sector, including the OFT's Review of High Cost Credit (2010) and Payday Lending Compliance Review (2013), the Bristol Report (2013), the FCA's Consultation Paper Proposals For a Price on High-Cost Short-Term Credit (2014) and the CMA's Payday Lending Market Investigation (2015).

As economic conditions worsened and the payday loan market grew in response, the relationship between financial exclusion and borrower vulnerability drove the price control and APR debate. For the first time in decades, politicians considered strictly regulating small loans.[63] The next section analyses, why, after refusing to do so for over a century, policymakers imposed price controls on small-value unsecured cash loans.

Price Controls

Parliamentary interest in the industry grew as the economic conditions of the working poor deteriorated. From 2010 to 2015 several initiatives sought to impose a limit on the total cost of small-value credit.[64] This is not surprising as price control measures gain support during periods of economic recession and increasing inequality (Glaeser and Scheinkman 1994). However, the implementation of price controls was not immediate or uncontroversial. From 2010 to 2013 the government rejected price controls. It was not until 2014 that a cap on the total cost of credit was approved.

One reason why the process took several years was because 'the problem', and by extension a definitive solution, was disputed. Whether or not payday loans helped or harmed consumers, the effectiveness of price controls was and remains contested (Caskey 2012; Lim et al. 2014). Major research studies have produced conflicting results. Some find that payday loans harm consumers as they create debt-traps and increases the risk of bankruptcy (Stegman and Faris 2008; Skiba and Tobacman 2011). Other studies have found no relationship between payday loan usage and 'debt-traps' or bankruptcies (Morgan and Strain 2007). Certain evidence argues that taking out a payday loan to pay a bill is less costly than missing the bill and incurring penalty fees.

Research on the impact of price controls on payday lending markets, while not unanimous is less divisive. While some studies have found that price controls help those at the lowest end of the market, others find interest rate caps harmed poorer consumers (Friedman 1970; Avio 1973; Zinman 2010). One of the most widely read research papers on the matter determined that without independent conditions such as high entry barriers or a monopolistic market structure, price controls 'is not only naive, it clouds the relevant issues by framing an economic problem in moralistic terms' (Cayne and Trebilcock 1973). Economists wonder how any government could legally define an 'excessive rate' or 'unconscionable transaction' (Staten and Johnson 1995). Milton Friedman suggested that he 'knows of no economist of any standing … who has favoured a legal limit on the rate of interest'.

The point is that the experts can't agree—are payday loans harmful, and if so, will price controls actually help? Tellingly, in 2014, the FCA admitted that 'there is no clear conclusion as to whether high-cost short-term credit is good or bad for consumers' or on 'the impact of bans, price caps or lending restrictions'.[65] The agency in charge of implementing price controls on payday loans publicly disclosed the inconclusiveness of the policy debate.

Few debated why consumers needed payday loans and what features were important to them. Payday loans were used for basic expenses, 'bills and everyday spending'.[66] Without payday loans and pawnbroking, borrowers were likely to default on other household bills. Borrowers cited convenience and speed as top priorities. Borrowers cited high satisfaction levels, even exceeding 95% among pawnbroker customers.[67] In comparison, only 38% of surveyed customers ranked NatWest Bank's service as 'good' (Christie 2014). In fact, so valued were small-loan products that many consumers indicated that they would choose to borrow at *higher* prices.[68] As before, borrowers were more concerned with speed and access than APRs and the total cost of credit. Supporting the speed and convenience theory, few borrowers shopped around. Approximately 80% of retail payday borrowers lived within 3.2 miles of the outlet they used.[69] The highest level of price comparison—46%—was conducted by online borrowers.[70] On average, this group had slightly higher incomes and were younger than retail borrowers.

That borrowers needed cash quickly to pay for unavoidable expenses and were price-insensitive is consistent across time. As is the fact that there were few if any borrowing alternatives. What differed this time was the political response. In this period policymakers felt the market had failed. Creasy, the most active and vocal MP seeking reform, argued that the debt cycle and high costs were grounds for market intervention.[71] Price controls were the only answer. The adoption of this measure took time and required a major policy reversal. In 2010, the OFT found that the high-cost short-term credit 'markets work reasonably well', but less than three years later it came to the opposite conclusion.[72] Even so, many consumer groups had not yet reversed their protest against price caps. Concerns over credit rationing and potentially drive borrowers to illegal providers kept Citizens Advice, the Association of British Credit Unions, the Institute of Public Policy Research, Which? and Advice UK from endorsing price caps.[73]

With the market approaching two billion pounds, price controls advocates gained the upper hand.[74] Creasy argued that without renewed regulation 'family debt, poverty and financial difficulties' could only get worse. The government had intervened in the water and energy industries and these precedents were understood as 'best practice market intervention'. Even self-described economic liberals, such as Nick Boles MP (Conservative), agreed that there was substantial market failure and sought new regulations.[75] Jenny Chapman MP (Labour) suggested that the only way to solve the problem of high prices was to implement price controls.

Pockets of resistance argued that an 'all-powerful regulator' was in no position to implement such 'draconian' measures.[76] Damian Hinds MP (Conservative) believed that regulating such a free and diverse market would lead to adverse consequences and growth in alternative products. Many more felt it the government's responsibility to prevent exploitation of the vulnerable who driven by desperation made harmful decisions. This paternalism is the opposite of prior themes echoed by Lord Elcho's who said it was impossible to save 'a fool from his folly'.

Hard-hitting reformers, along with more cautious voices, both drew on conflicting evidence from abroad. Jonathan Edwards MP (Plaid Cymru) cited the backlash against lenders in the US, where in thirty-five states price controls were operating, and that fourteen countries in Europe had restrictions of some sort.[77] James Sassoon, Lord Sassoon of Ashley Park (Conservative) softened the argument saying that while successful implementation of price caps and rollover limits in Japan had benefitted the poorest consumers, similar regulation in France and Germany had reduced access to credit and increased illegal lending.[78] Evidence from Japan suggests otherwise, as strict price regulation increased illegal lending and loan volumes fell from 8.5 trillion yen to 2.5 trillion yen resulting in a harmful impact on the working poor (Domoto 2012). The issue of price controls was far more complex than many of its advocates appreciated.

As the reform movement progressed, government authorities accessed far more accounting and statistical data than was available during previous episodes. One of the major hot-button issues was whether the payday lending model relied on repeat borrowing to bolster its already high profit margins. The answer is not so straightforward. On the one hand, yes, a majority of borrowers do so repeatedly. In 2012, the CMA found that among the eleven major lenders, 80% of loans (ex-rollovers) were issued to repeat borrowers.[79] However, Table 5.3 using data from the Association of Chartered Certified Accountants (ACCA), which was no friend of the industry, demonstrates that lenders often lose money on first time borrowers and multiple loans were required to remain profitable. Often new borrowers receive discounts, promotions and first-time borrowers are more likely than repeat customers to default. In this sense, repeat borrowers are part of a profitable business model, but not, perhaps, in the way that most policymakers appreciated.

The cost data contained in Table 5.3 demonstrate that first time fixed cost with new clients is considerable when compared with ongoing transactions. In comparison with the data below, in 1973 the National Association of Moneylenders estimated that the average cost of administering a loan was £9 which, adjusted for inflation, was £84.89 in 2010.[80]

Table 5.3 Cash America estimated UK loan p/l

2010–2011	
Revenue per first loan (after discounts)	£35.26
Cost per first loan	104.66
Average loss per first loan	**(£69.40)**
Revenue per repeat loan	£78.35
Total cost per repeat loan	22.01
	£56.34
Revenue total per three loans	£191.96
Cost total per three loans	148.68
	£43.28

Source 'Payday lending: Fixing a broken market', 18

Table 5.4 2012 Payday loan repayment

Repaid	*All (%)*	*Online (%)*	*High street (%)*
Early	14	16	7
On Time	50	51	48
Late	22	20	29
Never	14	13	16

Source CMA (2015, Fig. 2.5)

In 2005, it cost commercial and non-profit lenders approximately £30–£75 in set-up costs for a new customer (Collard and Kempson 2005, p. 19). The higher expenses shown below were driven by increased client acquisition costs.[81]

Estimates indicate that, on average, customers took out 3–4 loans a year.[82] Table 5.4 shows that of all loans issued in 2012, the majority were paid early or on time (64%) and that 84% were eventually paid in full. Under normal circumstances, delayed payment resulted in additional fees and charges. In 2012, approximately 36% of borrowers incurred penalty charges, the cost of which, as Table 5.5 demonstrates, varied. Like credit card companies, payday lenders earn more from clients who incurred interest and penalty fees but eventually paid off the principal in full. Whether payday lenders entrapped borrowers was debated. However, the data supported the assertion that repeat borrowing was necessary for a lender to remain profitable and that 86% of loans were repaid, with 22% having incurred penalty fees.

Table 5.5 Total cost of credit for the largest high street lenders

	Borrow for			
Lender (product)	*28 days*	*14 days*	*28 days 11 days late*	*28 days 28 days rollover*
Cheque Centres (payday)	£29.99	£29.99	£59.99	£59.98
The Money Shop (cheque)	29.85	29.85	58.85	59.70
The Money Shop (other)	29.99	29.99	58.99	59.98
H&T (cheque)	17.64	17.64	48.80	35.28
H&T (debit)	20.00	20.00	52.37	40.00
Speedy Cash (payday)	25.00	25.00	37.50	50.00
Speedy Cash (flex)	23.01	11.51	32.05	46.03
Speedy Cash (flex)	23.01	11.51	32.05	45.92
The Cash Store (payday)	38.24	34.06	66.74	76.48
Maximum	£38.24	£34.06	£66.74	£76.48
Minimum	17.64	11.51	32.05	35.28
Difference	£20.60	£22.55	£34.69	£41.20

Source CMA (2015, Table 4.1 and 5.6)

Debates on the debt cycle also led to questions concerning the high cost of payday loans, with headline rates of more than 5,800 APR.[83] The average amount borrowed was £260 and 50% of loans were for less than £200.[84] The average duration was twenty-two days and the most frequent amount borrowed was £100. Table 5.5 demonstrates that while headline prices tended to cluster around £30 for a £100 month-long loan, there was a great variation in fees.[85] As a point of comparison, under most scenarios these charges were considerably less than unauthorized bank overdraft fees.[86] As of 9 July 2016, for an unarranged overdraft of £100 outstanding for twenty-eight days, Lloyds TSB charged £80 and The Royal Bank of Scotland charged £90.

Major expenses for lenders included bad debts, client acquisition, advertising, retail operations and, for large lenders, the cost of capital. For online lenders client acquisition, including advertising, lead generation and the application process drove expenses higher. The Bristol Report suggested that these lenders, on average, screened one hundred customers for every ten loans, a rejection rate of 90%.[87] Dollar Financial estimated a conversion rate of 3.75%. A statistical outsider was industry leader Wonga, which rejected an estimated 60% of applicants, far fewer than the 90% online industry average.[88] At the end of line are customers who fail to repay. In 2011 and 2012, lenders incurred doubtful expense rates equal to 45% of total costs.[89] This rate is higher than the estimated 33% rate documented during the MLSC 1897 and MLSC 1925. The modern data confirms what much of the limited or anecdotal data suggested, lending small is an expensive and a risky business.

Parliament questioned the tactics of the 'very profitable' industry; often these critiques coincided with the industry's peak profitability in 2011.[90] From 2009 to 2013, the weighted average return on capital employed (ROCE) of the eleven major lenders ranged from 17 to 44%.[91] At the firm level there was variation between lenders, with larger lenders varying less than smaller providers, and their returns ranged from negative 175 to 170%. Returns peaked in 2011 and decreased thereafter. From 2009 to 2013, the CMA believed that the three largest lenders had returns in excess of what a competitive market should generate.[92] However, by 2013 the industry had begun to experience a downturn, and by this point of the 9 large lenders were no longer profitable. In 2013, ROCE averaged 17% compared to 33% in 2012. This decrease was primarily a result of shrinking loan volumes.

At the very least the CMA study demonstrated that the industry is cyclical and that returns vary by provider, with some having positive returns in the same period that others lost money. This is consistent across time, as the operations of any one business were influenced by market factors and company-specific operations. The assumption that high prices resulted in excessive profits is commonly held across time.

Whatever divergence between perceptions and reality, many policy-makers agreed that consumers borrow to pay for everyday necessities; demand was driven by inequality and rising prices; and lenders exploit borrowers and so unfairly profit and trap borrowers in a debt cycle:

> According to a recent report, 48 per cent of people who go to payday lenders are female, and the majority of females have borrowed for everyday necessities. They have borrowed to buy food for the family, or to pay the heating bills. Capping the cost of credit constitutes a welcome recognition that these companies are making profit from despair, but there is much more to be done. The root cause of rising prices and low incomes needs to be addressed if people are to be saved from being dragged into a spiral of debt … The people I represent are hard-working people who want the best for their families and who are doing the right thing.[93]

Categorizing female borrowers as 'hard-working people ... who do the right thing' is a far cry from the Chief Magistrate of the Metropolitan Police Courts, Thomas Henry's claim made in 1870: 'There is no doubt that a great number of the women in this town go into a pawnbroker's shop and pledge a shawl to get 4d to enable them to go into the public-house'.[94] Still, remnants of the Victorian-era ethic can be discerned when a financial commentator suggested that, instead of taking out a payday loan, borrowers should place a credit card in a tub of water and keep it frozen for emergencies. Jo Swinson MP (Liberal Democrat) hoped this technique 'might instil in them the discipline of not being tempted to use it for everyday spending'.[95] Unfortunately, for the working poor, emergency and everyday spending were often one and the same.

Despite all of this momentum, price controls were again rejected by the government in 2013.[96] Historical and contemporary research suggested that controls would lead to price clustering, credit rationing and less competition as lenders would quit the market. There was no clear evidence that controls reduce the actual cost of credit to the consumer.[97] The pressing issues of repeat borrowing, the high cost of credit and that lenders were not performing adequate affordability checks kept the regulatory momentum moving forward.

In 2013, the OFT condemned payday loan regulation as woefully insufficient and found significant breaches of the CCA 1974–2006.[98] They were particularly concerned with the systematic failure to perform affordability tests and excessive loan pricing.[99] The OFT issued a stark rebuke and required that fifty lenders, who made up approximately 90% of the market, prove compliance within twelve weeks or their licences could be revoked.

The OFT's sanctions were just the opening salvo, the government planned to overhaul the market by transferring oversight of to a newly created government agency, the FCA.[100] The government wanted to see a regulator that could 'keep pace with the innovative and fast-moving consumer credit market'.[101] In a break from the past, protecting the consumer was cited as more important than market efficiency. In 2012, Sassoon suggested that 'compared to the current regulatory regime under the OFT, the FCA will have a broader and more effective toolkit to monitor and tackle developments in the market and supervise practice among firms'.[102]

With the FCA in charge and 90% of the market sanctioned, price controls became a real possibility. The business response was decisive.

By July 2013, eleven of the fifty firms had ceased issuing payday loans and three more had their licences revoked.[103] Just as Isaac Gordon had feared in 1900, regulation had made it difficult to issue loans profitably. Comparing Q3 2014 to Q3 2013, for seven major lenders revenue and new lending decreased by 40% and profits by 30%.[104] Wonga attributed these declines to the changing regulatory environment and higher costs. CMA research agreed, stating that 'the contraction is likely to have been driven by a combination of lenders tightening their credit policies and the exit of some suppliers from the market as they adjust to and anticipate tighter regulatory conditions'.[105] Major lenders modified their participation in the market: Cheque Centres ceased offering single-instalment payday loans, CFO Lending stopped offering payday loans, EZCorp, a subsidiary of Ariste, ceased UK operations and Cash Store went into bankruptcy. By November 2014, an estimated fifty lenders had left the market. The Consumer Finance Association, an industry trade group, referred to 2013, a year during which members experienced a 68% decrease in loan volumes, as the 'perfect political, media and regulatory storm'.[106]

Three charges commonly held against the industry were that the market lacked price competition, granted credit too easily and exploited vulnerable people (Edmonds 2014). From 2013 to 2015 the OFT, University of Bristol, FCA and CMA released detailed reports on the payday lending market. More data became available in twenty-four months than in the previous 144 years. In 2014, the FCA gathered information from eight leading lenders and was able to amass data on 16 million loans. It analysed how a price cap would affect lending decisions and the financial position of borrowers.[107] They concluded that the industry's pricing was excessive, harmful to 'significant numbers' of borrowers and that these high-priced loans were of limited benefit.[108]

The debate was over. Damian Hinds, previously a vociferous opponent of price controls, had changed his mind:

> I was reluctant because, in this country, [apart from] natural monopolies ... we do not price control. It goes against the philosophy of our economy and our politics ... I believe in the efficacy of markets, in consumer sovereignty... I was trying to reconcile all those beliefs about what markets do ... and in many ways the normal laws of economics do not seem to apply [to payday loans].[109]

The verdict was clear: payday loans were a peculiar kind of credit warranting an aggressive regulatory response.[110] The FCA was not alone, as many consumer groups and charities reversed their earlier positions and sought price controls. Transact, StepChange, Association of British Credit Unions, Citizens Advice, Community Investment Coalition, Christians Against Poverty, Which?, Money Advice Trust, the Money Charity and the Trading Standards Institute supported capping the total cost of credit.[111] The CMA offered a lone voice of dissent. It believed that price controls limited competition owing to price clustering, decreased profitability and fewer market entries. Most troubling of all, since price controls could not stem borrower demand, where would needy borrowers turn for cash?[112] Their opposition wasn't enough and the FCA's cap on the total cost of credit came into effect on 2 January 2015.[113]

Figure 5.1 illustrates the FCA's three-part mechanism, including an initial cap, default fee maximum and limits on the total cost of credit. The cap ensured that customers would not pay more than £24 per £100 borrowed.[114] Perhaps for the first time ever, officially anyway, the government recognized that the pinnacle measure of cost, an APR calculation, was ill suited to short-term credit. After more than a century of policy advocating for annual percent cost disclosure, the 2015 cap was not stated in APR form. A later government publication revealed that under the FCA price cap a fourteen-day loan APR worked out at 1,492%, and for loans of

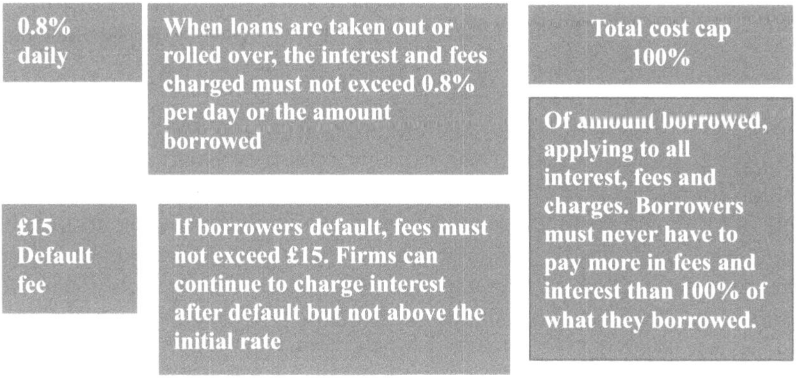

Fig. 5.1 Three-part price control (*Source* "FCA Confirms Price Cap Rules for Payday Lenders," FCA press release, 11 November 2014)

more than thirty days the APR was 1,270% (Edmonds 2014, p. 44). The FCA also limited repeat borrowing to two rollovers and lenders could not electronically access a borrower's bank account after two unsuccessful attempts.[115]

Regulators believed that the lowest segment of the market was better off without access to payday loans and that any decrease in the profitability of firms was required for borrower protection.[116] For those at the margin, it was expected that these changes would lead to an improved financial position, better mental health outcomes and less stress. These expectations demonstrate a broad understanding of the effects of poverty and parallel a much more expansive definition of vulnerability.

Finally, Edward Carson's belief in 1927, that moneylender loans provided little to no benefit, had found support in the twenty-first century. The goal was to restrict access to the wrong kind of credit. While the BCCA, an alternative finance trade group, agreed that 'given past behaviour, our sector does not get a lot of sympathy', it cautioned that the industry was now dramatically reshaped, with 700 fewer retail outlets and dozens of online providers having exited the market.[117] As many cautioned would be the case, major lenders clustered their pricing near to the cap, indicating that few lenders would undercut the regulatory pricing structure (Dunkley 2014). As predicted in both 2014 and 1900, price controls had forced lenders into higher-value loans with longer durations and instalment payments. Price controls forced lenders to make larger loans, thereby segmenting out borrowers in need of the smallest sums.

Disclosure Terms

Given the long and antagonist animosity towards them, it was not surprising that many sought the extreme option of banning loan advertising (Jones 2013). Advertising had grown considerably between 2008 and 2012, failed to offer clear and pertinent information and too easily permeated daily life in public transport, on websites and on the high street. Data indicated that advertising's impact had grown from 12 million in 2008 to 7.6 billion in 2012 or 152 loan advertisements per viewer annually.[118] The similarities between this period and the Victorian era are striking, as these hopes mirrored George Lewis's and Archie Lloyd's, who in 1898 had argued that if advertisements were 'attacked', then 'fewer people would come in contact' with moneylenders.[119] Crowther, however, took little issue with the normalization of advertising all consumer credit products. In the 1970s, it was taken for granted that advertising was a part of daily life and went mostly unchallenged.

To a surprising degree, there was agreement among politicians, industry, charities and borrowers—APR data were of little help to customers.[120] Again, a simple example was used to demonstrate why the use of APR was deceptive. According to Martin Lewis, a financial commentator, if someone were to lend £20 and asked the borrower to repay with a pint of beer next week, 'most people would see it as reasonable deal'; at £3 the APR is 141,000% (Lewis 2011). Instead, 89% of borrowers took into consideration the total cost of credit in cash terms and were well aware of the amount owed.[121] As moneylenders and pawnbrokers had argued over a century earlier, the amount owed in pounds and pence was of greater concern than percentage disclosure. Tellingly, when in 2015 the FCA implemented price controls, they did not specify an APR, but quoted a daily rate.

From at least the 1870s onward, a major component of the policy debates and plans to overhaul regulation pertained to disclosure. In the moneylending and pawnbroking markets there has long been a difference in focus between borrowers, who have ignored mandatory disclosure terms, lenders, who have claimed the terms do little to help consumers, and regulators, who relied on this mechanism even before the PBA 1872 came into effect. While mandated disclosure focuses on a real problem and rests on a credible assumption that the more information the better, it fails to appreciate how people actually make decisions and there is no evidence that disclosure improves the terms of borrowing (Ben-Shahar and Schneider 2011). John Battle was one of the few who questioned the entire rationale of information disclosure, saying, 'We have two images of the person taking out a loan. Sometimes we think that they can absorb incredible amounts of information and detail and analyse the fine print, and then are OK. That is not the reality' (Hilton 2003, p. 14).[122] It is difficult to know how many consumers are equipped to understand complex disclosure terms (Cartwright 2015).

In the scheme of things, disclosure requirements are relatively inexpensive and allow a certain degree of market freedom that other forms of regulations preclude, yet there is little evidence that consumers read and process the information when making decisions. Beginning with pawn tickets and evolving thereafter, policymakers hoped that they were one or two small changes away from effective disclosure requirements. Be it tweaks or overhauls, borrowers have found little meaning in the pages of fine print.

Conclusion

As early as 2003, policymakers were concerned about 'predatory' small-loan companies. The OFT began targeting 'irresponsible' lenders that trapped the poor into an endless cycle of payments. While the terms were new, the concepts mirror Victorian debates over what constituted helpful and harmful credit. Policymakers focused on protecting vulnerable borrowers. What constituted vulnerability vastly expanded to include debt impacted the financial, social and health outcomes of low-income families. Protecting vulnerable consumers began to outweigh concerns about interfering too much in the credit market. Many wondered whether limiting access to high-cost credit would benefit some borrowers. In 2006, that was a step too far, and price controls did not gain any serious traction.

Some of the hesitation concerning price controls and limitations on the credit markets stem from the priorities of the financial inclusion agenda. The idea was to increase access to 'proper' financial markets. More of the 'right' kind of finance would help to alleviate poverty. So long as proper financial institutions banked the poor, the government need not interfere in the market's pricing mechanism. With a little bit of guidance from the government, the market was best positioned to achieve the main goals of financial inclusion, poverty reduction and consumer protection.

Though price controls were shelved, the government intended to monitor the high-cost credit sector. The OFT placed lenders into risk categories with high-risk providers having to meet stringent business and filing requirements. Moneylenders turned payday lenders and pawnbrokers were once again regulated differently and no longer considered part of mainstream finance.

Compared to the loose enforcement of prior episodes, deviant lenders would be dealt with harshly. The first order of business was devising a legal test to determine whether a transaction had harmed a borrower. The CCA 2006 sought to root out 'unfair' transactions. Still, since 1900, each successive regulatory episode considered prior regulatory efforts to have failed and yet replaced each one with a largely similar measure. In 1974, the government provided an exhaustive list of test factors. In 2006, Parliament empowered the courts with wide latitude for review. In the end, low-income borrowers have shown little interest in seeking redress through the courts. Although strengthened by the ADR system, the failed policy of a case-by-case approach was again relied on.

As the payday loan market expanded and the Global Financial Crisis wore on, the CCA 2006 became a way station for more aggressive regulation to come. The implementation of price controls built on concerns raised during the 2006 debate, among them financial exclusion and borrower vulnerability. While most policymakers appreciated that the industry served a purpose, they believed that lower loan volumes and fewer market participants would benefit society. In 2014, Simon Danczuk MP (Labour) said, 'There are far too many of them [payday lenders], and better regulation will be critical in that regard'.[123] With the support of Parliament, HM Treasury and leading charities the FCA thought that the most effective way to protect borrowers was by controlling the price of credit. While in 2006 regulation was expected to create the 'right' market, by 2015 the market and its pricing mechanism were the problem. The FCA determined that 'excessive' charges 'contribute to borrowers' worsening financial situation' and they initiated price controls. More accurately they reinstated usury on a cash loan product, a move not seen since 1854.[124]

For decades, if not centuries, moneylenders were seen as evil, the product harmful and borrowers vulnerable. And yet, time and again, Parliament had rejected price controls. What had changed in 2015? Concerns over a lack of price competition harken to the Victorian market and were nothing new. The initial stages of changes began in 2004 with New Labour's financial inclusion agenda.[125] This policy embraced an expansive definition of poverty, vulnerability and harm, including financial, mental health and general welfare (Davis 2015).[126] The links between financial exclusion, poverty and payday loans were different from previous frameworks and facilitated the implementation of price controls. The issue was not solely a government response to a market failure but an intervention on social grounds. It was an attempt to create a fairer and more just economic society.

Crowther relied on consumer protection through market competition and easily accessible credit was viewed positively. By 2014, policymakers sought market limitations through price controls. This position is far different from Thomas Chambers MP's (Liberal), who in 1870 argued that freedom of contract provided far better borrower protection than regulation.[127] The FCA was convinced that price controls would usher in lower costs for those borrowers who could afford the loan payments.

They believed that those segmented out of the market would be better off without a loan. Price controls were implemented to protect marginal borrowers. Reduced loan volumes and lower profitability were the price of such harsh measures.[128] The market contracted quickly.[129]

Controlling the price of credit through government decree does not suspend the laws of economics—risk and return still matter. Once the market became aware of the cap, firms began adjusting their pricing or withdrawing from the market. On the demand side it is unclear where customers such as Edward, who took out a £100 loan to pay his final notice electricity bill, would turn without access to payday lending (Rowlingson et al. 2014, p. 5). It was predicted that borrowers would turn to other forms of credit (pawn, doorstep, overdrafts, etc.) that were not subject to price controls.[130] Some MPs suggest the working poor could once again borrow from friends and family.[131] In addition to being historically inaccurate, it is unlikely that friends and family would have sufficient capital to supply the multi-billion pound market. Regardless, the FCA was aware of the risks; in fact, smaller loan volumes and a less attractive market were stated intentions of the reform.

The initial results suggest that higher-income borrowers are paying less for payday loans and that credit availability for marginal borrowers has decreased.[132] On the other hand, the demand for emergency credit has not fallen and 40% of the British population have less than one week's income in savings. Debates continue as to whether payday loan users are vulnerable or are sophisticated and proactive managers of their financial resources (Ali et al. 2015). Whether marginal borrowers are better off remains unclear. What is clear is that price controls dramatically impacted the market.

The financial inclusion agenda influenced the regulation and development of the payday loan market, first through the CCA 2006 and its segmentation of high-risk lenders and then through price controls. By the twenty-first century the link between finance, poverty and vulnerability had expanded to include 'unemployment, poor skills, low income, poor housing, high crime environments, bad health and family breakdown' (Kempson et al. 2000, p. 7). Whereas targeted measures enacted in the CCA 2006 were expected to encourage price competition, by 2015 the FCA was intervening in the market's pricing mechanism. This evolution conflicted with Crowther's belief that regulation could not protect those 'who through no fault of their own' experience insufficient incomes.[133]

Justifying the implementation of price controls based solely on market failure itself also fails to appreciate the influence of social justice concerns, especially those related to inequality and economic fairness (Stephen 2005).[134] Whereas it was suggested that 'proper' finance would reduce poverty, payday loans were considered to have contributesd to it. This wasn't a matter of Victorian morality nor was the issue solely a government response to market failure. It was a social justice intervention driven by the government's role in constructing the 'right' kind of market participation. In this case it was not morals that had failed, but the market—and the government set out to right the wrong.

Notes

1. HC deb. 9 June 2005, vol. 434.
2. HC deb. 13 January 2005, vol. 429.
3. "The Consumer Credit Market in the 21st Century: Fair, Clear and Competitive," Department of Trade and Industry (6040), 2003, 4.
4. HL Select Committee on European Union 36th Annual Report 2007, Chapter 4 UK Consumer Credit Legislation, 64–5.
5. "The Consumer Credit Market in the 21st Century: Fair, Clear and Competitive," Department of Trade and Industry (6040), 2003, 10.
6. Responsible lending was understood as 'more than just meeting the minimum legal requirements. It is also about driving forward best practice and treating customers fairly'. See "Transparency of Credit Charges," House of Commons Treasury Committee First Report of Session 2003–2004 vol. 1, section 83.
7. According to the FSA, the financial inclusion agenda was stimulated by the 1997 Labour government's Social Exclusion Unit initiative, see Kempson 'In or Out?' The first government strategy report, 'Promoting financial inclusion', was issued by HM Treasury in 2004. While the initial focus was on increasing access to basic banking facilities, ATMs and affordable credit, it was expected that insurance and related products would follow. Alternatives to the banks were also promoted, including the Post Office, Community Development Finance Initiatives and credit unions. Financial illiteracy was to be addressed in school-based programmes and money advice centres.
8. "Promoting Financial Inclusion," HM Treasury, 2004, 3; "Access to Financial Services," HM Treasury, 1999; "Promoting Financial Exclusion," HM Treasury, 2004, 3.
9. "Promoting Financial Inclusion," HM Treasury, 2004, 12.
10. HL Select Committee on Financial Inclusion, Evidence, Session 11, 25 October 2016; HC Library, "The Consumer Credit Bill," Research

Paper 05/03, 11 January 2005; "Financial Inclusion: Credit, Savings, Advice and Insurance," House of Commons Treasury Committee Twelfth Report of the Session 2005–2006 vol. 1, 3.

11. "The Consumer Credit Market in the 21st Century: Fair, Clear and Competitive," Department of Trade and Industry (6040), 2003, 3, 24, 74.
12. "Financial Inclusion: Credit, Savings, Advice and Insurance," House of Commons Treasury Committee Twelfth Report of the Session 2005–2006 vol. 1, 21.
13. The Social Fund was established in 1987 to provide loans for immediate and exceptional need. The fund did not effectively compete with the alternative loan industry as it was limited in scope and required a lengthy application process.
14. "Memorandum of Association," H&T Group, May 2006, 6.
15. "Pawnbroking Customers in 2010," A report for the National Pawnbrokers Association prepared by the Personal Finance Research Centre, University of Bristol, 2010, 20.
16. A 42 DIR 57, London Yellow Pages, Guildhall Library, 1975–1990.
17. "The Pawnbrokers Guide," The National Pawnbrokers Association, 1999, 20; "Annual Report," Albemarle & Bond Holdings, 2005 and 2006; "Memorandum of Association," H&T Group, May 2006, 8–11; "Information Package," The National Pawnbrokers Association, March 2017, 6. Similar developments occurred in the modern American market, see Woloson (2009, pp. 1–20).
18. "Memorandum of Association," H&T Group, 1 May 2006, 6, 10. Cash flow as measured by earnings before interest, taxes, depreciation and amortization.
19. "Memorandum of Association," H&T Group, 1 May 2006, 13.
20. "Memorandum of Association," H&T Group, 1 May 2006, 15.
21. "Annual Report," Albemarle & Bond Holdings, 1989 and 30 June 2006.
22. Before the CCA 1974, the Yellow Page trade directory provided a moneylender's category. By 1980, moneylenders were listed within the 'Credit and Finance Companies' section. As a result, it is impossible to determine which companies offered small-value unsecured loans. See A 42 DIR 57, London Yellow Pages, Guildhall Library, 1975–1990.
23. "The True Cost of Credit," Office of Fair Trading, 1990; 'Unjust Credit Transactions," Office of Fair Trading, 1991; "Consumer Credit Regulation," Office of Fair Trading, 1994; "Extortionate Credit," Office of Fair Trading, 1998.
24. "The Consumer Credit Market in the 21st Century: Fair, Clear and Competitive," Department of Trade and Industry (6040), 2003, 3.

25. "Financial Inclusion: Credit, Savings, Advice and Insurance," House of Commons Treasury Committee Twelfth Report of the Session 2005–2006 vol. 1, 3.
26. "Fair, Clear and Competitive" followed the Task Force on Tackling Over-indebtedness and preceded The Ministerial Group on Over-indebtedness Action Plan 2004.
27. "The Consumer Credit Market in the 21st Century: Fair, Clear and Competitive," Department of Trade and Industry (6040), 2003, 19.
28. HC deb. 9 June 2005, vol. 434.
29. "The Consumer Credit Market in the 21st Century: Fair, Clear and Competitive," Department of Trade and Industry (6040), 2003, 62–63; HC deb. 9 June 2005, vol. 434.
30. HC deb. 9 June 2005, vol. 434.
31. See Consumer Credit (Advertisements) Regulations 1989 and the House of Commons Treasury Committee inquiry into the transparency of credit card charges, first report of session 2003–2004; "The Consumer Credit Market in the 21st Century: Fair, Clear and Competitive," Department of Trade and Industry (6040), 2003, 37.
32. HC deb. 9 June 2005, vol. 434.
33. HC Standing Committee D, 15 June 2005.
34. "Consumer Credit Regulation: Guidance on the Regulations Implementing the Consumer Credit Directive," Department for Business, Innovation and Skills, August 2010; "The Consumer Credit (Total Charge for Credit) Regulations 1980," The Department of Trade, 28 April 1980.
35. "Consumer Credit Regulation: Guidance on the Regulations Implementing the Consumer Credit Directive,"; HC Standing Committee D, 23 June 2005; "The Consumer Credit Market in the 21st Century: Fair, Clear and Competitive," Department of Trade and Industry (6040), 2003, 52.
36. "Consumer Credit Regulation: Guidance on the Regulations Implementing the Consumer Credit Directive,"; HC Standing Committee D, 23 June 2005; HL deb. 23 April 1926, vol. 194.
37. HC Standing Committee D, 23 June 2005.
38. "The Consumer Credit Market in the 21st Century: Fair, Clear and Competitive," Department of Trade and Industry (6040), 2003, 46; More technically, the OFT 'lacked flexibility in the imposition of intermediate measures to promote compliance'.
39. "Consumer Credit Act 2006," Slaughter and May, October 2008. See also "Irresponsible Lending – OFT Guidance for Creditors," Office of Fair Trading 1107, February 2011.
40. HC deb. 9 June 2005, vol. 434; HC deb. 14 July 2005, vol. 434.
41. HC deb. 9 June 2005, vol. 434.

42. "Financial Inclusion: Credit, Savings, Advice and Insurance," House of Commons Treasury Committee Twelfth Report of the Session 2005–2006 vol. 1, 3.
43. "The Consumer Credit Market in the 21st Century: Fair, Clear and Competitive," Department of Trade and Industry (6040), 2003, 24.
44. "Payday Lending: Fixing a Broken Market," Association of Chartered Certified Accountants, May 2014, 10; Company websites and statistica.com.
45. "Payday Lending Market Investigation: Final Report," Competition and Markets Authority, February 2015), 16.
46. "Pawnbroking Customers in 2010," A report for the National Pawnbrokers Association prepared by the Personal Finance Research Centre, University of Bristol, 2010, 7–9.
47. "Pawnbroking Customers in 2010," A report for the National Pawnbrokers Association prepared by the Personal Finance Research Centre, University of Bristol, 2010, 7–9; "Key Facts," The National Pawnbrokers Association, 8 October 2015, thenpa.com.
48. "The Impact on Business and Customers of a Cap on the Total Cost of Credit," A Report for the Department for Business, Innovation and Skills prepared by The Personal Finance Research Centre, University of Bristol, 2013, 10.
49. HC deb. 20 January 2014, vol. 574.
50. HC deb. 4 July 2011, vol. 530; HC deb. 10 December 2012, vol. 555.
51. HC deb. 2 July 2013, vol. 565; "Consultation Response: FCA Proposals for a Price Cap on High-cost Short-term Credit," Money Advice Trust, August 2014.
52. "Payday Lending Market Investigation: Final Report," Competition and Markets Authority, February 2015, 4.
53. NOP Research.
54. HL deb. 20 June 2013, vol. 746.
55. HC deb. 3 February 2011, vol. 522.
56. Mabel Robinson, "Pawnbroking in England and Abroad," *Fortnightly Review*, 1888, 44(259):70–71, 86–87.
57. HC deb. 16 May 2012, vol. 545.
58. HC deb. 3 February 2011, vol. 522; HC deb. 17 February 2011, vol. 523; HC deb. 4 July 2011 vol. 530; HL deb. 11 June 2012, vol. 737; HL deb. 13 September 2012, vol. 550; HL deb. 24 October 2012, vol. 740; HL deb. 28 November 2012, vol. 741; HL deb. 9 December 2012, vol. 750.
59. HC deb. 3 February 2011, vol. 522.
60. HC deb. 3 February 2011, vol. 522; HC deb. 4 July 2011, vol. 530; HC deb. 20 January 2014, vol. 574.
61. HL deb. 5 December 2012, vol. 741.

62. HC deb. 3 November 2010, vol. 948; HC deb. 3 February 2011, vol. 530; HC deb. 12 July 2013, vol. 566; HC deb. 20 January 2014, vol. 574; HL deb. 29 November 2012, vol. 741; HL deb. 28 November 2012, vol. 741.
63. HL deb. 20 June 2013, vol. 746.
64. Unlike an interest rate cap, a total cost credit limits the total amount of paid over the life of a loan.
65. "Proposals for a Price Cap on High-cost Short-term Credit: Consultation Paper," Financial Conduct Authority CP 14/10, July 2014, 74.
66. "The Impact on Business and Customers of a Cap on the Total Cost of Credit," A Report for the Department for Business, Innovation and Skills prepared by The Personal Finance Research Centre, University of Bristol, 2013, i, viii.
67. "Pawnbroking Customers in 2010," A report for the National Pawnbrokers Association prepared by the Personal Finance Research Centre, University of Bristol, 2010, 3.
68. "The Impact on Business and Customers of a Cap on the Total Cost of Credit," A Report for the Department for Business, Innovation and Skills prepared by The Personal Finance Research Centre, University of Bristol, 2013, ii.
69. "Payday Lending Market Investigation: Final Report," Competition and Markets Authority, February 2015, 181.
70. "The Impact on Business and Customers of a Cap on the Total Cost of Credit," A Report for the Department for Business, Innovation and Skills prepared by The Personal Finance Research Centre, University of Bristol, 2013, ii.
71. HC deb. 3 November 2010, 948.
72. "Review of High Cost Credit Final Report," Office of Fair Trading (1232), 2010, 4–6; "Payday Lending Compliance Review Final Report," Office of Fair Trading (1481), 2013, 2.
73. HC Written Statements, 22 March 2010, 146; HL deb. 17 June 2010, vol. 719.
74. HC deb. 3 February 2011, vol. 552.
75. HC deb. 1 December 2011, vol. 536.
76. HC deb. 3 February 2011, vol. 522.
77. HC deb. 3 February 2011, vol. 522.
78. HL deb. 28 November 2012, vol. 741.
79. "Payday Lending Market Investigation: Final Report," Competition and Markets Authority, February 2015, 47.
80. Cost data for first loans are unavailable.
81. "Payday Lending Market Investigation: Final Report," Competition and Markets Authority, February 2015, 139.

82. "Payday Lending Market Investigation: Final Report," Competition and Markets Authority, February 2015, 5, 14, 139.
83. HC deb. 3 February 2011, vol. 522; Emma Dunkley, "Wonga Caps Fees on Payday Loans," *Financial Times*, 16 December 2014.
84. "Payday Lending Market Investigation: Final Report," Competition and Markets Authority, February 2015, 35.
85. "Payday Lending Market Investigation: Final Report," Competition and Markets Authority, February 2015, Tables 4.1 and 5.6.
86. "Overdraft Charges More Expensive than Payday Loans," Which?, 9 July 2016.
87. "The Impact on Business and Customers of a Cap on the Total Cost of Credit," A Report for the Department for Business, Innovation and Skills prepared by The Personal Finance Research Centre, University of Bristol, 2013, 10.
88. "Payday Lending: Fixing a Broken Market," Association of Chartered Certified Accountants, May 2014, 22.
89. "Payday Lending: Fixing a Broken Market," Association of Chartered Certified Accountants, May 2014, 131.
90. HC deb. 3 February 2011, vol. 522.
91. "Payday Lending Market Investigation: Final Report," Competition and Markets Authority, February 2015, 6, 130–34, 146–50. Profitability as measured by the weighted average annual return on capital employed (ROCE). ROCE is calculated by dividing EBIT by the capital employed. The eleven lenders studied by the CMA comprised 90% loan volume.
92. "Payday Lending Market Investigation: Final Report," Competition and Markets Authority, February 2015, 150.
93. HC deb. 27 November 2013, vol. 571.
94. PBSC 1870, 3663.
95. HC deb. 12 July 2013, vol. 566.
96. HL deb. 28 November 2012, vol. 741.
97. "The Impact on Business and Customers of a Cap on the Total Cost of Credit," A Report for the Department for Business, Innovation and Skills prepared by The Personal Finance Research Centre, University of Bristol, 2013, v–vi, 83, 98–99.
98. "Payday Lending Compliance Review Final Report', Office of Fair Trading (1481), 2013.
99. HL 12 July 2013, vol. 566, 4.
100. "Government Response to the Bristol University Report on High Cost Credit," Department for Business, Innovation and Skills, March 2013, 3–4; On 1 April 2014 enforcement of the CCA 1974 would be transferred from the OFT to the FCA. The Financial Services and Markets Act 2000 (FSMA) replaced the provisions of the CCA that dealt with licensing. On 1 April 2013, the FCA was established and took over

responsibility from the FSA for the conduct and relevant prudential regulation of financial services firms and financial markets. Parliament directed the FCA to introduce some form of price control under section 137C of the FSMA and section 131 of the Financial Services Banking Reform Act 2013. The FCA is funded by the firms it regulates and held accountable to the Treasury and Parliament. Consumer credit firms are regulated by the FCA and subject to the CCA 1974.

101. "Government Response to the Bristol University Report on High Cost Credit," Department for Business, Innovation and Skills, March 2013, 3–5.
102. HL deb. 5 December 2012, vol. 741.
103. HC deb. 12 July 2013, vol. 566.
104. "Payday Lending Market Investigation: Final Report," Competition and Markets Authority, February 2015, 134, 142.
105. "Payday Lending Market Investigation: Final Report," Competition and Markets Authority, February 2015).
106. "Annual Report 2014," The Consumer Finance Association.
107. The FCA mandate to investigate the industry began on 1 April 2014.
108. "Proposals for a Price Cap on High-cost Short-term Credit: Consultation Paper," Financial Conduct Authority CP 14/10, July 2014, 6.
109. HC deb. 20 January 2014, vol. 574.
110. HC deb. 20 January 2014, vol. 574.
111. Found on each respective website: "Transact Response to FCA Price Cap," Transact (August 2014); "StepChange Debt Charity Response to FCA," StepChange (September 2014); "Credit Union Association Response to Caps," Association of British Credit Unions (undated letter); "FCA's Proposals for a Price Cap on High-cost Short Term Credit," Citizens Advice Bureau (August 2014); "Proposals for a Price Cap on High-cost Short-term Credit," Community Investment Coalition (undated letter); "Proposals in Response to the CMA's Recommendations on High Cost Short Term Credit," Christians Against Poverty (October 2015); "Hope for Millions of Borrowers Stuck in a Cycle of Debt, Response to the FCA Announcement on a Price cap for Payday Lenders," Which? (11 November 2014); "Consultation Response: FCA Proposals for a Price Cap on High-cost Short-term Credit," Money Advice Trust (August 2014); "Response to the FCA's Proposals for a Price Cap on High-cost Short-term Credit," The Money Charity (August 2014); "Proposals for a Price Cap on High-cost Short-term Credit," Trading Standards Institute (August 2014).
112. "Payday Lending Market Investigation: Final Report," Competition and Markets Authority, February 2015), 149–60.

113. For dissenting voices see HC deb. 12 July 2013, vol. 566; HC deb. 11 December 2013, vol. 572; HC deb. 20 January 2014, vol. 574; HL deb. 20 June 2013, vol. 746.
114. "Detail Rules for the Price Cap on High-cost Short-term Credit, Including Feedback on CP 14/10 and Final Rules," Financial Conduct Authority PS 14/16, November 2014, 7–8.
115. "Tougher Rules for Payday Lenders Take Effect," FCA Press Release, 1 July 2014. See also the FCA's Consumer Credit Sourcebook 6.7 Rules on refinancing.
116. "Detail Rules for the Price Cap on High-cost Short-term Credit, Including Feedback on CP 14/10 and Final Rules," Financial Conduct Authority PS 14/16, November 2014, 14–17.
117. "Our Quarterly Magazine," BCCA 73, July 2016.
118. HC deb. 20 January 2014, vol. 574.
119. MLSC 1898, 140–142.
120. "Payday Lending Market Investigation: Final Report," Competition and Markets Authority, February 2015, 209–11.
121. "Payday Lending Market Investigation: Final Report," Competition and Markets Authority, February 2015, 209–11.
122. HC Standing Committee D, 15 June 2005. Hilton asked a similar question, 'How much responsibility ought to be expected of the individual in the exercise of his or her consuming duties and how much should the state seek to protect the rights of the collective mass of all consumers?' Like this research, Hilton was trying to understand the inherent tension between a consumer's freedom of choice and the role of the state in structuring such decisions.
123. HC deb. 20 January 2014, vol. 574.
124. "Proposals for a Price Cap on High-cost Short-term Credit: Consultation Paper," Financial Conduct Authority CP 14/10, July 2014, 22. The FCA considered charges excessive if those charges resulted in an unacceptable risk of harm such that the borrower's financial situation was made worse by loan repayment.
125. "Promoting Financial Inclusion," HM Treasury, 2004; Financial Inclusion an Action Plan 2008–2011," HM Treasury, 2007; "Financial Inclusion the Way Forward," HM Treasury, 2007.
126. "Proposals for a Price Cap on High-cost Short-term Credit: Consultation Paper," Financial Conduct Authority CP 14/10, July 2014, 61–63.
127. PBSC (1870, pp. 261–262).
128. "Proposals for a Price Cap on High-cost Short-term Credit: Consultation Paper," Financial Conduct Authority CP 14/10, July 2014, 50–51.

129. "Detail Rules for the Price Cap on High-cost Short-term Credit, Including Feedback on CP 14/10 and Final Rules," Financial Conduct Authority PS 14/16, November 2014, 1–6, 13.
130. "Detail Rules for the Price Cap on High-cost Short-term Credit, Including Feedback on CP 14/10 and Final Rules," Financial Conduct Authority PS 14/16, November 2014, 1–6, 13.
131. HC deb. 5 September 2013, vol. 567.
132. "A Modern Credit Revolution: An Analysis of the Short-term Credit Market," By the Social Market Foundation on behalf of the Consumer Finance Association (2016).
133. Crowther, 6.1.8–6.1.9.
134. Additionally, while HM Treasury stated that financial inclusion was intended to improve the market's efficiency, it believed that financial inclusion was a matter of social policy and social justice. See "Financial Inclusion: An Action Plan for 2008–11," HM Treasury, December 2007 and "Promoting Financial Inclusion," 2004. On p. 3 of the latter, The Treasury claimed that beyond market failures, government intervention was warranted based on equity.

Bibliography

Archives

The British Library, London.
PP2501—The Moneylenders' Federation Manual and Directory, 1913.
The Guildhall & City Business Library, City of London.
332.34—The Pawnbroker, 2005–present.
A 42 DIR 57—London Yellow Pages.

Official Publications

Consumer Credit (Advertisements) Regulations 1989.
Consumer Credit. 1971. Report of the Committee (4596).
"Financial Inclusion: Credit, Savings, Advice and Insurance." 2006. House of Commons Treasury Committee Twelfth Report of Session 2005–06, vol. 1, November.
"Government Response to The Bristol University Report on High Cost Credit." 2013. Department for Business, Innovation and Skills, March.
House of Lords Select Committee on Financial Inclusion. Evidence Session 11, 25 October 2016.
House of Lords Select Committee on European Union 36th Annual Report 2007, Chapter 4: UK Consumer Credit Legislation.
Report from the Select Committee on Moneylending 1897 (364).

Report from the Select Committee on Moneylenders 1898 (260).
The Pawnbrokers Select Committee 1870 (377).
The Consumer Credit Act 1974, c. 39.
The Consumer Credit Act 2006, c. 14.
"Transparency of Credit Charges." House of Commons Treasury Committee First Report of Session 2003–04, vol. 1.

Sources

"A Modern Credit Revolution: An Analysis of the Short-term Credit Market." 2016. Social Market Foundation on Behalf of the Consumer Finance Association.
"Access to Financial Service." 1999. HM Treasury.
Aldohni, Abdul Karim. 2013. "Loan Sharks v. Short-term Lenders: How Do the Law and Regulators Draw the Line?" *Journal of Law and Society* 40 (3): 420–29.
Ali, Paul, Cosima McRae, and Ian Ramsey. 2015. "Payday Lending Regulation and Borrower Vulnerability in the UK and Australia." *Journal of Business Law* 3: 223–25.
"Annual Report." 1989. Albemarle & Bond Holdings.
"Annual Report." 2006. Albemarle & Bond Holdings.
"Annual Report." 2014. The Consumer Finance Association.
Avio, Kenneth. 1973. "An Economic Rationale for Statutory Interest Rate Ceilings." *Quarterly Review of Economics and Business* 13: 61–72.
Ben-Shahar, Omir, and Carl Schneider. 2011. "The Failure of Mandated Disclosure." *University of Pennsylvania Law Review* 159 (3): 647–749.
Berthoud, Richard, and Elaine Kempson. 1992. *Credit and Debt*. London: Policy Studies Institute.
Boggan, Steve. 2016. "Pawn Again." *Guardian*, October 20.
Burton, Dawn. 2008. *Credit and Consumer Society*. Oxford: Routledge.
Cartwright, Peter. 2015. "Understanding and Protecting Vulnerable Financial Consumers." *Journal of Consumer Policy* 38 :119–38.
Caskey, John. 2012. "Payday Lending: New Research and the Big Question." In *The Oxford Handbook of the Economics of Poverty*, edited by Philip Jefferson, 681–708. Oxford: Oxford University Press.
Cayne, David, and Michael Trebilcock. 1973. "Market Considerations in the Formulation of Consumer Protection Policy." *University of Toronto Law Journal* 23: 396–430.
"Changing Household Budgets." 2014. Money Advice Trust, June.
Christie, Sophie. 2014. "Rated: The Best and Worst Banks This Year for Customer Service." *Telegraph*, August 28.

Collard, Sharon, and Elaine Kempson. 2005. "Affordable Credit: The Way Forward." The Joseph Rowntree Foundation.
Collard, Sharon, Elaine Kempson, and Claire Whyley. 2011. "Tackling Financial Exclusion: An Area-based Approach." The Policy Press.
"Consultation Response: FCA Proposals for a Price Cap on High-cost Short-term Credit" 2014. Money Advice Trust, August.
"Consumer Credit Act 2006." 2008. Slaughter and May.
"Consumer Credit Regulation." 1994. Office of Fair Trading.
"Consumer Credit Regulation: Guidance on the Regulations Implementing the Consumer Credit Directive." 2010. Department for Business, Innovation and Skills, August.
Consumer Credit Sourcebook (CONC) Release 8. 2016. Financial Conduct Authority.
Consumer Credit Sourcebook (CONC) Release 1. 2013. Financial Conduct Authority.
"Credit Union Association Response to Caps." Undated. Association of British Credit Unions.
Cribb, Jonathan. 2013. "Income Inequality in the UK." Institute for Fiscal Studies.
Davies, Richard, and Peter Richardson. 2010. "Evolution of the UK Banking System." *Bank of England Quarterly Bulletin* Q4.
Davis, Philip. 2015. "Economic Theories of Poverty." Joseph Rowntree Foundation, June.
"Detail Rules for the Price Cap on High-Cost Short-Term Credit, Including Feedback on CP 14/10 and Final Rules." 2014. Financial Conduct Authority PS14/16.
Domoto, Hiroshi. 2012. "The Risk of Yamikin Market, Which is Spreading Quietly in Japan." *Institute for Research on Credit Business* 12 (003): 1–18.
Dunkley, Emma. 2014. "Wonga Caps Fees on Payday Loans." *Financial Times*, December 16.
Edmonds, Timothy. 2014. "High Cost Consumer Credit." House of Commons Library Briefing Paper 05849, July 15.
"Fair, Clear, and Competitive: The Consumer Credit Market in the 21st Century." 2003. Department of Trade and Industry, December.
"FCA's Proposals for a Price Cap on High-cost Short Term Credit." 2014. Citizens Advice Bureau, August.
"Financial Inclusion: An Action Plan for 2008–11." 2007. HM Treasury, December.
"Financial Inclusion: The Way Forward." 2007. HM Treasury, March.
Friedman, Milton. 1970. "Defense of Usury." *Newsweek*, April 6.

Glaeser, Edward, and Jose Scheinkman. 1994. "Neither a Borrower nor a Lender Be: An Economic Analysis of Interest Restrictions and Usury Laws." National Bureau of Economic Research Working Paper 4954: 1–45.
Hilton, Matthew. 2003. *Consumerism in Twentieth Century Britain: The Search for a Historical Movement*. Cambridge: Cambridge University Press.
"Hope for Millions of Borrowers Stuck in a Cycle of Debt, Which?" 2014. Response to the FCA Announcement on a Price Cap for Payday Lenders, Which? November 11.
"Information Package." 2017. The National Pawnbrokers Association, March.
"Irresponsible Lending – OFT Guidance for Creditors." 2011. Office of Fair Trading, February.
Jenkins, Jamie. 2010. "The Labour Market in the 1980s, 1990s and 2008/09 Recessions." *Economic & Labour Market Review* 4 (8): 29–36.
Jones, Rupert. 2013. "Crackdown on Payday Loans Advertising." *Guardian*, July 1.
Kempson, Elaine. 2002. "Over-Indebtedness in Britain." A Report to the Department of Trade and Industry by The Personal Finance Research Centre, University of Bristol, September.
Kempson, Elaine, and Claire Whyley. "Extortionate Credit in the UK." 2009. A Report for the Department for Trade and Industry by the Personal Finance Research Centre, University of Bristol, 1999.
Kempson, Elaine, Claire Whyley, Sharon Collard, and John Caskey. 2000. "In or Out? Financial Exclusion: A Literature and Research Review." Financial Services Authority.
"Key Facts." 2015. National Pawnbroker Association, October 2.
Lewis, Martin. 2011. "Don't tell MPs I'm against payday loan regulation!" moneysavingexpert.com, January 28.
Leyshon, Andrew, and Nigel Thrift. 1993. "The Restructuring of the UK Financial Services Industry in the 1990s: A Reversal of Fortune?" *Journal of Rural Studies* 9 (3): 223–41.
———. 2005. "Geographies of Financial Exclusion: Financial Abandonment in Britain and the United States." *Transactions of the Institute of British Geographers* 20: 312–341.
Lim, Youngee, Trey Bickham, Cassie M. Dinecola, Julia Broussard, Brittany E., and Martin Lewis. 2014. "Don't Tell MPs I'm Against Payday Loan Regulation!" moneysavingexpert.com, January 28.
Marron, Donncha. 2013. "Governing Poverty in a Neoliberal Age: New Labour and the Case of Financial Exclusion." *New Political Economy* 18 (6): 785–810.
"Memorandum of Association." 2006. H&T Group, May 1.
Morgan, Donald, and Michael Strain. 2007. "Payday Holiday: How Households Fare After Payday Credit Bans." Federal Reserve Bank of New York Staff Reports 309.

Nickell, Stephen. 2003. "Two Current Monetary Policy Issues." Bank of England Monetary Policy Committee, September 16.

Offer, Avner. 2007. *The Challenge of Affluence*. Oxford: Oxford University Press.

Osborne, Hillary. 2013. "Payday Lenders May Vanish Within a Year as Result of Price Cap, Says Economist." *Guardian*, November 10.

"Our Quarterly Magazine." 2016. BCCA 73, July.

"Overdraft Charges More Expensive than Payday Loans." 2016. Which? July 9.

Palmer, Guy, Tom MacInnes, and Peter Kenway. 2006. "Monitoring Poverty and Social Exclusion 2006." The Joseph Rowntree Foundation and the New Policy Institute.

"Payday Lending Compliance Review Final Report." 2013. Office of Fair Trading 1481.

"Payday Lending: Fixing A Broken Market." 2014. The Association of Chartered Certified Accountants, May.

"Payday Lending Market Investigation: Final Report." 2015. Competition and Markets Authority, February 24.

"Pawnbroking Customers in 2010." 2010. A Report for the National Pawnbrokers Association Prepared by the Personal Finance Research Centre, University of Bristol.

"Promoting Financial Inclusion. 2004. HM Treasury.

"Proposals for a Price Cap on High-cost Short-term Credit: Consultative Paper." 2014. Financial Conduct Authority CP 14/10, July.

"Proposals for a Price Cap on High-Cost Short-Term Credit." 2014. Financial Services Consumer Panel, August 2.

"Proposals for a Price Cap on High-Cost Short-Term Credit." 2014. Trading Standards Institute, August.

"Proposals in Response to the CMA's Recommendations on High Cost Short Term Credit." 2015. Christians Against Poverty, October.

"Response to the FCA Consultation CP 14/10: Proposals for a Price Cap on High-Cost Short-term Credit." Undated. Community Investment Coalition.

"Response to the FCA's Proposals for a Price Cap on High-cost Short-term Credit. 2014. The Money Charity, August.

"Review of High Cost Credit. 2010. Office of Fair Trading (1232).

Robinson, Mabel. 1888. "Pawnbroking in England and Abroad." *Fortnightly Review* 44 (259): 69–88.

Rose, Nikolas. 1999. *Power of Freedom: Reframing Political Thought*. Cambridge: Cambridge University Press.

Rossiter, Jenny, and Niall Cooper. 2005. "Scaling Up for Financial Inclusion." Debt on Our Doorstop Campaign.

Rowlingson, Karen, Lindsay Appleyard, and Jodi Gardner. 2014. "Capping the Cost of Payday Lending in the UK: What Will the Impact Be?" A Paper for the Financial Conduct Authority, July.

Skiba, Paige, and Jeremy Tobacman. 2011. "Do Payday Loans Cause Bankruptcy?" *Vanderbilt Law and Economics Research Paper* 11 (13): 1–32.

Staten, Michael, and Robert Johnson. 1995. "Case for Deregulating Interest Rates on Consumer Credit." Credit Research Center, Purdue University, Indiana: 1–60.

Stegman, Michael, and Robert Faris. 2008. "Payday Lending: A Business Model that Encourages Chronic Borrowing." *Economic Development Quarterly* 17 (1): 8–32.

"StepChange Debt Charity Response to FCA." 2014. StepChange, September.

Stephen, Timms MP. 2005. "Labour, Financial Secretary to the Treasury." In 'Scaling up for financial inclusion', Church Action on Poverty: Debt on Our Doorstep.

Tebbutt, Melanie. 1983. *Making Ends Meet: Pawnbroking and Working-Class Credit*. Leicester: Leicester University Press.

"The Consumer Credit Bill." 2005. House of Commons Library Research Paper 05/03, January 11.

"The Consumer Credit (Total Charge for Credit) Regulations." 1980. The Department of Trade, April 28.

"The Impact on Business and Customers of a Cap on the Total Cost of Credit." 2013. A Report for the Department for Business, Innovation and Skills by The Personal Finance Research Centre, University of Bristol.

"The Pawnbrokers Guide." 1999. The National Pawnbrokers' Association.

"The True Cost of Credit." 1990. Office of Fair Trading.

"Tougher Rules for Payday Lenders Take Effect. 2014. Financial Conduct Authority Press Release, July 1.

"Transact Response to FCA Price Cap." 2014. *Transact*, August.

"Unjust Credit Transactions." 1991. Office of Fair Trading.

Woloson, Wendy. 2009. *In Hock: Pawning in America from Independence Through the Great Depression*. Chicago: The University of Chicago Press.

Zinman, Jonathan. 2010. "Restricting Consumer Credit Access: Household Survey Evidence on Effects Around the Oregon Rate Cap." *Journal of Banking & Finance* 34 (3): 546–56.

CHAPTER 6

Fintech to the Rescue or Predators in Disguise?

Financial crises create a wave of redundancies, administrations and new regulation. Typically, the worse the collapse the more aggressive the policy response. Payday lenders and pawnbrokers rode the market boom leading up to 2007, grew during the economic bust phase as borrowers needed short-term loans, and soon enough new rules and turbulent market conditions ended years of profit and growth. Embodying all that was wrong with the industry, Wonga collapsed under the weight of regulatory fines and price controls. Wonga owed 358,000 borrowers a collective £460 million in compensation (Makortoff 2020). Now bankrupt, it is unlikely that claimants will receive much, if anything from the defunct lender. Ironically, Britain's once-largest payday lender could not pay its debts. Its reckless behaviour is exactly why centuries of policymakers have targeted small-loan providers. Hundreds more payday and pawn lenders have also closed up shop. Strict regulation and a challenging market environment have altered the small-loan market almost beyond recognition.

One thing that has not changed, affordable credit remains out of reach for many low-income households. Mainstream banks provide few options for those surviving on irregular and low incomes. While over 97% of adults have a current account, banks suggest the same responsible lending criteria that has shrunk the payday loan market precludes them from issuing small loans to vulnerable borrowers (Lane and Rodrigues).[1]

© The Author(s), under exclusive license to Springer Nature Switzerland AG 2021

C. McMahon, *Taming the Fringe*, Palgrave Studies in the History of Finance, https://doi.org/10.1007/978-3-030-70615-9_6

Lending small sums is expensive, risky and the product invites negative publicity and criticism. Given all the trouble, entering the market is hardly worth it for well-known financial service companies. Yet, borrowers need cash, and payday lenders and pawnbrokers still lend £1.6 billion a year fulfilling that demand.[2] More altruistic lenders, such as Credit Unions and Community Development Financial Intuitions (CDFIs) have slowly, and only in a limited way, expanded into lower market segments. Nearly fifty years since Crowther's hopes of outcompeting them, borrowers keep returning to pawnbroking and payday loans. Financial inclusion efforts and regulation have largely failed to expand credit or offer alternative products.

Technological innovation may unlock new opportunities to profitably and responsibly provide financial services to low-income households and vulnerable borrowers. Many options have developed outside of traditional financial channels (Chambers et al. 2020). Consumer lending, cryptocurrencies, fund-raising platforms and microfinance companies offer services unimaginable only a few years ago. Fintech on-demand wage companies are disrupting the annual 5.4 million payday loan industry and the overall £3.3 billion high-cost credit sector.[3] For a fee, these companies allow an employee access to earned daily wages before the traditional monthly pay cycle. Other companies, such as Koyo and its competitors, use data-driven technology to expand credit eligibility to help customers with poor credit profiles access funding. My-Quick online platform matches borrowers with the lowest rate offering within the high-cost short-term small-loan sector. Whether these technologies offer a long-term and financially viable alternative to payday loans is unknown. Some consumer advocates wondered if these new models are simply yet another form of predatory lending profiting off of those least able to afford it.

The FCA's price cap has left many marginal borrowers without access to much need cash. Fintech, credit unions, CDFI's and familial and social networks have only partially fulfilled the excess demand. It is not clear whether those locked out of the small-loan market are better off without a loan. Two questions remain unanswered: What does financial inclusion actually mean for the poor and is there a way to responsibly overcome the inherent tension in pricing risk for a market segment that has experienced financial difficulties before seeking credit.

Market and Policy Developments

From Victorian pawnbrokers to today's Internet lenders, competitive markets have encouraged speedier loan approvals, accommodative trading hours, aggressive collateral valuations, and product innovation. While during times of plenty business acumen influenced the fortunes of any given lender, it also pushed companies to cut corners and lend irresponsibly. After the 2015 regulatory tsunami, many payday companies exited voluntarily or through administration. Financial penalties, price caps and rollover limits pushed them to the brink. Major pawnbroking players also folded alongside their payday loan counterparts. In September 2019, one of Britain's largest operators, Albemarle & Bond, abruptly ceased trading after years of operational struggles and bad bets on gold prices.

Analysing Wonga's downfall provides meaningful insights. Knowing which factor contributed more to its demise, lower profits from price caps or regulatory fines is anyone's guess. Wonga never adjusted to the FCA's strict regime. It admitted that its algorithm underwriting standards had lent money to people who could not afford to pay back.[4] It wrote off 330,000 loans and waived interest and fees on an additional 45,000. In 2016, its revenue fell by £146 million and it posted a £64 million loss, half of which came from regulatory fines. This on the heels of £80 million in losses the year before. Making matters worse, the company suffered a major data breach in 2017 impacting 250,000 UK customers.[5] It looked like things might turn for the embattled company in 2018 when investors provided a £10 million emergency investment to stem losses from customer compensation claims over legacy loans (Marriage 2018). Those efforts were not enough and Wonga soon collapsed. Though at first some companies including QuickQuid, Pounds to Pocket, On Stride, Wage Day Advance, Juo Loans and Sunny Loans benefitted from Wonga's demise, their revenue gains were short-lived, and many entered administration (Makortoff 2020).

The 2015 regulations incentivized US-owned Wage Day Advance away from single payday loan towards instalment loan products and small wage guarantor loans under its Juo Loans brand.[6] Its UK single loan product contribution fell from 4% of total revenue in 2015 to 1% 2017. Total UK revenue across all loan categories was $33.7 million for 2016, a decrease of $20.9 million, or a 38.3% decline compared to 2015.[7] Since 2015 it lost money every year at the EBITDA and Net Incomes levels. With provision for loan losses exceeding 43% of revenue, CURO, the parent company of Wage Day Advance and Juo Loans, found profiting in the British market near impossible.[8] Under the weight of affordability complaints and millions of pounds in customer compensation, CURO ceased operations in 2019.

In 2015, US-based Enova derived almost 20% or $142 million of its revenue from UK operating subsidiaries QuickQuid, Pounds to Pocket and On Stride.[9] This result was dramatically lower than its 2014 UK revenue of $335 million. New regulations forced the company to change its affordability assessment and underwriting standards, leading to lower loan volumes and less aggressive debt collection techniques.[10] A short-lived revenue bump after Wonga's decline wasn't enough to save the company and by October 2019 the UK's third largest lender with 25% market share and 1 million customers closed its doors. Only months before in June, the second largest lender, the Money Shop had too.

At the 2013 market peak, over 400 firms had issued 10 million loans valued at £2.5 billion to 1.6 million customers.[11] By 2018, loan volume had near halved to 5.4 million as had their value to £1.3 billion a year issued by only eighty-eight firms. The average loan amount increased to £284 in 2018 from £260 in 2012. Price controls drove up average loan sizes as payday lenders could no longer profitably service smaller loans. The loan duration also increased from 30 days in 2012–2013 to 80 days in 2015 (Edmonds 2018). The geographic distribution of loans remains little change from the Victorian era as depicted by Fig.2.1. From July 2017–June 2018, the North West, North East and London had the highest concentration of loans per 1,000 person and the South West and Northern Ireland tallied the lowest. This speaks volumes about long-term structural poverty and small-loan demand (Gregory et al. 2000).

Borrower statistics are also relatively consistent compared to pre-FCA regulation. The bulk of payday loan borrowers, 59%, are 25–44 years old, which is far higher than their share of the total UK population at 38%.[12] The average payday loan user took out almost five loans per year with 60% taking out three or fewer.[13] In total, 14.6% of UK adults are considered over-indebted, compared to 67.3% of payday loan borrowers. While low-income households are less likely to use consumer credit compared to higher-income households, when they do they are more likely to use high-cost providers (Davies et al. 2019). Even users of retail finance have better credit profiles than high-cost credit users. The 2016 median retail finance credit score was sixty-nine compared to forty-two for high-cost credit users.[14]

High-cost credit borrowers earn between £18,000–£31,000 annually, with most averaging between £20,400–£25,000, which is below the UK median of £28,400.[15] Those number conceal the fact that 40% of the working-age population have less than £100 pounds in savings (Russell 2019).[16] A large percentage of the British population have almost no financial buffer. The household savings ratio has declined from 13.2% in 1997 to 6.2% in the fourth quarter of 2019. This is why over 3 million adults, or 6% of the UK population, have or had a high-cost loan in the past twelve months.[17] Several highly-reliable data confirm that low-income households use high-cost credit to pay household bills (Davies et al. 2019, p. 7; Bow 2017).[18] Estimates suggest that 70–77% of payday loans are taken out for everyday living expenses including food. Income shocks drive borrowers towards high-cost credit. Often, these consumption-smoothing loans are spent on essential needs (Dobridge 2018).[19]

Millions of British adults have saved little and millions of loans once available from payday lenders have vanished under the weight of the FCA's affordability requirements, price controls and rollover limits. Are those vulnerable and marginal borrowers better off without a payday loan? Have consumers benefitted from the price caps? Before the price caps took hold, reformers insisted that a smaller and better regulated market benefitted both marginal and qualified small-loan borrowers. The former was better off without a loan, and the latter gained from lowered pricing and enhanced regulatory compliance. Detractors argued that payday lenders were a necessary, albeit most unwelcomed financial provider. High-cost providers, they argue, fulfil a market need without which borrowers face worse alternatives such as missed bill payments.

The FCA's regulatory impact on the small-loan market is mixed. The FCA found that loans are less expensive, and that firms are less likely to lend to customers who cannot afford repayment.[20] Before the cap borrowers paid over £100 per loan. The cap drove that cost down to £60, saving approximately £150 million for 760,000 borrowers. Table 6.1 illustrates the average revenue per loan before and after the cap.

While with the rise of instalment loans technical defaults increased owing to one missed payment, overall defaults decreased suggesting that repayment issues were temporary in nature. It is too soon to know whether longer-term instalment loans help or harm consumers. The FCA also found no negative consequence for marginal borrowers turned down for a payday loan. The main determinant of harm depended on whether a

Table 6.1 Pre- and post-cap average revenue per loan

Revenue source	*2013*	*2016*
Contract interest	£70	£50
% of loans with rollover or early lending	28%	10%
Rollover or early relending revenue	£32	£8
Late fees	£8	£2
Average revenue per loan	£110	£60

Source "High–cost Credit: Including Review of the High-cost Short-term Credit Price Cap," Financial Conduct Authority FS 17/2, July 2017

borrower or rejected applicant experienced a negative credit report event within twelve months of the application or loan. There was no significant rise in illegal lending or increased use of other high-cost products nor are lenders avoiding the cap through creative product structures.

The profile of denied applicants reveals much about marginal low-income households. Denied applicants are more likely to be female, receive government benefits, less likely to work full time and have lower incomes (£15,900) than accepted borrowers of £20,400.[21] While the share of denied and accepted applicants with absolutely no savings is the same, denied applicants with savings have £117, which is 33% less than approved applications. Twenty-two percent of denied applicants were falling behind on bills. The FCA found no evidence that this group experienced a continued trajectory of increased debts resulting from their inability to take out a payday loan. Of the 40% of denied applicants seeking out funds, only 15% went on to take out formal credit. Many obtained funds from family and friends. Less than 1% actually missed a bill payment. A majority of 63% believed they were in a better position having been denied a payday loan.

Those borrowers able to take out a payday loan owe debts to all sorts of companies. Table 6.2 depicts the web of debt held by low-income households. The top three categories are credit card, current account overdraft and telecommunication debt.

Since approved borrowers utilize so many credit products it is hard to believe that those unable to access payday loans manage without any credit whatsoever. The FCA's findings conflict with research on the American market which finds that payday loan bans led to an increase in supply of other high-cost credit providers and especially pawnbrokers (Ramirez

Table 6.2 Debt held by high-cost credit borrowers as of November 2016

Catalogue credit	32%
Retail finance	8%
Store card	7%
Home credit	15%
Rent-to-own	4%
Other running account	9%
Guarantor loan	4%
Logbook loan	<1%
Mortgage	9%
Credit card	57%
Overdraft	50%
Charge card	<1%
Unsecured personal loan	29%
Motor finance	12%
Telecommunications	41%
Other household bills	10%

Source "High-cost Credit: Including Review," FCA, July 2017, 16. Data as a per cent of consumers taking out product December 2015–November 2016

Table 6.3 Other credit usage in same period as denied payday loan

42%	Had used credit cards
35%	Had used an overdraft
26%	Had borrowed from doorstep lenders
14%	Had used catalogue or online retail credit
12%	Had turned to pawnbrokers
12%	Purchased goods through rent-to-own stores

Source "Payday Loans After the Cap," Citizens Advice, August 2016, 23

2019). Unlike the FCA, Citizens Advice finds that nearly half of denied applicants missed payment on a household bill or priority debts and 35% sold an item to raise cash.[22] A similar study found that 27% of approved payday loan applicants would have gone without an essential if not for the loan.[23] Decreased levels of consumer credit as a percentage of all debt issuance led to higher levels of missed priority debt payments.[24] Table 6.3 shows the type of credit products that denied applicants received during the same period as their unsuccessful application.

While consumer issues related to payday loans have fallen, debt advice services report a significant rise in problems related to rent arrears, telephone, energy and water bills, and council taxes.[25] Only 22% felt they were better off financially, while 37% felt they were worse off without a payday loan.[26] A leading community development finance association speaks of a 'credit desert' resultant from the crackdown on payday lenders (Gregory and Hughes 2014). Untangling and assigning weight to how much of these changes resulted from market regulation, as opposed to continued struggles with inadequate income and welfare reform is near impossible.

Where there is agreement: approved borrowers are paying less for payday loans. Moreover, the majority of the revenue comes from interest payments which are restricted by the price cap.[27] Lenders rely less on roll-overs, late fees or loan extensions. Profits and loan volumes have fallen and far fewer lenders participate in the market. A portion of the highest-risk borrowers are segmented out of the market. According to the FCA, the loan acceptance rate fell from 50% pre-cap to 30% after implementation. The FCA periodically reviews the cap levels, and although the market contracted further than initially projected, it left the price controls at the 2015 level. It might have to revisit that decision, as its deliberations concluded before some of the early price survivors had exited the market.

Until recently, the pawn landscape was not radically different from its composition before the 2007 Global Financial Crisis. In 2018, 290 firms earned £125 million in revenue operating just over 1,050 shops which lent £300 million annually to approximately 350,000 customers.[28] Since 2005, the industry added approximately 200 shops while industry-wide revenue and APRs remained relatively consistent. These results were driven by the seven firms commanding 80% of the market. The two largest were H&T and Albemarle & Bond. Table 6.4 depicts an average pawnbroker based on the FCA's 2018 sector investigation. The 1970s trend towards multi-locations has continued. Even with increased Internet business, with twenty-three staff per pawnbroker, the model remained salary heavy as in the old Victorian days. Their 6% profit margin is remarkably

Table 6.4 Average pawnbroker in 2018

Trading since 2008	5,400 loans per year
23 members of staff	£300 average loan
Operates 4 stores	£2,000 maximum loan
£1.5 million in revenue	Advance rate 50%
£100,000 in profit	120% APR

Source "Pawnbroking Sector Review," FCA, 10 July 2018

similar to the average 5% return on invested capital earned by Victorian pawnbrokers. For what it is worth, this may indicate a long-term efficient and competitive market. The shift from pawning everyday essentials to gold and jewellery did not provide a profit windfall for pawnbrokers.

In many ways, the twists and turns of Albemarle & Bond's story mirror that of the entire high-cost credit sector. At one moment, some of the biggest firms were flush with cash only to see profits vanish. While the growth of payday loans occurred at the expense of pawnbrokers, certain businesses dabbled in both business lines—a decision they came to regret. At the time of its 2014 administration filing, the Albemarle & Bond group operated 183 shops serving over 100,000 customers and employed 900 staff.[29] From 2012–2013, profit fell from £15.7 to £3.5 million. The fall resulted from a decline in gold prices and increased competition in secured and unsecured lending. Its woes had little to do with the ancient practices of pawning. Instead of advancing cash based on pledged collateral, senior managers pivoted towards outright purchases of gold, unsecured lending, and borrowed heavily for new store acquisition (Burgess 2014). With gold prices falling 28%, its asset base diminished and revenue from gold sales dwindled, paying their debtors grew increasingly problematic. The allure of higher profits led the company away from the low margin but steady pawnbroking business.

After a failed turnaround plan, Japanese pawnbroker Speedloan Finance purchased the group in 2014. Profitability worsened in the coming years with the group's 116 stores losing £11.4 million in 2015 and its 114 stores lost £3.6 million in 2016.[30] Its pawn book was worth £15.6 million, which is not dramatically different from its 2006 value of £11 million. After 2016, having jettisoned unsecured lending, the chain focused on pawn and auxiliary services including jewellery buying, cheque cashing, foreign currency exchange and money transfers. Reduced overheads and conservative lending practices stemmed losses during the period. Still, regulatory uncertainty and heightened competition for small-loan customers inhibited a return to profitability. Operational struggles continued into 2018 and the business collapsed in 2019 when losses approached £11 million.[31] Panicked customers of their 116 closed shops wondered the fate of their pledged goods. Overtures to the company from the NPA fell on deaf ears (Hall 2019). Chaotic store closures and mass firings of employees left customers 'sick to their stomachs' by the sudden collapse (Hadfield 2019). Unable to secure the return of her family heirlooms, a Liverpool woman was left in tears. Like

Mrs Vincent in Chapter 2, she had pawned for much-needed cash to help her ill husband.

She and others were relieved when H&T Group, with its 248 shops spread across the UK, purchased Albemarle & Bond's £8 million pledge book and guaranteed return of pledged item (Butler 2019).[32] Shortly before, H&T had acquired sixty-five stores and twenty-nine pledge books from another failed lender and pawnbroker, the Money Shop. With its £72 million pledge book and 252 stores, H&T actually distributed profits of 11.7p in dividends per share. A major factor in driving profits is their centralized collateral review process. Expert Eye technology transmits high-quality images to remotely stationed experts. According to the company, the technology and centralized expertise improves the quality of decisions and extends the type of accepted assets. Nor was their good fortune at the expense of consumers, as the company complied with the FCA's affordability and creditworthiness assessments. H&T did suspend unsecured lending and has worked with the FCA to improve borrower assessment methods. The company assured investors and customers that its core business would remain pawnbroking.

Though the FCA found little substitutability between products, pawnbrokers regularly cite significant competition from payday lenders and other credit providers. On the other hand, Albemarle & Bond's demise and H&T's troubles with unsecured lending were unrelated to the traditional business of pawnbroking. Even with its Victorian heyday long since passed, perhaps the old-fashion pawn model augmented by modern technology will survive after all.

Financial Inclusion Policy Developments

By most accounts official financial exclusion policy dates to the 1999 founding of the Policy Action Team of the government's Social Exclusion Unit. This and related efforts led to a Basic Bank Account programme and a financial inclusion taskforce, which ran from 2005 until its disbandment in 2011. Financial firms, charities and policymakers bemoaned the loss of the Treasury led government body and the related £130 million Financial Inclusion Fund. Both demonstrated a clear degree of priority for the financial inclusion agenda. In 2016, the House of Lords Select Committee on Financial Exclusion was appointed to consider access to financial services with a broad remit of understanding the social and economic implications of exclusion. The report's eight chapters were organized around three topical areas including increased access to banking, accessing affordable credit and improved access to financial advice. Focal points included reanimating the government's coordination efforts, proactive FCA regulation, and individual and private sector capacity building.

Those on low incomes and living in poverty remain at high risk of financial exclusion.[33] Other population groups include the elderly and disabled persons, and, with an estimated 40% of persons age 25–35 having been turned down for credit in the past twelve months, young people are not immune from exclusionary risk either. The growing divide between those with digital access and those without also warrants special attention. The issue is all the more pressing since 53% of bank branches have closed from 1989–2016, with rural and poor areas especially hard hit. Those geographies also tend to have less reliable Internet access. Financial exclusion impacts people from all walks of life. Many still lack basic, safe and affordable financial services inhibiting them from participating fully in modern society, or they meet unexpected expenses.

Even after decades of regulatory and voluntary efforts, the financially excluded pay a 'poverty premium' for the acquisition of goods and services. From pay-as-you-go mobile service to insurance products, inadequate financial services leave the poor paying more. Estimates suggest that in 2016, an average low-income household paid a poverty premium approaching £500.[34] In the late nineteenth and early twentieth centuries, certain policymakers blamed the poor for their lot in life. Many believed government policy could counter, if not, correct their immoral and frivolous ways. By 2016, much of the thinking on poverty had changed, and the select committee believed that causes of financial exclusion were clear, 'free markets do not always serve the financial needs of these consumers effectively'.[35]

In a January 2017 speech entitled 'The shared society', Prime Minister Theresa May argued that while a prosperous society requires the supportive role of government towards free markets, so too the government must 'repair' markets when they are not 'functioning as they should'.[36] The select committee provided a host of remedies for the persistent 'injustices' of financial exclusion and in support of the government's goal of 'delivering a fairer society'. As seen during the FCA's implementation of price controls, concepts of fairness and justice framed a government corrective of the market. The overt recognition, if not criticism, that markets fail low-income consumers is a meaningful and significant evolution in financial inclusion policy and is in line with the rationale behind the FCA's aggressive regulation of high-cost credit.

Despite the FCA's sweeping powers, implementing financial inclusion policy is outside of its statutory remit of market regulation.[37] Certain policymakers want the FCA to require inclusionary and duty of care requirements under its consumer protection mandate.[38] The select committee supports the FCA's legal basis both as a way to change market behaviour, and to provide political cover for anticipated push back from financial institutions (Wilson and Barker 2003). Even so, advancing financial inclusion requires a multi-stakeholder approach of which regulation plays only one part.

Banks, Credit Unions and Community Development Financial Institutions

Reliable and low-cost transaction services through the standard banking system is a critical step towards financial inclusion. Great strides have been made by the government and private banks since efforts began in the mid-1990s—now more people than ever have a basic current account with a mainstream bank. Millions of people have opened accounts based on industry agreements with the government and in compliance with the European Union Payment Accounts Directive. As the needs of low-income households evolve, banks have adjusted their basic product offerings.[39] Despite this progress, barriers to entry still keep many low-income persons from obtaining current accounts.

Many front-line bank staff are unaware of the accounts and those that are sometimes lack knowledge of the eligibility requirements. These conditions likely stem from low levels of internal and external advertisement and promotion. Basic economics plays a part too. The British Bankers Association estimates that basic accounts cost the industry between £300 and £350 million per year. These costs are borne by the banks servicing such accounts, and the distribution between banks is highly uneven. Barclays, Lloyds and the Co-operative Bank shoulder much more of the burden than some of their competitors, some of whom do not offer basic accounts. The Co-operative estimates that 20% of all of their current accounts are basic.[40] Despite these challenges, that a number of major banks treat the loss-making product as a societal commitment is a far cry from early decades when the mere idea of banking low-income households was unimaginable.

Other barriers are more easily addressed, such as personal identification requirements under anti-money laundering laws. Many of the financially excluded lack suitable identification or the documents they do have are met with scepticism by front-line bank employees. Certain electronic verification procedures and an expansion of suitable forms of identification would go a long way towards a more efficient and secure system. Efficiencies, however, also present the more inextricable problem of branch closures. As of 2014, with 180 branches per million persons, the UK had much lower concentration levels than Spain's 718 and Germany's 521 branches per million.[41] While chastising banks for closures is rather easy, the fact is that many of the now closed branches serviced a shockingly low number of customer transactions, often between 50 and 100 a week.[42] It would be unreasonable to expect a bank to keep a branch open under such conditions. From banks to payday lenders, economic fundamentals and profit motives are not so easily cast aside.

Less ambiguous is the cost of unarranged overdrafts. According to the FCA, in 2017 firms generated £2.4 billion in revenue from overdrafts, £720 million or about 30% were unarranged.[43] More than half of that £720 million came from 1.5% of its customer base. Vulnerable people in deprived areas were most impacted by these charges, some of whom were paid upwards of ten times the cost of payday lenders. Since most overdrafts result from standing payments such as utilities, council tax and rent, this is a similar, if not the same market, as payday lenders.[44] The frequency of usage also resembles the pre-price cap payday loan market. Between 30 and 65% of unarranged users 'went over' fifteen times during the prior twenty four months.[45] Like payday loans and pawn, the sums borrowed are small and relatively expensive, as most unarranged borrowing is for less than £50. At the typical £5 a day fee this equates to 10% the amount borrowed vs. the payday loan cap of 0.8% a day or 40p on a £50 loan.

With its small sums, high-cost and frequent usage, the product draws much criticism. Many urged the FCA to include overdrafts within its price cap system. Like the payday loan market, the FCA used its powers to collect data and undertook a wide-reaching study of overdrafts. It studied millions of transactions spanning six of the largest UK banks. Published in 2018, the 'High-cost Credit Review – Update' provided much of the data above. In April 2020, the FCA implemented reforms aimed at simplifying and limiting charges. Firms are compelled to use a simple annual interest rate and charge no addition fees. For example, an unarranged £100 overdraft outstanding for seven days from NatWest Select accounts would see charges drop from £56 to 65 pence and HSBC Advance accounts would see charges drop from £35 to 65 pence. While lowering prices is helpful, like the payday loan price cap, some borrowers will be segmented out of the market and it is unclear where those borrowers will turn for much-needed cash. Since a portion of unarranged overdrafts result from being turned down for a payday loan, certain borrowers may find themselves with even fewer credit options.[46]

When it comes to financial inclusion, mainstream banks present a mixed record. Certainly, unarranged overdrafts were expensive. It is too early to know how the new regulation will impact bank's willingness to offer unarranged overdrafts to higher risk borrows. On the positive side, banks have made headway in improving access to basic current accounts. There is no doubt that many millions of low-income consumers benefit from these low-to-no fee accounts. Accessing transactional services removes a significant financial exclusionary barrier. These accounts are a major historical reversal of an industry that ignored the many millions living on insufficient incomes and irregular employment. Further promotion of these accounts will reduce the number of unbanked. Still, challenges remain. Stemming the tide of physical branch closures is likely beyond any government programme. Even with advancing digital technology, banks maintain high fixed costs and for the most part cater to customers with a higher deposit base than low-income customers can reasonably maintain. Providing basic current accounts is a money losing activity. Short of a radical change in their cost structure and a complete adjust to their business model, that dynamic will not likely change. This presents a difficult situation, how much financial loss should the banking sector bear in pursuit of societal goals? Can other financial institutions more efficiently and effectively provide transactional services and increase affordable credit options to the financially excluded.

One such institution, credit unions, has long been touted as the remedy against high-cost credit providers and vehicles for widespread financial exclusion. Their failure in achieving those ends are well documented (O'Connell 2005; Berthoud and Hinton 1989; Jones 1999, 2006, 2008; Drakeford 2002; McKillop et al. 2007, 2011; Goth et al. 2006; Gregory and Drakeford 2011). Credit unions are self-help, non-profit, co-operative financial institutions (McKillop et al. 2011). Perhaps their most distinctive feature is their restrictive membership to those persons sharing a local 'common bond', typically through geographic, communal or employment concerns. They are membership-driven savings and loan institutions and are prohibited from providing services to the general public. Traditionally, volunteer-run, community-based credit unions provided low-cost credit options capped at 1 per cent monthly in areas underserved by banks. Members are permitted to make loan application after a defined period of savings contribution. Supported by the 1979 Credit Union Act, the sector began growing in the 1980s, as volunteers across Britain opened credit unions in support of the poor and financially excluded (Jones 1999). In the mid-1990s, there were ninety-four credit unions and that number reached 700 by 2000, the supermajority of which provided financial services to disadvantaged and excluded persons in low-income neighbourhoods (Jones 2006, 2008).

Despite the growth in the number of credit unions, their overall market impact was limited. Average membership hovered around 200, and all but four of them were financial failures (Jones 2008, p. 2142). The critiques were many. A host of researchers questioned whether linking credit unions with poverty reduction could ever work (O'Connell 2005; McKillop et al. 2007). Even as non-profits supported by government subsidies, it was hard to imagine how financial institutions serving the poor with a limited deposit base could impact the community and generate sustainable financial returns. An all too familiar dynamic was at play, whether analysing payday loans or credit unions: there is very little money in poor communities. From basic current accounts to lending small sums, providing financial services to low-income communities is expensive.

These realities were met with reform efforts which included public investment and easing of regulatory restrictions. Credit unions also shifted towards a business model characterized by expanded membership, professional managers, financial sustainability and national scale. The issue was not the social mission or target market, but the organizational structure and narrowed product focus of Britain's credit unions (Jones 2006, 2008). Where the original credit union movement provided low-cost credit options, later reforms focused on asset building and savings schemes. This shift is seen as moving from a focus on poverty reduction through better lending terms to a broad-based financial inclusion strategy.

Once again, the financial inclusion agenda framed the path forward. The Treasury identified a modernized credit union sector as a primary vehicle for reducing financial exclusion.[47] Whether that path was and remains the appropriate strategy is debated (Gregory and Drakeford

2011; Sinclair 2014). One camp argues that the financial inclusion movement and regulatory updates sparked a growth in credit unions and has enhanced their sustainability (Jones 2008; Ryder 2009). Regulatory updates included permission to charge up to 3% monthly (42.6% APR) on loans, an expansion in the definition of common bonds and removing limits on dividend payments to members. While assets, loans outstanding and membership have grown since 2010, British credit unions have not penetrated the market anywhere near levels needed to transform the financial fortunes of low-income households.[48] In Britain, credit unions provide services to just over 4.3% of the population compared to 55% in the United States. After decades of disappointment, some argue that the current model can never serve the poor in a sustainable manner (McKillop et al. 2011; McKillop and Wilson 2003). Requiring minimal savings contributions before qualifying for a loan and concentrating on poor neighbourhoods minimizes the ability to attract a diversified membership. Long-term sustainability requires competing with traditional banks and an expansive model beyond financial inclusion, only then will membership increase and lessen stigmas associated with joining 'poor person' banks (Gregory and Drakeford 2011).

The twin-track reform of credit unions to serve poor communities while operating under professional management fostering sustainable practices is a difficult, if not impossible, task. Government funding to credit unions in support of new members unable to meet the pre-loan savings requirements have helped, but over the long term the industry needs to create a profitable model without public monies.[49] With decades of lacklustre market penetration, many still feel that focusing on diversified business practices within poorer communities remains the best hope for the credit union movement.[50] For the House of Lords Select Committee on Financial Exclusion, the answer was increased government funding and expanded product offerings. Other stressed the importance of long-term patient capital alongside customer deposits and grant programmes.[51] Several witnesses suggested automatic 'jam-jarring' schemes would help low-income households increase their savings. The Centre for Responsible Credit advises a model based on the United States Community Reinvestment Act that requires banks to fund and support third-sector lenders such as credit unions.

The British credit union movement was a grass-roots activist model to help alleviate poverty and encourage self-help solutions to local community problems. At first, providing low-cost credit to low-income communities was a top priority. As the financial inclusion agenda evolved, credit unions widened their mission. Though the reformed model is controversial, mainstream research finds that they remain the best placed financial institution to serve low-income communities (Jones 2008). As it has for decades, the long-hoped-for holy grail of providing financial products that poor households need while also serving customers with larger deposits seems just within reach. Perhaps recent recommendations suggesting the government invest with long-term capital rather than grants will help credit unions operate sustainably. Optimism aside, the record is clear: credit unions have not meaningfully challenged the payday lending sector. Whatever their faults, failures, and drawbacks, of which there are many, payday lenders and moneylenders before them, tailor their products to the unique borrowing needs of low-income households in a way that credit unions have not.

The contraction of the payday lending market has also generated opportunities for Community Development Financial Institutions (CDFIs). These non-profit social enterprises provide affordable and accessible finance to individuals, businesses, and even to other social enterprises that otherwise struggle in obtaining funds from mainstream lenders. They were founded to channel credit to underserved communities for purposes of local economic development and regeneration. Unlike credit unions, they do not have membership requirements or a deposit base. They rely on investment from public and private sector sources. With a higher cost of capital, their lending rates exceed credit unions but are lower than the commercial sector. At present, around seventy CDFIs provided £254 million in personal and small business loans to over 52,100 customers.[52] In 2018, the sector provided 45,903 personal loans worth £26 million, averaging £569 per loan with a 10-month term carrying a 129.45% APR.[53] From 2014–2018, CDFIs averaged a 9.66 % bad debt expense, which is far higher than the 1.6% of all consumer loans written off in 2018. The APR and bad debt rate losses are yet more proof of the expense related to serving low-income and financially struggling communities.

CDFIs are loss-making enterprises and upwards of 80% of their total source funding comes from government grants.[54] CDFIs cannot survive without government grants nor is there an agreed upon path towards long-term sustainability. Perhaps owing to this, studies suggest that there is a mission creep from serving local community social ventures towards lending more broadly to small and medium enterprises (Thiel and Nissan 2008).[55] CDFIs, like their credit union counterparts will continue to struggle to address the conflicting goals of supporting low-income communities and financial sustainability. Based on studies of the American market, there is some agreement that consistent levels of government funding and a legislative framework that incentives private sector investment could spur more CDFI activity. Even so, there is no end in sight for the sector's dependency on government funds.

While credit unions and CDFIs have saved low-incomes households and communities money and alleviated certain financial pressures, neither is financially stable and both are reliant on government funding. Providing affordable and readily accessible finance to low-income communities presents many challenges, doing so profitability has proven impossible. The high-cost credit market is complicated, expensive and risky. Driving existing high-cost providers from the market seems outside the capabilities of banks. Government funds support third-sector lenders, but their operating costs are high, and their lending processes are not totally dissimilar from that of traditional banks. Perhaps only a radically different model, less reliant on taxpayer money and embracive of disruption, can provide affordable finance for small sums borrowers. For the first time in any meaningful way, technology wedded with finance (fintech) may offer low-income borrowers the right balance between product features and price.

Fintech and Innovation

The world of fintech is a wide one, encompassing everything from payment services to health insurance, digital wallets, online banks and brokerages. Modernization of the payment system has received considerable attention and funding. From 2018–2019, global funding for payment services received the most money within the fintech sector jumping from $12 to $15 billion (Kauflin 2020). Many of these companies offer considerable cost savings for businesses reliant on traditional credit and debit card providers. The global upheaval will likely impact almost every aspect of consumer banking too. Like their business-focused peers, these companies have attracted considerable investment and attention. Insights into consumer behaviour from deep data analysis should offer less expensive and more customer-friendly products. Fintechs promise creative solutions to savings, investing and lending. What's less is clear whether low-income consumers will benefit from the fintech revolution.

Unless fintechs offer products that the poor want and need, they will join a playing field littered with failed attempts at circumventing high-cost credit providers. Payday lenders and pawnbrokers generate millions in revenue because they offer services demanded by low-income borrowers. Payroll advance companies believe their product might just offer an appropriate balance between speed, flexibility and cost that could very well displace payday lenders. With 85% of UK workers paid monthly, these companies provide employees with access to their earned wages in-between paycheques (Flinders 2019). Many work through smartphone apps and position themselves as affordable alternatives to high-cost credit. UK-based Wagestream, partners with employers who view the service as a staff retention programme and one way to reduce reliance on payday lenders. Employee funds are distributed through partner banks with Wagestream recouping the money on the next pay cycle. The company charges £1.75 per withdrawal and a £1 monthly service fee per employee. Early data suggests the average user borrows £80 'from themselves' about twice monthly. While the embedded infrastructure of payment methods is hard to change and the compliance and tax costs significant, wage advance companies offer a route to a faster payday.

While many first-generation fintech companies tended to focus on businesses and affluent customers, today's entrants are thinking through ways to serve low income clients. Some consumer advocates are not impressed, arguing that wage advance single balloon repayments too closely resemble the payday loan sector before the 2015 FCA regulations. Others worry that the service encourages a cycle of early spending (Tergesen 2019; Fussell 2019). Whether accelerated pay apps are an innovative alternative or just another predatory financial product is unclear. Fintech companies believe they are addressing the needs of low-income households. While technology may reduce costs and respond to certain of the unique demands of the poor, it may also encourage chronic borrowing and a diminished capacity to meet other financial obligations similar to payday loans. Disruptive fintech companies offering new payment and borrowing platforms may very well be the long-sought solution to helping the poor achieve better financial outcomes. At some point, policymakers will decide whether fintechs are appropriately and fairly serving low-income households, until then experimentation and innovation offer the best hope for solving the historically intractable problem of banking the poor (Chambers et al. 2020).

Conclusion

Lending to poor people is expensive. While banks, credit unions and CDFIs offer financial products to low-income households, they do so at a considerable loss. Though large financial institutions offer basic current accounts, they are a 'million miles away from being able to offer' a small sum, short-term loan product (Lane and Rodrigues 2016). A lending model reliant on a substantial deposit base, almost by definition, excludes low-income households. Similarly, lending small sums will never cover the high fixed costs associated with traditional bank loans. Even if one day a public-private partnership solves the sustainability conundrum, lending to people experiencing financial difficulties carries great reputational risk and niche operational procedures that are hardly worth the trouble for the likes of NatWest and Barclays.

Regulation and the financial inclusion agenda have gone a long way in shaping the provision of basic banking facilities, its impact on lending is less impressive. Predatory behaviour, bad decisions and regulatory burdens drove many payday lenders and pawnbrokers from the market. While on the one hand the exodus created an opportunity ripe for credit unions and CDFIs to fill the void, the laws of basic economics remain at play. Without government subsidies or a completely new way of pricing, allocating and collecting debts, lending small sums to poor people remains an expensive affair. The jury is out on whether technology companies can offer affordable products and do so sustainably.

It is unclear if the private markets can ever reasonably satisfy the demands of the financial inclusion agenda and anti-debt advocates. Despite the success of price controls in bringing down loan costs and forcing a market contraction, providing a clear answer as to what financial inclusion means for poor borrowers, and, more directly, what should reasonable profits look like for fintechs is a social objective determined by policymakers. History demonstrates that policymakers have spent far more time concentrating on altering the supply of credit without due consideration for the underlying factors impacting the demand for small sums in the first instance. If fintech lenders profitability and sustainably reduce costs for low-income borrowers, there is nothing stopping policymakers from targeting them. However politically fraught, limiting the profits of private companies is far easier than solving the complexities of poverty and low incomes. How much more effective would policy be if it engaged both the supply and demand sides simultaneously? Britain has avoided this question thus far.

Notes

1. "Sector Views," Financial Conduct Authority, 9 April 2018, 16.
2. "Pawn Sector Review," Financial Conduct Authority, 10 July 2018; "Consumer Credit – High-cost Short-term Credit Lending Data," Financial Conduct Authority, 24 January 2019.
3. "Consumer Credit – High-cost," Financial Conduct Authority, 24 January 2019; "Sector Views," Financial Conduct Authority, 9 April 2018, 24.
4. "Post Wonga Collapse, FCA Scrutinizes Payday Lenders," *PYMTS Alternative Finance*, 16 October 2018.
5. "Why Wonga," *PYMTS Alternative Finance*, 4 September 2018.
6. "Annual Report," CURO Group, 2018, 10.
7. "Annual Report," CURO Group, 2016, 81.
8. "Annual Report," CURO Group, 2018, 61.
9. "Annual Report," Enova International, 2015, 1.
10. "Annual Report," Enova International, 2015, 5, 17.
11. "Proposals for a Price Cap on High-cost Short-term Credit: Consultation Paper," Financial Conduct Authority CP 14/10, July 2014.
12. "Consumer Credit – High-cost Short-term Credit Lending Data," Financial Conduct Authority, 24 January 2019.
13. "High-cost Credit: Including Review of the High-cost Short-term Credit Price Cap," Financial Conduct Authority FS 17/2, July 2017, 13–14.
14. "High Cost Credit Review Technical Annex 1," Financial Conduct Authority, July 2017.
15. "Annual Report," CURO Group, 2018, 5 and 8.
16. "Tackling Financial Exclusion: A Country that Works for Everyone?" HL Select Committee on Financial Exclusion Report of 2016–17 Session, HL Paper 132, 25 March 2017, 15.
17. "The Financial Lives of Consumers Across the UK," Financial Conduct Authority, 20 June 2018, updated January 2020, 62.
18. "High-cost Credit: Including Review," Financial Conduct Authority, FS 17/2, July 2017, 13–14; "Tackling Financial Exclusion," HL Paper, 25 March 2017, 15.
19. For an econometric treatment of consumption smoothing and high-cost credit, see (Dobridge 2018).
20. "High–cost Credit: Including Review of the High-cost Short-term Credit Price Cap," Financial Conduct Authority FS 17/2, July 2017, 4–5, 10–14.

21. "High-cost Credit: Including Review of the High-cost Short-term Credit Price Cap," Financial Conduct Authority FS 17/2, July 2017, 17.
22. "Payday Loans After the Cap," Citizens Advice, August 2016, 4, 24.
23. "A Modern Credit Revolution: An Analysis of the Short-term Credit Market," Social Market Foundation on Behalf of the Consumer Finance Association, 2016.
24. "Citizens Advice Impact Report 2015/16," Citizens Advice, 2016.
25. "Tackling Financial Exclusion: A Country that Works for Everyone?" HL Select Committee on Financial Exclusion Report of 2016–17 Session, HL Paper 132, 25 March 2017, 41.
26. "Payday Loans After the Cap," Citizens Advice, August 2016, 28.
27. "Impact of Regulation on High Cost Short Term Credit: How the Functioning of the HCSTC Market has Evolved," Consumer Finance Association, March 2017, 2.
28. "Pawnbroking Sector Review," Financial Conduct Authority, 10 July 2018.
29. "Joint Administrators," Albemarle & Bond Holdings – in Administration High Court of Justice, Chancery Division, Companies Court Case No. 2321 of 2014, 23 October 2014.
30. "Annual Report," Speedloan Finance Limited, 2016.
31. "Annual Report," Speedloan Finance Limited, 2019.
32. "Annual Report," H&T Group, 2019.
33. "Tackling Financial Exclusion: A Country that Works for Everyone?" HL Select Committee on Financial Exclusion Report of 2016–17 Session, HL Paper 132, 25 March 2017, 14, 19.
34. "Making the Poverty Premium History," Personal Finance Research Centre, the University of Bristol, November 2017.
35. "Tackling Financial Exclusion: A Country that Works for Everyone?" HL Select Committee on Financial Exclusion Report of 2016–17 Session, HL Paper 132, 25 March 2017, 9–10.
36. "Tackling Financial Exclusion: A Country that Works for Everyone?" HL Select Committee on Financial Exclusion Report of 2016–17 Session, HL Paper 132, 25 March 2017, 9–10.
37. "Access to Financial Services in the UK," FCA, May 2016, 58–59.
38. "Tackling Financial Exclusion: A Country that Works for Everyone?" HL Select Committee on Financial Exclusion Report of 2016–17 Session, HL Paper 132, 25 March 2017, 30–31.
39. "Tackling Financial Exclusion: A Country that Works for Everyone?" HL Select Committee on Financial Exclusion Report of 2016–17 Session, HL Paper 132, 25 March 2017, 57.
40. "Tackling Financial Exclusion: A Country that Works for Everyone?" HL Select Committee on Financial Exclusion Report of 2016–17 Session, HL Paper 132, 25 March 2017, 58.

41. "Need a Bank Branch? Then Head to Europe," This Money, 25 February 2015.
42. "Tackling Financial Exclusion: A Country that Works for Everyone?" HL Select Committee on Financial Exclusion Report of 2016–17 Session, HL Paper 132, 25 March 2017, 63.
43. "FCA Confirms Biggest Shake-up to the Overdraft Market for a Generation," FCA, 7 June 2019.
44. "Tackling Financial Exclusion: A Country that Works for Everyone?" HL Select Committee on Financial Exclusion Report of 2016–17 Session, HL Paper 132, 25 March 2017, 74.
45. 'High-cost Credit Review – Update," Financial Conduct Authority, January 2018, 6.
46. "Tackling Financial Exclusion: A Country that Works for Everyone?" HL Select Committee on Financial Exclusion Report of 2016–17 Session, HL Paper 132, 25 March 2017, 74.
47. "Access to Financial Services," Report of the Policy Action Team 14 Social Exclusion Unit, HM Treasury, November 1999.
48. 2018 Statistical Report World Council of Credit Unions, *Association of British Credit Unions*.
49. The Financial Inclusion Growth Fund was part the government's strategy as outlined in *Promoting Financial Inclusion*, 2004. Other programs have followed since, including £38 million of new funding in 2012 under the Credit Union Expansion Project established by the Department for Work and Pensions.
50. The government reiterated its support in its 2014 Treasury publication, "British credit unions at 50: response to the call for evidence."
51. "Tackling Financial Exclusion: A Country that Works for Everyone?" HL Select Committee on Financial Exclusion Report of 2016–17 Session, HL Paper 132, 25 March 2017, 84.
52. "Annual Report," Responsible Finance, 2018.
53. "Annual Report," Responsible Finance, 2018, 28–29, 32; Consumer Lending in the UK, Statistica, 2020.
54. "The Sustainability of Community Development Financial Institutions," *PWC*, December 2015.
55. "The Sustainability of Community Development Financial Institutions," *PWC*, December 2015.

Bibliography

2018 Statistical Report World Council of Credit Unions. *Association of British Credit Unions.*

"A Modern Credit Revolution: An Analysis of the Short-term Credit Market." 2016. Social Market Foundation on Behalf of the Consumer Finance Association.

"Access to Financial Services." 1999. Report of the Policy Action Team 14 Social Exclusion Unit. HM Treasury, November.

"Access to Financial Services in the UK." 2016. Financial Conduct Authority, May.

"Annual Report." 2016. CURO Group.

"Annual Report." 2018. CURO Group.

"Annual Report." 2015. Enova International.

"Annual Report." 2019. H&T Group.

"Annual Report." 2018. Responsible Finance.

Berthoud, Richard, and Teresa Hinton. 1989. *Credit Unions in the United Kingdom.* London: Policy Studies Institute.

Bow, Michael. 2017. "The FCA Killed Payday Loans But What Followed Could Be Just as Bad for Borrowers." *Evening Standard*, March 14.

Burgess, Kate. 2014. "New Albemarle & Bond Owners Bank on Tradition." *Financial Times*, April 20.

Butler, Sarah. 2019. "Albemarle & Bond Pledge Book Bought by Rival Pawnbroker." *Guardian*, September 30.

Chambers, David, Rasheed Saleuddin, and Craig McMahon. 2020. "Innovations in Alternative Finance in Historical Perspective." In *Palgrave Handbook of Technology Finance*, edited by Raghavendra Rau and Robert Wardrop. London: Palgrave Macmillan.

"Citizens Advice Impact Report 2015/16." 2016. Citizens Advice.

"Consumer Credit – High-cost Short-term Credit Lending Data." 2019. Financial Conduct Authority, January 24.

"Consumer Lending in the UK." 2020. Statistica.

Davies, Sara, Andrea Finney, Sharon Collard, and Lorna Trend. 2019. "Borrowing Behaviour." Personal Finance Research Centre, the University of Bristol on behalf of the Standard Life Foundation, August.

Dobridge, Christine. 2018. "High-Cost Credit and Consumption Smoothing." *Journal of Money, Credit and Banking* 50 (2–3): 407–33.

Drakeford, Mark. 2002. "Co-ordinating Policies and Powers to Reduce Social Exclusion: The Welsh Approach to Credit Union Development." *The Wales Law Journal* 1 (3): 246–55.

Edmonds, Tim. 2018. "High-cost Consumer Credit: The New Regulatory Regime." House of Commons Library CBP–07978, May 31.

"FCA Confirms Biggest Shake-up to the Overdraft Market for a Generation." 2019. Financial Conduct Authority, June 7.

Flinders, Karl. 2019. "Wagestream Gives Staff Alternative to Payday Lenders: Fintech 30." *ComputerWeekly*, November 13.

Fussell, Sidney. 2019. "The New Payday Lender Looks a Lot Like the Old Payday Lender." *Atlantic*, December 18.

Gregory, Dan, and Ben Hughes. 2014. "Just Finance." *cdfa*.

Gregory, Ian, Humphrey Southall, and Daniel Dorling. 2000. "A Century of Poverty in England and Wales, 1898–1998: A Geographical Analysis." In *Researching Poverty*, edited by Jonathan Bradshaw and Roy Sainsbury, Chapter 7. London: Routledge.

Gregory, Lee, and Mark Drakeford. 2011. "Just Another Financial Institution? Tensions in the Future of Credit Unions in the United Kingdom." *Journal of Poverty and Social Justice* 19 (2): 117–29.

Goth, Peter, Donal McKillop, and Charles Ferguson. 2006. *Building Better Credit Unions*. Bristol: The Policy Press.

Hall, Archie. 2019. "Albemarle & Bond Pawnbrokers Cease Trading." *Financial Times*, September 13.

Hadfield, Charlotte. 2019. "Families Sick to Their Stomachs by 'Sudden Closure' of 100 Pawnbroker Shops." *Liverpool Echo*, September 14.

"High-cost Credit: Including Review of the High-cost Short-term Credit Price Cap." Financial Conduct Authority, FS 17/2, July 2017.

"High Cost Credit Review Technical Annex 1," Financial Conduct Authority, July 2017.

"Impact of Regulation on High Cost Short Term Credit: How the Functioning of the HCSTC Market has Evolved." 2017. Consumer Finance Association, March.

"Joint Administrators." 2014. In Administration High Court of Justice, Chancery Division, Companies Court Case No. 2321. Albemarle & Bond Holdings.

Jones, Paul. 1999. *Towards Sustainable Credit Union Development: A Research Project*. Manchester: Association of British Credit Unions.

———. 2006. "Giving Credit Where It's Due: Promoting Financial Inclusion Through Quality Credit Unions." *Local Economy* 21 (1): 36–48.

———. 2008. "From Tackling Poverty to Achieving Financial Inclusion – The Changing Role of British Credit Unions in Low Income Communities." *The Journal of Socio-Economics* 37: 2141–54.

Kauflin, Jeff. 2020. "The Future of Payments: Fintech 50 2020." *Forbes*, February 12.

Lane, Pippa, and Laura Rodrigues. 2016. "Filling the Gap: Can Banks Step into the Gap Left by Payday Loans – and if so, How?" *Citizens Advice*, 2016.

"Making the Poverty Premium History." 2017. Personal Finance Research Centre, the University of Bristol, November.

Makortoff, Kalyeena. 2020. "Wonga Claimants to Get Just 4.3% Payout for Mis-sold Loans." *Guardian*, January 30.

Marriage, Maddison. 2018. "Wonga Receives £10m Lifeline from Investors." *Financial Times*, August 5.

McKillop, Donal, and John Wilson. 2003. "Credit Unions in Britain: A Time for Change." *Public Money & Management* 23 (2): 119–24.

McKillop, Donal, Anne Marie Ward, and John Wilson. 2007. "The Development of Credit Unions and Their Role in Tackling Financial Inclusion." *Public Money and Management* 27: 37–44.

———. 2011. "Credit Unions in Great Britain: Recent Trends and Current Prospects." *Public Money & Management* 31 (1): 35–42.

"Need a Bank Branch? Then Head to Europe." 2015. This Money, February 25.

O'Connell, Sean. 2005. "Alternatives to Money Lenders? Credit Unions and Their Discontents." *History & Policy.org*. May 3.

"Pawn Sector Review." 2018. Financial Conduct Authority, July 10.

"Payday Loans After the Cap." 2016. Citizens Advice, August.

"Payday Price Cap Consultation." 2014. Financial Conduct Authority, July.

"Post Wonga Collapse, FCA Scrutinizes Payday Lenders." 2018. *PYMTS Alternative Finance*, October 16.

Ramirez, Stefanie. 2019. "Pay-day Loan Bans: Evidence of Indirect Effect on Supply." *Empirical Economics* 56: 1011–37.

Russell, Harriet. 2019. "As QuickQuid Collapses, Is It All Over for Payday Lenders?" *Telegraph*, October 26.

Ryder, Nicholas. 2009. "The Credit Crunch – The Right Time for Credit Unions to Strike?" *Legal Studies* 29 (1): 75–98.

"Sector Views." 2018. Financial Conduct Authority, April 9.

Sinclair, Stephen. 2014. "Credit Union Modernisation and the Limits of Voluntarism." *Policy & Politics* 42 (3): 403–19.

"Tackling Financial Exclusion: A Country that Works for Everyone?" 2017. House of Lords Select Committee on Financial Exclusion Report of 2016–17 Session, House of Lords Paper 132, March 25.

Tergesen, Anne. 2019. "Some Companies Offer a New Benefit: Payroll Advances and Loans." *Wall Street Journal*, September 2.

"The Financial Lives of Consumers Across the UK." 2018 (updated 2020). Financial Conduct Authority, June 20.

"The Sustainability of Community Development Financial Institutions." 2015. *PWC*, December.

Thiel, Veronika, and Sargon Nissan. 2008. "UK CDFIs From Surviving to Thriving: Realizing the Potential of Community Development." New Economics Foundation.

Wilson, Graham, and Anthony Barker. 2003. "Bureaucrats and Politicians in Britain." *Governance: An International Journal of Policy, Administration, and Institutions* 16 (3): 349–72.

"Why Wonga Finally Called it Quits." 2018. *PYMTS Alternative Finance*, September 4.

CHAPTER 7

Conclusion: Perceptions Matter

Policy has largely failed to tame the small-loan market and old struggles have yet to be resolved. Affordable credit remains out of reach for many low-income households. Industry supporters have long argued that small loans serve borrowers overlooked by banks and other financial institutions. Since borrowers know the repayment amount in pounds and pence, lenders champion their process as the ultimate form of transparency. Reformers, on the other hand, have not let them cast off the predatory loan shark moniker. However divergent the viewpoints, the core issue is little debated: poor people face a near-permanent shortage of money.

Supplying small cash loans to poor borrowers is risky and expensive, especially on a cost-per-pound-lent basis. Much of the originating and service costs are fixed and covering those expenses over such small sums lent is different from traditional banks accustomed to dealing with larger loans. Banks deal with people who have more assets and earn higher and steady incomes. Low and irregular wages place small-loan borrowers on the economic margins. The difficulty for policy is not so much pointing out the distinctions, but in figuring out how those realities should inform small-loan policy (Fleming 2018).

Chronicling over 150 years of state intervention reveals the complexities of the small-loan market. Some policymakers argued for fewer legal restraints and more competition, while others wanted regulation to significantly decrease loan volumes. Both groups sought their vision of fairness

© The Author(s), under exclusive license to Springer Nature Switzerland AG 2021

C. McMahon, *Taming the Fringe*, Palgrave Studies in the History of Finance, https://doi.org/10.1007/978-3-030-70615-9_7

and justice within the world of small-time capitalism. Each balanced a desire for enhanced safety without unduly restricting access for those in need. Though the future will differ from the past, and nor does history tell us how to solve our current problems, it does reveal several patterns that can inform our understanding of this market.

The first issue for policymakers is drawing appropriate boundaries. Blurry boundaries between small loans and other financial products have created a host of issues and policy failures. Often, avoiding caps and restrictions required only a slight modification in a loan feature. For much of the twentieth century, price controls were shunned because they are easily evaded. While the FCA's three-part price cap system is well designed, millions in potential profit provide ample incentive to test the legal frontiers. Similarly, the proliferation of the high-cost credit sector makes understanding product distinctions all the more important. The moment price caps impacted payday loans, reformers demanded similar measures on other fringe products including overdrafts, rent-to-own and auto title loans. Policymakers need to create boundaries and decide which products necessitate regulation, especially those that closely mirror forms of mainstream household credit (Fleming 2018).

Banks define what is considered appropriate finance. Financial inclusion policy relies on the products and services offered by high-street banks. While the boundary between 'right' and 'wrong' finance seems clear enough, in reality, society has not determined what financial inclusion means for the poor. Too often, 'good' citizenship means accepting a level of finalization that poor people will never reach (Marron 2007; Berry 2015). This is not mere academic speculation, as the continued failure of credit unions demonstrate. 'Good' financial institutions reliant on savings will struggle precisely because they require what the poor do not have—spare cash. Continued reflection on the boundaries of financialization and inclusion should be based on the lived realities of lower-income households.

The second issue is the relationship between poverty, state welfare and small loans. *Taming the Fringe* has established that none of the examined reform episodes dealt with the root causes of poverty. Small-loan providers receive such high customer satisfaction marks because they provide what is needed and demand by low-income households. The private markets respond to the lived realities of their customers. Tackling predatory lending is one thing, but the next step is addressing how income insecurity and cutbacks in state welfare drive demand for small loans in the first place (Rowlingson et al. 2016). Reductions in state welfare provision coincided with an increased reliance on private credit to fill the gap (Rowlingson et al. 2016). Regulating high-cost small-value credit shifts the state from relief 'provider' to the 'enabler' of the 'finalization of everyday life' (Aitken 2010; Rowlingson et al. 2016). Evolutions in the poverty debate, from a Victorian moral matrix to today's individualized credit-as-safety-net system, should more readily be recognized as a formative force behind small-loan usage.

Similarly, today's hope—fintech companies—operate at the intersection of 'good' banking, poverty and increased finalization. If rigorous and innovative data analysis can bring down costs and sustainable profits, lenders and borrowers will be better off. A potential result of their success could be a further shift away from the state's role of welfare provider towards an increased reliance on private markets. While it is too early to know whether these firms reduce or exacerbate the conditions of poverty, such important trends should occur as well-vetted policy and not as a resultant accident of tightened high-cost credit regulation.

The third issue is about the policy tools themselves. Small-value credit is expensive and can cause issues for some borrowers. Parliament has struggled to design adequate tools for the unique demands of poor borrowers or the lenders supplying them much-needed cash. Figuring out how to supply affordable credit to vulnerable borrowers is no easy task. *Taming the Fringe* has identified and analysed the main policy responses to the many problems associated with small loans. That the same tools resurface decade after decade is telling in and of itself. More revealing is why the tools were sought and why some ended up in the final legislation while others did not.

The road towards justice within small-time capitalism has relied on some combination of price controls, information disclosure and licensing. Concerns over the high cost of loans, advertising, the use of an annual percentage rate (APR) and the legitimacy of small-value lenders in the financial system focused policy responses. Each of the tools brings strength and weaknesses in smoothing out the rough edges of capitalism for low-income borrowers. Deeper still, the tools reveal much about how policymakers viewed borrowers and lenders. Requiring disclosure and APR data assumes that borrowers are capable of understanding and interested in such information. Are borrowers helpless or sophisticated consumers? Has individual failure or systemic economic conditions created the demand for small loans? Time and again the actual and perceived capabilities of borrowers impacted the course of regulatory reform. Too often reform proceeds without carefully identifying policymakers' position on borrower capabilities. Policymakers' underlying desire to protect through regulatory tools changes regularly, from limiting the 'immoral passions' of the 'degenerate poor' to empowering 'rational adults' towards competition-enhancing decision making. Some degree of consensus concerning borrower competences would go a long way towards effective policy outcomes.

This leads to the tricky question of the lenders themselves. Like some accounts of the small-loan market, on the surface, *Taming the Fringe* may seem overly sympathetic to pawnbrokers, moneylenders and their modern payday lending colleagues (Smith 1983). Analysing the revenues, expenses, profits, business model, trade group publications, internal memos and lobbying efforts of lenders provides valuable insights into the world of small-time capitalism. Their viewpoints and experiences are worth knowing. If they conduct predatory practices, the law should respond accordingly. However, demonizing these lenders as 'evil' prejudices the investigatory proceedings. When determining whether these lenders peddle harmful products, derogatory terms should be avoided.

However, small the amounts, pricing risk for borrowers in financial difficulties is just one of the many peculiarities of this market. The role of money and its regulation is complicated. This reality helps to explain why, whether framed in economic terms or social policy, motivations to limit the supply of funds and restrict the working poor's access to high-cost credit have varied so dramatically.

The final issue is recognizing how much perceptions matter. Even with millions of data points, the FCA failed to determine if small loans are good or bad for consumers. Each in their own way, generations of policymakers believed that small-loan pricing was high and that the product was harmful. This moves beyond whether APR is an appropriate measure of cost. Small-loan policy is shaped by strongly held convictions. Lenders have wanted legitimacy and a real sense of belonging and acceptance. Many have rebuked them on the grounds that their loans simply 'feel' wrong. Research reports and studies arrive at differing conclusions. Passionate spirits motivated a protective ethic. The entangled relationship between capitalism, poverty and the state's response is complex. The end results matter for people living on the economic edge and desperately in need of cash. Since the private markets will continue to innovate, and the demand for loans is unlikely to disappear anytime soon, admitting how much we know, and the aspects of reform that remain subjective can help open up new pathways of defining fairness within capitalism for the poor and vulnerable.

Bibliography

Aitken, Rob. 2010. "Regul(ariz)ation of Fringe Credit: Payday Lending and the Borders of Global Financial Practice." *Competition and Change* 14 (2): 80–99.

Berry, Craig. 2015. "Citizenship in a Financialised Society: Financial Inclusion and the State Before and After the Crash." *Policy & Politics* 43 (4): 509–25.

Fleming, Anne. 2018. *City of Debtors: A Century of Fringe Finance*. Harvard, MA: Harvard University Press.

Marron, Donncha. 2007. "Governing Poverty in a Neoliberal Age: New Labour and the Case of Financial Exclusion." 2013. *New Political Economy* 18 (6): 785–810.

Rowlingson, Karen, Lindsey Appleyard, and Jodi Gardner. 2016. "Payday Lending in the UK: the Regul(aris)ation of a Necessary Evil?" *The Journal of Social Policy* 45 (3): 527–43.

Smith, Harold. 1983. Review of "Making Ends Meet: Pawnbroking and Working-Class Credit by Melanie Tebbutt." *Journal of Economic History* 44 (3): 856–7.

Principal Persons

George Attenborough, Alfred Hardaker and John Telfer
Pawnbrokers
Reform advocates, 1860-1870s

Acton Smee Ayrton
Member of Parliament, Liberal
Chairman, PBSC 1870

Edward Carson
Peer, Member of Parliament, Irish Unionist
Lead sponsor, MLA 1927

Stella Creasy
Member of Parliament, Labour
Reform advocate, 2006-present

Geoffrey Crowther
Economist, journalist
Chairman of the Committee on Consumer Credit 1968-1971

Thomas Farrow

© The Editor(s) (if applicable) and The Author(s), under exclusive license to Springer Nature Switzerland AG 2021

C. McMahon, *Taming the Fringe*, Palgrave Studies in the History of Finance, https://doi.org/10.1007/978-3-030-70615-9

Reform advocate, MLSC 1897

George Gillman
London City Missionary, Charity worker
Witness, PBSC 1870

Royston Goode
Emeritus Professor of Law, St John's College, Oxford
Member, Committee on Consumer Credit 1968-1971

Issac Gordon, John Kirkwood and Isaac Samuel
Moneylenders
Witnesses, MLSC 1897
Archibald Orr-Ewing
Member of Parliament, Conservative
Member, PBSC 1870

Thomas Russell
Member of Parliament, Liberal
Chairman, MLSC 1897

Richard Wells
Member of Parliament, Conservative
Lead sponsor, MLA 1927

Index

A
advertising, 6, 10
  circulars, 80, 84
  fraudulent, 71–72
  limits on newspaper, 84, 89
  by moneylenders, 57, 60
  by pawnbrokers, 144
  payday lending, 2, 166
Advice UK, 158
Airedale, Oliver Kitson, Lord, 127
Albemarle & Bond, pawnbrokers, 3, 145, 146
  collapse of, 187, 194
alcohol, consumption by poor, 34
Alternative Dispute Resolution (ADR) scheme, 151, 169
Anson, William, MP, 74
anti-Semitism, and moneylenders, 57, 75, 84
APR, 6, 215
  and Consumer Credit Act (1974), 127
  and Crowther Committee disclosure programme, 117–119, 121
  debate (1920s), 85–86
  problems of calculating, 118, 150, 165
  resistance to use of, 61–62, 71–72, 89
  unsuitable for short-term credit, 165–166
  see also interest rates
Association of British Credit Unions, 158
Association of Chartered Certified Accountants, 159
Attenborough, George, pawnbrokers, 23, 24, 46, 144
Ayrton, Acton Smee, MP, 35, 41, 44

B
Balfour, Arthur, Prime Minister, 71
bank accounts
  access to, 139, 141, 143
  basic current accounts, 139, 141, 196–198
Bank of England
  interest rate, 119

© The Editor(s) (if applicable) and The Author(s), under exclusive license to Springer Nature Switzerland AG 2021

C. McMahon, *Taming the Fringe*, Palgrave Studies in the History of Finance, https://doi.org/10.1007/978-3-030-70615-9

and low-income group debt, 153
view of unsecured debts, 141
banks, 9, 109, 196–199
account minimums, 142
borrowers' dissatisfaction with, 157
branch closures, 142, 195, 197, 198
costs of basic accounts, 196, 198, 204
and financial inclusion, 198, 214
high fixed costs, 198, 204
included in licensing, 119–120
moneylenders and, 74–76
overdrafts, 161, 197, 214
pawnbroking compared with, 30
personal identification requirements, 197
and small loans, 11, 185
Barclays
basic accounts, 196
credit cards, 140
Barnett, Mr, pawnbroker, 38, **38**, 101
Battle, John, MP, 150, 152, 167
BCCA trade group, 166
Beneficial Financial Company, small-loan lender, 112
Bentham, Jeremy, *Discourse on Usury*, 27
Betting and Loans (Infants) Act (1892), 75
Beveridge Report, 108
Birrell, Augustine, MP, 70
Blackwell, Ernley, Home Office, 77
Blackwood, Benjamin, pawnbroker, 5
Blenkinsop, Tom, MP, 156
Board of Trade, 109
and moneylenders, 78
Boles, Nick, MP, 158
borrower rationality, 8, 34
borrowers
avoidance of courts, 114, 150
better off without loans, 140, 166, 170, 189, 190
competence of, 78, 216
Crowther Committee view of, 149
female, 162–163
loans to cover living expenses, 154, 157, 162, 189
misled by advertisements, 71–73
preference for convenience over cost, 113, 143, 157–158
preference for monetary costing for loans, 85, 89, 144, 166
profile of, 189, 190
rejected for loans, 161, 189–190, 192
and risk of exposure, 73
as vulnerable, 149, 151, 159, 168, 169
see also households, low-income
Bosanquet, Helen, social reformer, 33
Bouverie Society, 25
Bristol Report (2013), 156, 161
British Bankers Association, 196
Broomfield, F.J., Board of Trade, 123
Burt, Lorely, MP, 156

C

Cardiff Advance Bank, moneylenders, 78
Carson, Edward, Lord, 80, 84, 88, 166
Carter, Robert, MP, 23
Cash America Inc, 145
loan costs and revenues, **160**
Cash Store, 164
Centre for Responsible Credit, 200
CFO Lending, 164
Chalmers, Mackenzie, Judge, 81
Chambers, Thomas, MP, 169
Chapman, Jenny, MP, 158
Chappell & Co, instrument makers, 26
Charitable Organisation Society, 33

charities
  charitable loan funds, 83
  testimony to MLSC (1925), 80–81
  view of small loans, 9
charity, indiscriminate. *See* 32â€“34
charity workers, on management of budgets by poor, 34
Chaytor, David, MP, 148
Cheque Centres, 164
cheque traders, 5
  pawnbrokers, 144
Church of England, on payday lenders, 2
circulars, moneylenders', 80
  ban on, 84, 89
Citizens Advice Bureaux, 148, 158. *See also* National Citizens Advice Bureau Council
CMA (Competition and Markets Authority), Payday Lending Market Investigation (2015), 156
Collier, Judge, 116
community development financial institutions (CDFIs), 11, 186, 201–202, 204
  bad debts, 201
  government grants, 201, 204
  loss-making, 201
Companies Act (1967), 108
competition
  CCA 1974 and, 100, 122–124, 127
  CCA 2006 and, 142
  government support for, 141, 169, 213
  and regulation, 27
Consumer Council, 105
consumer credit, 140–141
  access to, 11
  expansion of, 128
  growth of, 99
  and market reform, 108
Consumer Credit Act (CCA) (1974), 100, 122–127
  and APR, 125
  market background, 100–107
  political background, 107–108
  and price controls, 124–125
  and small-loan agreements, 123
Consumer Credit Act (CCA) (2006), 6, 139
  and competition, 142
  and disclosure, 150
  and financial inclusion, 147–153
  and high-risk lenders, 152–153
  licensing and enforcement, 151–152
  and price controls, 148–149
  unfair relationships, 150–151, 168
Consumer Credit Commission
  and licensing, 119–120, 126–127
  proposed, 117, 120, 123
Consumer Finance Association, 164
Consumer Focus, 154
consumer protection, 100
  role of market, 100, 142, 147, 169
Consumers Association (Which?), 112, 148, 158
contract, freedom of, 8, 78
contracts, moneylending, 61–63, 88
Co-operative Bank, basic accounts, 196
counterfeit goods, 24
courts
  borrowers avoidance of, 114, 150
  moneylending cases, 61
  see also judiciary
Creasy, Stella, MP, 156, 158
credit
  access to, 116, 170, 186, 214
  for consumer goods, 143
  for immediate needs, 141
  rationing, 8, 42, 43, 158
  types, 5–6

usage when denied payday loan, 192
credit card system, 140–141
credit markets
expansion of, 100, 127–128, 140, 153–156
government and, 111, 127
range of products, 144, 146, 147
size of (by 2005), 144
see also small-loan market
credit reports, negative, 189
Credit Union Act (1979), 199
credit unions, 11, 186, 198–201, 204
changing business model, 199
limited market impact, 199
need for public investment, 199, 204
restrictive membership, 199
savings requirements, 200
Crowther Committee (1968–71), 99, 108–122, 127–128, 169
and borrowers, 112–114
and competition, 121
evidence before, 109
and price controls, 115–117
recommendations, 122–124
Report, 122
view of borrowers, 149
Crowther, Geoffrey, Lord, 109–110
cryptocurrencies, 186
customers, 5

D
Daily Telegraph
and moneylending, 60
on pawnbroking reform, 30, 48
Danczuk, Simon, MP, 169
Davies, Howard, Lord Davies of Leek, 122
Davies, John, Secretary of State for Trade and Industry, 122
debt
categories of, 191, **191**
household bills, 139, 143, 157, 190, 191
of low-income groups, 153
and morality, 43, 49, 162, 171, 215
personal, 139, 141, 188
rising, 147
see also poverty
debt spiral, 18, 19, 43
default, 20, 23, 24
concept of honest, 113–114
fees, 165
Dennison, Robert, MP, 84
Department for Trade and Industry (DTI)
on Consumer Credit bill, 123
on debt, 141
and disclosure, 147
and licensing, 119
Derby, pawnbrokers' meeting on reform (1869), 29
Derby scale, proposed pawnbroking charges, 29, **30**, 47
deregulation
1970s, 108
financial (1980s), 140
Dicker, John, London pawnbroker, 42
bulky goods, 42
business analysis, 36, **37**, 39
customer relations, 43
revenue, 22, 24
sale of forfeited goods, 45
transactions, **23**
disclosure, 215
2006 reforms and, 147, 148, 150
2015 reforms, 167–168
in advertisements, 72
and borrowers' decision-making, 167
and competition, 125, 126
Consumer Credit Act and, 122–123

Crowther Committee and, 117–118, 121
MLA (1900) and, 76
of moneylending costs, 59, 85
see also APR
dolly-shops, 25
Dudley Herald and Wednesbury Borough News, 40

E

economic inequality, 142–143, 171. *See also* financial exclusion; poverty
The Economist, 26
economy
changes since 1800, 25
globalization, 140
Education Act (1944), 108
Edwards, Jonathan, MP, 159
Elcho, Lord, 159
employment, casual urban, 21
enforcement, 6
and licensing, 119–120, 126, 127, 151–152
Enova, 188
EU (European Union)
Payment Accounts Directive, 196
price controls, 148, 159
Expert Eye technology, 194
extortionate terms
definition, 123
test for, 115–116
and unfair relationships, 150–151
EZCorp, 164

F

'Fair, Clear and Competitive', DTI White Paper (2003), 147, 150, 152
fairness
concept of, 196
and unfair moneylending contracts, 62–64
and unfair relationships, 150–151, 168
Fair Trading Act, 126
Farrow, Thomas
on advertising, 72
The Moneylender Unmasked, 60–61
and reform of moneylending, 63
Faux, John, borrower, 72
Fieldings Limited, moneylenders, 66
Finance Act (1949), licensing, 100–102
Finance Houses Association, 109
Financial Conduct Authority (FCA), 6, 163, 196
analysis of payday lending, 164–166, 169–170
and concept of fairness, 196
Consultation Paper Proposals For a Price on High-Cost Short-Term Credit (2014), 156
'High-cost Credit Review - Update' (2018), 197
payday lending price controls, 2, 6, **6**
price control mechanism, 165–167, *166*, 186, 214
financial exclusion
categories of people, 194
and poverty premium, 195
financial inclusion, 169, 186
banks and, 196–199, 214
Basic Bank Account programme, 194
costs to lenders, 204
and community development financial institutions (CDFIs), 201–202
and Consumer Credit Act (2006), 147–153
and credit unions, 198–201

Labour government and, 141–142
policy developments, 194–196
Financial Ombudsman Service, 151
financial sector
1970s regulation, 99, 111
expansion, 139
Finlay, Robert, lawyer, 71–72
Fintech (on-demand wage companies), 186, 202–204
and low-income consumers, 202
possibilities for, 215
First World War, and register of moneylenders, 78
forfeiture of goods, 20, 23, 44–46, 145
Consumer Credit Act and, 122–124
Fovargue, Yvonne, MP, 155
France, non-profit pawnbrokers, 41
free trade, arguments on regulation, 26–27
friendly societies, 5, 33
fund-raising platforms, 186

G

Gedge, Sydney, MP, 70
Gibbs, Vicary, MP, 68
Gillman, George, London City missionary worker, 21, 44, 45
Gilmore, Sheila, MP, 156
Glasman, Maurice, Lord, 2, 156
Global Financial Crises (2007), 5, 153, 169
and campaign against payday lending, 140
and market expansion, 153–156
and price controls, 156–166
globalization, 140
gold and silver, pawned, 145, 193
Goldsmiths Company, and counterfeit goods, 26
Goode, Sir Royston, 116, 124
goods
counterfeit, 24
forfeited, 20, 23, 24, 41, 44–46
heavy/bulky, 25, 42
holding period, 44, 46
pawned, 34, 101–103, 145, 193
redemption rates, **45**
sold to raise cash, 191
Gordon, Isaac, 75, 164
Gorell, Ronald Barnes, Lord, 84
government
role in credit market, 110, 127
role in economy, 108
role in poverty mitigation, 8
role in regulation of moneylending, 58, 86
see also financial inclusion; policymakers; welfare state
Guardian, on pawnbrokers (2016), 3

H

H&T Group, pawnbrokers, 145, 192
and unsecured lending, 194
Haldane, Richard, Lord, 82
Ham, Arthur, Sage Foundation, 83–84
Hambro, Charles, MP, 33
Hames, Duncan, MP, 156
Hancock, William, pawnbroking expert, 35
Hardaker, Alfred, pawnbroker, 45
Harris, Rebecca, MP, 156
Hawkins, Henry, Judge, 76
Heath, Edward, Prime Minister, 99, 108
and Crowther Report, 122
Hector, William, public prosecutor, Renfrewshire, 21, 40, 44
Hendry, Charles, MP, 151
Henry, Thomas, Metropolitan Police Courts (1870), 163

Hepburn, Stephen, MP, 148
Heys, Mr, Manchester pawnbroker, 27
Hinds, Damian, MP, 158, 164
hire-purchase, 5
Hire Purchase Association, 122
Hollick, Clive, Lord, 154
Home and Social Affairs Committee, 118, 123
household savings, 1
  lack of, 143, 146, 170, 188
households, low-income
  arrears and debts, 139, 143, 154, 190, 192
  and debt spiral, 18
  financial management, 7, 34
  as high-risk borrowers, 8, 12, 188
  see also poor, the
House of Commons Treasury Committee, on financial inclusion, 147
House of Lords Select Committee on Financial Exclusion (2016), 195, 200

I

illegal lenders, 19th-century, 25, 47
illegal lending, as result of price controls, 148, 153, 159
Inland Revenue
  and moneylenders registry, 77
  and moneylending problems, 78–79
  and powers of prosecution, 110
Institute for Fiscal Studies, 154
Institute of Public Policy Research, 158
interest rates, 8, 10, 24
  and Bank rate, 119
  calculation of, 20, 125–126, **126**
  guidance rate, 105, 116–117, 121–122, 124
  moneylenders, 57, 60, 65–67, 79–81
  for moneylending, 67–71, **71**, 81, 83
  payday lenders, 2
  preference for cash price, 144, 167
  resistance to use of APR, 61–62, 72–73, 84–85, 89
  and return on capital, 40–41, 66–67, 81–83, 86
  unsecured loans, 105, **104–107**
  see also APR; price controls
Internet, and pawnbroking, 144
Ireland, non-profit pawnbrokers, 41
Isaacs, Rufus, lawyer, 78
Islington Consumer Group, 106, 110
IT (information technology), 146
  and payday lending, 147

J

Japan, price controls, 159
Jews
  and anti-Semitism, 75, 84
  as moneylenders, 61
John Hilton Bureau, 105
Johnston, Robert, MP, 34, 35
Jones, Susan, MP, 156
Joynson-Hicks, William, MP, 80
judiciary, judges
  and guidance interest rates, 70–71
  and review of consumer credit transactions, 124–125
  role in control of moneylending, 60–61, 68–70, 77–78, 88
  and unfair moneylending contracts, 62–64
  and unfair relationships, 150–151, 168
  see also courts
Juo Loans, 187, 188

K

Keeling, Dorothy, charitable loan fund, 83
Kenworthy, Joseph, 84
Kirkwood, John, 70
Knight, William, judge, 35
Koyo company, 186

L

Labour government (from 1997), social and financial inclusion, 141–142, 195
labour markets, 19, 32, 143
Lamb, Norman, MP, 152
Lancashire and Cheshire Moneylenders Association, 107
Latest News, on pawnbroking reform, 30
leaving shops, 25
Lewis, George, solicitor, 65–67, 74
Lewis, Martin, 167
licenses
  (1870–1930), 47, 48
  distribution (1909), *21*
licensing, 6, 10, 139
  of all financial institutions, 119–120
  Consumer Credit Commission and, 119–120, 126–127
  and enforcement, 119–120, 128, 151–152
  by local authorities, 100–101
  of moneylenders, 59, 77, 86–87
  of new lenders-of-money (1960s), 107–108
  and power of suspension, 110
Linnell, Robert, moneylender, 73, 74
Liverpool, pawnbrokers, 28–29, 102
Lloyds, basic accounts, 196
loan applications
  moneylenders and, 61–62
  rejected, 161, 189–191
loan consolidations, moneylenders and, 75–76
loan defaults, 23, 112–114
loan rollovers, 73
loans
  connected and unconnected, 119
  demand for, 11, 80, 112–114, 121
  geographic distribution, 188
  as harmful or beneficial, 32, 168, 189, 216
  informal, 171, 190
  instalment, 106, 187
  length of, 24, 40, 41, 188
  numbers of, 8, 21, 23, 187–188
  purpose of, 31–32
  size of, 21, 23, 38, 39
  small-value from moneylenders, 79–86
  unsecured, 58, 194
  to wealthy clients, 58, 62
  see also payday loans
London
  pawnbrokers, 21, 101, 102
  production of counterfeit goods, 24

M

Manchester
  pawnbrokers trade association proposals, 27–29
  production of counterfeit goods, 24
Manchester Examiner and Times, on pawnbroker loans, 35
Mansfield, Horace, MP, 78, 110
Marks, Henry, MP, 65
Mathew, James, Judge, 62
May, John, Salford pawnbroker, 21, 34
May, Theresa, Prime Minister, 195
McCall, Alexander, Chief Constable of Glasgow, 33, 34, 48
McKay, John, Glasgow pawnbroker, 3, **38**, 38, 43

Mersey Financial, moneylenders, 86
Metropolitan Police, and moneylenders, 78
microfinance companies, 186
Midland Bank, 118
 and Crowther Committee, 118
Miller, William, MP, 40
Mitchell, Parry, Lord, 156
Money Advice Trust, 154
moneylenders and moneylending, 57–87, 146–147
 1900 reforms, 59–60
 1927 reforms, 60
 administration expenses, 66, 70
 associated with crime, 87
 and bad debts, 62, 82
 bills of sale, 65, 66
 compared with banks, 74–76, 89
 contracts, 61–63, 84
 definition, 77, 85
 financial data, **82**
 legitimized (1974), 100
 licensing, 100–101, 103–105, **104**, 127
 numbers of, 75, 78, 99
 parliamentary definition of, 79–81
 public view of, 57, 60, 83–84, 215
 registration, 76–78, 86–87
 restrictions on trade names, 59, 74–76
 return on interest rates, 65–66, 81–83
 and risk, 66–68
 and self-regulation, 87
 see also National Association of Moneylenders; payday lending; usury
Moneylenders Association, 84
Moneylenders Select Committee (MLSC 1897), 60–71
 and advertising, 71–72
 and disclosure, 71–72
 and price controls, 67–69
Moneylenders Select Committee (MLSC 1925), 60, 80–83
Moneylending Act (1900), **6**, 7, 59, 60
 draft bill, 70–71
 failures of, 81, 88, 89
 and fraud and transparency, 75
Moneylending Act (1927), **6**, 10, 59–60, 85, 87–88, 99
 failures, 103, 110
 licensing, 103, 108
 price controls, 88
 registration, 86–87
 standard contract, 85
Money Shop, 188, 194
Moore, Alfred, 70
morality, debt and, 33, 34, 49, 162, 171, 215
Murphy, Phil, Albemarle & Bond, 3
My-Quick online platform, 186

N

National Association of Moneylenders, 104–107, 109, 159
 and guidance rate, 116, 117
 and licensing, 120
National Citizens Advice Bureau Council, 110
 and APR, 118
National Consumer Council, 148
National Health Service (NHS), 108
National Pawnbrokers Association (NPA), 101–103, 109
Newcastle United football club, Wonga and, 2
newspapers
 coverage of moneylending, 57
 and pawnbroking reform (1870), 31
New Towns Act (1946), 104

'Nottingham Sessions' (1868), pawnbrokers' meeting on reform, 28

O

Observer, on Crowther Report, 122
Office of Fair Trading (OFT)
  and consumer credit, 140–141
  on credit market, 158
  and high-risk lenders, 168
  investigation of small-loan providers, 147, 168
  and licensing penalties, 151–152
  on payday lending regulation, 163
  Review of High Cost Credit (2010), 156
On Stride, 187, 188
Orr-Ewing, Archibald, MP. *See* 32â€“34, 45
overdrafts, 161, 214
  fees for unarranged, 197
Owen, Stevenson, Judge, 66

P

Parish, Neil, MP, 156
Parker, James, London City missionary, 34
Parliamentary Pawnbroking Select Committee (1870), 30–47
Parliamentary Select Committee (1897), 10
Pawnbroker Act (1800), 18, 25
Pawnbroker Parliamentary Reform Association (PPRA), reform proposals, 29–31
Pawnbrokers Act (1872), **6**, 47
Pawnbrokers Gazette (PBG), 20, 26, 30, 44
pawnbrokers and pawnbroking, 7, 8, 194
  in 2018, **192**
  bookkeeping, 37, 45
  calls for regulatory reform (1860s), 18–19, 25–30
  capital sources, 146
  Consumer Credit Acr and, 123–124
  credit cap (1546), 6
  customer relationships, 43, 144
  decline of, 99, 104, 107, 186, 187
  as financial service, 31
  legitimized (1974), 100
  licensing, **101**, 101–102, 103, **104**
  loan volumes, 101
  market estimates, **5**
  market size (by 2005), 3, 154, 144–147
  new services, 145, 146, 193
  non-profit (Ireland and France), 41
  operating expenses, 20, 24, 36, 39
  Parliamentary reform, 31–47
  pledge analysis, **103**, 103–104, 107
  price caps
    ended, 100, 121–122
    schedule (1800), 1
  profitability, 19, 39–41, 43, 45, 47, 193
  and redemption rates, **45**, 103
  reputation of, 26, 40, 156, 216
  revenues, 22, 24, 145–146
  seasonality, 21, 24, 46
  size of Victorian industry, 18, 42, 47
  and special contracts, 29, 47
  testaments to Parliament, **37**, 38, 39, **40**
  trade organization, 26
  weekly pledges, 17, 21
Pawnbroking Select Committee (1870), 6, 8
pawn tickets
  fees, 24
  regulations, 20, 46
pawn transactions, 3

speed of, 20
payday lenders and payday lending, 2, 7, 146–147
campaign against, 140
collapse of, 164, 185, 187–188
expenses, 161–162
exploitation, 159, 164
interest rates, 2
lack of price competition, 164
loan acceptance rate, 192
market expansion, 153–155, **154–156**, 169
online, 158, 161
retail outlets, 153, 166
return on capital, 162
revenues and profits, 159–162, 192
Payday Lending Compliance Review (2013), 156
payday loans
costs, **161**, 192
to cover living expenses, 154–156, 161, 162–163
as harmful, 140, 157
instalment loans, 146, 187
penalty fees, 160
price caps, 214
repayments, **161**
payroll advances, 203. *See also* Fintech
Percy, Andrew, MP, 156
Pery of Limerick, Lord, 124
policymakers
campaign against payday lending, 140, 169
and causes of poverty, 214–215
and competition, 121–122, 141, 169, 213
and credit market expansion, 147
and credit supply, 3, 204–205
and disclosure, 118, 121
and financial inclusion, 147
and market failure, 158
and moneylenders (1920s), 81
need for boundaries, 214
and price controls, 140, 163, 165–166, 170
and regulation, 5, 213
role of pawnbrokers, 7
shift to deregulation, 108, 113
and social justice, 153, 171
tools of, 215
view of borrowers' capabilities, 114, 119, 216
see also government
Poor Law (1834), 34
poor, the
ability to negotiate, 32, 62
consumption of alcohol, 34
decline in real income, 142–143
deserving and undeserving, 32, 43, 48
household debt, 139, 143, 154, 191
as intellectually inferior, 33
lack of bank accounts, 139, 141–143, 185
lack of savings, 1, 143, 146, 170, 189
management of budgets, 34, 112, 114
use of credit, 142–144, 170
working, 143
see also households, low-income; poverty
Pounds to Pocket, 187, 188
poverty
causes of, 214–215
and crime, 33
effect of small loans on, 11–12, 33
end of destitution, 111–112
expansive definition of, 169
and role of government, 8, 9
structural, 9, 143, 171, 188
varying views of, 36, 43
and welfare state, 99, 107

see also debt; households, low-income; poor, the
poverty premium, 195
price controls, 7
1974 (CCA), 124–125
2006 reforms and, 148–149, 168
2010–2015 initiatives, 156–166
Crowther Committee and, 115–116, 128
default fee maximums, 165
effect on payday loans, 2, 214
effect on small-loan market, 189, **190**
evidence for reform (1870), 36–44
FCA and, 140, 163–165
mechanism, *165*, 165–166
'guidance interest rates, 67–71
and higher-value loans, 166, 170
and illegal lending, 148, 159, 170
lifted (1872 Act), 47
moneylending, 66–67, 87
practical difficulties of, 68
price cap schedule (1800) on pawnbroking, 1, 25, 41
research into payday loan costs, 156–158
resistance to, 58, 67
total cost limits, 165
see also interest rates
profitability
and interest rates, 8
for lenders, 159–162, 192, 215–216
of pawnbroking, 18, 19, 39, 40, 45, 193
public opinion
against moneylenders, 58, 60, 86–87, 216
and reputation of pawnbrokers, 26, 40, 156, 216

Q
QuickQuid, 188

R
Reeves, Rachel, MP, 156
'Reform of the Law on Consumer Credit', 1971 White Paper, 122–123
registration, of moneylenders, 76–78, 86–87
regulation, 4, **6**, 110, 111, 114
and competition, 27
enforcement, 6
increased, 11, 21
independent regulator, 119, 126–127
of moneylending, 80–82
policymakers and, 169
see also deregulation; financial regulation; licensing; registration
risk-based monitoring, 151
Robinson, Mabel, 155
Roxburgh, Francis, Judge, 66
Royal Statistical Society, 21
Russell, Terrance, MP, 70–72
Russell, Thomas, pawnbroker, 38, **38**
Rutland Partners, 145

S
Sage (Russell Sage) Foundation, America, 83–84
sale
of forfeited goods, 20, 23, 24, 46
public auctions, 23
Samuel, Isaac, moneylender, 61
and interest rates, 65, 66, 69
and licensing proposal, 77
Sassoon, James, Lord, 159, 163
savings. *See* household savings
savings institutions, 5
Scrutton, Justice, 78
Second World War, 107
Shaw, William, assistant pawnbroker, 35

shop credit, 5
Simon, John, Board of Trade, lawyer, 78
Simon, John, MP, 45
Simpson & Co., moneylenders, 60
Slater, Arthur, railway fitter, 60
small-loan market, 1, 3, 8, 9, 12
  1870s view of, 8–9
  1970s–2006, 142–147
  impact of price cap on, 189, **190**
  place in financial system, 9–10, 214, 216
  as 'predatory', 168
  see also credit markets
smartphone apps, fintech, 203
Social Exclusion Unit, Policy Action Team (1999), 194
Social Fund, 144
social justice, 153, 171
Spectator
  on moneylending contracts, 63
  on pawnbroking reform, 30
Speedloan Finance, Japanese pawnbroker, 193
Standard newspaper, and moneylending, 60
Standing Conference on Organisation of Social Workers, 113
StepChange, 154
stolen goods, 24
Storr, Raynor, auctioneer, 46
Stubbs, Lucas, Liverpool magistrate, 114
Sunny Loans, 187
Sutton, T.M., pawnbrokers, 144
Swinson, Jo, MP, 163

T
tallymen, 5
Tebbutt, Melanie, *Making Ends Meet*, 18
Telfer, John, Whitechapel pawnbroker, 24, 38, 45
Tomlinson, Justin, MP, 156
trade associations, moneylending, 80, 87
trade names, moneylenders, 74–76

U
unfair relationships, judicial evaluation of, 150–151, 168
United States (US)
  CDFIs, 202
  Community Reinvestment Act, 200
  credit unions, 199
  payday loans ban, 190
  price controls, 148, 159
  Sage Foundation, 83–84
usury
  Bentham on, 27
  moral concept of, 74
  see also moneylenders
Usury Repeal Act (1854), 3, 27, 58, 61

V
Vaizey, Edward, MP, 148

W
Wage Day Advance, 187
wage labour, and cash loans, 6
wages
  1970s, 99, 107
  irregular, 21
  low, 19
  stagnant, 142–143, 154–155
Wagestream, fintech company, 203
Webb, Fred, borrower, 80
Wedgwood, Josiah, MP, 86, 88
wee-pawns, Scotland, 25

welfare benefits, and access to bank accounts, 141
welfare state, 1
  cutbacks, 214
  and poverty, 99, 107
  and social change, 108
Wells, Richard, MP, 80, 84
Which?. *See* Consumers Association (Which?)
Williams, Alan, MP, 125
Wilson, Harold, Prime Minister, and Consumer Credit Act (1974), 108
Wilson, Mark, moneylender, 83
women
  as borrowers, 163
  rejected for loans, 190
  as small-scale moneylenders, 79
Wonga, 2, 4
  collapse of, 185, 187
  lending decline, 164
  rejection of loan applications, 161
working class
  judicial treatment of, 62
  see also households, low-income; poor, the
work-place loans, 80
Wormersley, Walter, MP, 150
Wright, Ian, MP, 152

Y

Yerburgh, Robert, MP, campaign against moneylenders, 64–65
Yorkshire Discount Bank, moneylenders, 78
Yorkshire Moneylenders' Association, 84, 86–87

The manufacturer's authorised representative in the EU is Springer Nature Customer Service Centre GmbH, Europaplatz 3, 69115 Heidelberg, Germany. If you have any concerns regarding our products, please contact ProductSafety@springernature.com

Printed and bound by CPI Group (UK) Ltd, Croydon, CR0 4YY

30/09/2026

02225702-0006